Post/modern Dracula

Post/modern Dracula
From Victorian Themes to Postmodern Praxis

Edited by

John S. Bak

CAMBRIDGE SCHOLARS PUBLISHING

Post/modern Dracula: From Victorian Themes to Postmodern Praxis, edited by John S. Bak

This book first published 2007 by

Cambridge Scholars Publishing

15 Angerton Gardens, Newcastle, NE5 2JA, UK

British Library Cataloguing in Publication Data
A catalogue record for this book is available from the British Library

For Nathalie, Margaux and James

TABLE OF CONTENTS

Part III: Postmodernism in Coppola's *Bram Stoker's Dracula*

LIST OF FIGURES

PREFACE

BAD BLOOD; OR, VICTORIAN VAMPIRES IN THE POSTMODERN AGE OF AIDS

"Blood in Stoker's novel is visualized; blood in the book's criticism is signified."

—William Hughes, 2006 conference in Nancy, France

Among the classic Victorian themes Stoker addresses in *Dracula*—from the woman question to colonialism, from scientific innovation to psychosexual transgression—one certainly has important ramifications in the postmodern age: the contamination and commoditization of blood. In the Reaganomic 1980s, when AIDS was a gay or user's disease unworthy of governmental research funding, to the Jean Chrétien 1990s, when the Canadian government underwent its own AIDS scandal involving the Red Cross's negligent distribution of HIV-tainted blood that resulted in at least 3000 deaths and some 20,000 cases of Hepatitis C, few postmodern readers of *Dracula* could escape recognizing the fact that blood today is as synonymous with political hegemony as it was back in Stoker's day.[1] This is something Australian scientist Geoffrey Robertson surely considered back in 1986 when he organized a panel of AIDS experts, which included Prof. Luc Montagnier (the co-discoverer of the HIV-strain in 1981), under the hypothetical title, "Does Dracula Have AIDS?" Brian Wilson Aldiss certainly thought so when he made the vampire HIV positive in his 1991 novel, *Dracula Unbound*.[2] So too did the Illinois Department of Public Health (IDPH) in its decision to adopt Dracula as its 1993 poster-child to warn sexually-active teenagers against going "batty over someone" and risk contracting AIDS.[3]

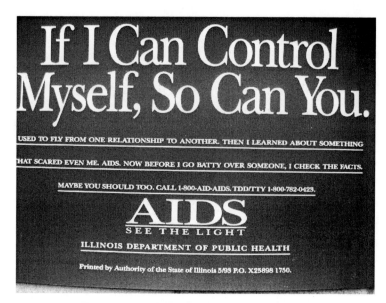

Figure 0-1: 1993 IDPH AIDS Campaign Poster
(Courtesy of the Illinois Department of Public Health)

A certain amount of criticism—some serious, some not—has already been devoted to answering Robertson's question. While it is not my intent here to suggest whether or not a postmodern vampire could transmit HIV, I do want to stress that Stoker's postmodern audiences, conscious or not, have been sensitive to the novel's imported AIDS subtext. It seemed only natural to link a bloodthirsty vampire with the common mosquito as a potential transmitter of the AIDS virus, a theory that took health authorities over a decade to prove erroneous. In fact, though none of the seventy-nine films and media resources David Skal cites that have been adapted from Stoker's novel since 1981 alone directly raises the specter of an HIV-infected world, few could have avoided reminding their viewing publics that Dracula was perhaps more terrifying as a political metaphor for the spread of contaminated blood than as a mythic creature of the night preying on unsuspecting victims.[4] Vampires were fiction after all; AIDS a reality.

Figure 0-2: 1993 IDPH AIDS Campaign Brochure
(Courtesy of the Illinois Department of Public Health)

Perhaps it is not coincidental either that several of those films Skal lists were hard- and soft-core porn films, gay and straight alike, for sexuality, like blood, oozes from the many pages and stills of *Dracula,* and filmmakers certainly knew how to adapt Victorian sexual fantasies to postmodern tastes. Despite these films' hedonistic messages, however, the 1980s still proved to be a decade of rediscovered morality if only out of fear that, left unchecked, sex would spread AIDS from Reagan's social pariahs to his self-ordained heteronormative society. With health officials eventually debunking the myth that heterosexuals were immune to AIDS, *Dracula* in effect restored the Victorian sex taboo that had been all but lost on post-Freudian readers. In other words, if "unprotected sex" had become the shibboleth of a panic-stricken gay community, it soon gained currency among skittish heterosexuals as well, wary more than ever of the sexual Russian roulette that awaited them in the various night clubs or singles' bars they frequently haunted. One did not sleep with one partner, health officials were preaching, but with all of the partners that that person had had over the past few years. If a vampire's bite was a clever metonymy for phallic penetration, it is rather easy to see how knowing who that "vampire's" recent partners were was of vital importance to the preservation of the self and of the body politic. It took little effort, then, to move from "unprotected love bites" back to "unprotected sex," though the sight of George

Hamilton wearing tiny condoms over his fangs in Stan Dragoti's *Dracula* pastiche, *Love at First Bite* (1979), would hardly have been the stuff of Hollywood, horror spoofs or otherwise.

Given this argument, all postmodern praxes on *Dracula*'s themes of blood and sexuality, including Francis Ford Coppola's 1992 film, are "HIV positive," for even if they could not address the subject material directly (Jonathan Demme's award-winning AIDS-inspired film *Philadelphia* would not come out for another year), indirectly they could not have entirely avoided the subject either.[5] Even Coppola admitted to having used vampirism as a metaphor for the spread of AIDS, inserting jump cuts of blood samples being examined under a microscope both to document the new science of blood typing that materialized a few years after Stoker's novel *and* to recall for contemporary audiences the dark truth of HIV-testing being played out all-too-frequently in laboratories across the planet. Van Helsing's comment to his medical students in the operating theatre that "civilization" is becoming "syphilization" (*BSD* 88) is as much a commentary on Coppola's times as it was on Stoker's (who perhaps even died from the disease, as Daniel Farson suggests in his biography of the novelist[6]).

As such, if Keanu Reeves's *ménage à quatre* in Coppola's film could be read as an *ad hoc* call for a return to the free-sex pleasures that would come to define the Bill Clinton administration, Lucy's failed blood transfusions can equally be interpreted as a postmodern gloss on the Red Cross's tainted-blood scandal just then coming to public light. As many critics have already mentioned, several of whom are represented in this book, the blood of every major male character has passed through Lucy's veins, whether directly through Seward's having transfused "the blood of four strong men" (*D* 138) in her (Holmwood's, his own, and then that of Van Helsing and Morris), or indirectly through the bites she receives from Dracula, who has already sucked the blood of Jonathan Harker, not to mention the crew members aboard the *Demeter* and countless other victims. In fact, the blood coursing through Lucy represents the better part of twenty or more men, many of whom are foreigners—a conservative figure at best given the centuries that Dracula, like some nightclub barfly, has been cruising. In more ways than one in Stoker's novel, then, blood *is* patrimony, and its theft (a crime which Dracula also perpetrates in the novel) or contamination provides justification alone for its jingoistic preservation.

If the Victorians believed seriously in the corruption of blood, literal and figurative alike, then the postmodernists have understood it to its fullest, epidemic extent. In the age of AIDS and widespread HIV—that postmodern plague not only of sexual transgression but also, and if not more so, of Third-World poverty and postcolonial wreckage—Dracula seems as poised as ever to haunt humanity. Like some human-size mosquito threatening the spread of bad blood across time and space, Stoker's antagonist, even after a hundred years, has become the perfect metaphor for a planet divided by a common agenda—survival. Stoker's having that evil force chased out of London and potentially killed in the exotic clime from whence it came holds frightening connotations to the manner in which the First World has disproportionately dealt with AIDS at home and in Africa. In the United States, the American Medical Association (AMA) propped up Nancy Reagan's naïve "Just Say No" campaign in the 1980s with a potent AZT cocktail; in Botswana, the population was simply being taught their ABCs: "Abstain, Be faithful, Condomise."

Figure 0-3: AIDS Prevention Billboard in Botswana

The havoc that AIDS has caused throughout sub-Saharan Africa stands as a testament to the colonialist racism we have inherited from our Victorian forefathers and which we, perhaps, practice more virulently. Dracula simply haunted the 1980s as ubiquitously as he had the 1890s, and continues to do so to this day.

"Post/modern *Dracula*" comprises a selection of essays based on papers given at the international conference "Victorian Themes/Postmodern Praxes: *Dracula* from Stoker to Coppola" held at Nancy-Université in France in 2006. While the conference's goal was not to proclaim both works in the name of postmodernism, nor to apply strict postmodernist tools of analysis through which to understand their wide-ranging appeal, certainly one of the residual elements of the conference was—to which each essay in this collection will lay testament—the revelation that *Dracula* is a postmodern novel *avant la lettre*. Instead, the conference had as its main objective the intent of negotiating the two works per their opposing eras in synchronic rather than diachronic terms in order to understand more clearly how the Victorian novel could be viewed in a postmodern light and how the postmodern film could be seen as upholding Victorian aesthetics. To be sure, while postmodernist features in Coppola's *Bram Stoker's Dracula* are readily traceable through his pastiche of the silent film era and of the spaghetti Western, the authors represented in this book will demonstrate, as I have tried to do in this brief preface, how the century that separates the two artists binds them more than it divides them.[7] What are the postmodern elements of Stoker's novel? Where are the Victorian traits in Coppola's film? Is there a postmodern gloss on those Victorian traits? And can there be a Victorian directive behind postmodernism in general?[8] The various essays in this collection will address to some extent these and other pertinent questions per the novel and the film, whether comparatively or separately, at three distinct periods: (post)modern Victorianism, post/modernism (that period neither fully modernist nor consciously postmodern), and finally post-modernism. Therefore, while each essay may concentrate on a particular period of the nineteenth or twentieth century, it keeps postmodernism as its critical touchstone.

    This book is thus divided into three parts, reflecting the movement away from Victorian themes and into modernist then postmodernist praxes. Though scholars of *Dracula* and Gothic literature in general will find some of the essays innovative and engaging per today's literary criticism, the book is also intended in addition for both the informed general reader and the novice student of the novel and of the film. As such, a few essays are highly specialized in postmodern theory, whereas others are more centered around the socio-historical context of the novel and film and use various postmodern theories as inroads into the novel's or the film's study. It is my hope to reach, and please, as many readers as possible.

    Part I on (post)modernist issues in Stoker's novel establishes the link between Victorian themes and postmodern praxes that begins with colonialist concerns and ends with poststructuralist signification. *Dracula* expert William Hughes suggests in his essay, "On the Sanguine Nature of Life: Blood, Identity, and the Vampire," that criticism of the novel alone has been responsible for this paradigm shift in reading the novel's obsession with blood (this preface's epigraph came from the Q/A session after his talk). In examining how the epistemological differences in the notions of materialism and spiritualism at the turn the century sparked a trend in reading blood more in symbolic than in purely materialist terms, Hughes notes:

This inscription of a broadly spiritual value to blood in the novel initiates a principle of signification whereby criticism is enabled to accrete further meanings to the substance, meanings which have often eclipsed the debate upon materialism within the script with the cultural symbolisms current in a society of sanguinity which is paradoxically located within that with sexuality.

Postmodern praxes evident in the novel's criticism have thus turned the novel's central theme of Victorian spirituality into a blood science that, "once brought into pre-eminence in postmodernity," has become "the emblem of a praxis, a preoccupation of the twentieth-century practice of criticism, rather than a theme that is discretely Victorian." At the "heart of *Dracula* criticism," Hughes concludes, "is blood": "If blood means something to those who merely appreciate or defend it, the vampire hunters and the modern critics, then it has quite another set of associations to those who physically consume it."

After charging recent new historicist critics of *Dracula* for having imposed a "Balkanizing" reading on the novel, one that problematizes "the legitimacy and 'naturalness' of traditional conceptual frameworks," Ludmilla Kostova proffers a postcolonial perspective that reads the novel against other "terrorist novels" of the late Victorian era. Joseph Hatton's *By Order of the Czar* (1890), Richard Henry Savage's *My Official Wife* (1891), and L. T. Meade's *The Siren* (1898) all demonstrate a western fascination with "transgressive" Eastern European (anti)heroines who "successfully infiltrate key areas of western life" because they have mastered its cultural codes and understand the workings of its political and economic institutions. Like Stoker's *Dracula*, these terrorist novels were marked by "the constellation of fears" of "reverse colonization" of Eastern Europeans into Great Britain and America. Viewed against this background, Stoker's vampiric Count "stands for the dangers posed by Eastern Europeans without any of the fascinating characteristics of the terrorist *femmes fatales*," thus demonstrating that the closer the East moved toward the West via advances made in communication and in travel, the more it threatened western "purity" and "nativeness" and, paradoxically, the more "foreign" (and thus typed) it became.

Picking up upon this relationship of communication and culture, renowned Gothic scholar David Punter examines in "Bram Stoker's *Dracula*: Tradition, Technology, Modernity" how the complexity of *Dracula* can be found in its engagement with traditional and "modern" means of communication. Contrary to the usual reception of *Dracula* as a traditional Gothic text, Punter argues, *Dracula* is almost aggressively contemporary, both in its habitation of events and in its deployment of means of "recording" those events for the reader. Arguably, this is what gives *Dracula* much of its force and its postmodern appeal; certainly, it is what has provided the basis for much of its filmic potential. We do not experience the plights of the women in the text as matters to do with "long-dead" social and political regimes, Punter concludes, but rather as consequences of modern technological and familial structures, which can be continually remade—just as Dracula is himself, in one sense, continually remade according to the epoch in which he finds himself. In *Dracula*, the dead indeed come to life, not only in terms of content but also in terms of the (narrative) form necessary to house, to reveal, or to bury that content.

Part II looks at the post/modernist concerns in Stoker's *Dracula*, that is, at those issues obviously influenced by modernism but also, with the help of the novel's plasticity vis-à-vis the media over the last century, by postmodernism. To be sure, modernism's rapid advances in science, sociology, and technology laid the groundwork for postmodern inquiries of the novel years later, helping to form a historical continuum between the Victorian novel and its many screen and media adaptations rather than the typical rupture frequently encountered in fin-de-siècle works and their contemporary film treatments.

Punter's notion of Dracula having been made by modernism and remade by postmodernism is explored more fully in Nathalie Saudo's essay, "Every speck of dust [...] a devouring monster in embryo": The Vampire's Effluvia in *Dracula* by Bram Stoker." Saudo argues that *Dracula* can be read as an aesthetic and scientific exploration of the modalities of vampiric circulation that are "determined historically and betray a universal fear of indifferentiation [...]." These modalities, which Saudo calls "vampours," represent the vampire's quest for endless disseminations and mutations. Dracula's effluvia reveal the social fears and scientific queries of the fin-de-siècle—such as the fascination with supernatural forms of communication like magnetic phenomena and mesmerism, and the influence of evolutionary discourse on nascent sociological theory—and create an area where belief and reason, science and superstition overlap. In *Dracula*, however, scientific discourse does not so much legitimatize the narrative as it does unsettle it, which is what gives the novel its postmodern gloss. As *the* Gothic metanarrative par excellence, Saudo concludes, *Dracula* in its preoccupation with vampiric circulation has proven "the ideal playground for the postmodern reader," who has seen that circulation transcend the book's pages to nearly every media form known today.

While Saudo concentrates on how the "body" changes shape and circulates in *Dracula*, Françoise Dupeyron-Lafay looks at how the "body" itself deconstructs the novel. Her essay, "Fragmented, Invisible, and Grotesque Bodies in *Dracula*," posits that *Dracula* is dissimilar from many Victorian narratives in that it offers little in the way of description of its characters' physical appearances. In fact, what evidence the novel does provide of its four young male "heroes" serves only to establish them as the embodiment of a virile and racially pure ideal threatened by the fin-de-siècle specters of degeneration.

Ubiquitous and obsessive, even when invisible or absent, the body is a central theme in *Dracula*, Dupeyron-Lafay contends, becoming the locus of territorial power struggles that arouse ambiguous feelings in the reader. *Dracula*, as a novel of grotesque bodily metamorphoses and anamorphoses, expresses a sense of insecurity, disorientation, and alienation that heralds postmodernism. Cut up and fetishized, the body is thus turned into a synecdoche of evil that, like the fragmented text of *Dracula* itself, gradually builds itself up while the human bodies slowly disintegrate. Like any good postmodern text, Dupeyron-Lafay concludes, the fragmented body is more meaningful or "eloquent" than it would be if it were whole.

 If bodies in the novel become fragmented and fetishized, so too has the myth of Dracula itself, and Monica Girard reveals just how Vlad Țepeș represents today a postmodern commodity about which Romanians themselves are ambivalent. "Teaching and Selling Dracula in Twenty-first-Century Romania" begins with a series of surveys that Girard recently carried out in Romania asking high school students: "What do you know about Vlad Țepeș?" Their answers, which depict the historical figure of Vlad Țepeș as a national hero—a symbol of justice protecting national interests, a defender of the independence and autonomy of his country, and a tireless fighter of Islamism—are based largely on information found in their school textbooks, but also on their exposure to Stoker's *Dracula*. Girard documents how the power of myth over historical fact as it is taught in Romanian schools represents the limits of teaching history when truth becomes so shrouded in temporal mythical references that the boundaries between ancient myth and reality blur, even to the point of contributing to the making of modern Romanian popular culture. Romanians have begun taking advantage of the West's fascination with the Dracula myth and are currently developing an economy based on "Dracula tourism" which paradoxically promotes the stereotypes that, elsewhere, they are trying to debunk. "Selling" Dracula to foreign consumers, Girard concludes, "evinces postmodernism's tendency to produce historicity through the disappearance of the 'real'" by marketing its "simulacrum not as a representation of the "real" but as the real itself," demonstrating clearly how postmodern life imitates art.

 While Parts I and II explore how the novel looks forward to postmodernism, though firmly planted on the cusp of late Victorianism/early modernism, Part III examines more closely the novel's postmodern characteristics, particularly with respect to Coppola's film, *Bram Stoker's Dracula*. Jean Marigny explores the basic paradoxical shifts found in the novel that have been responsible for the paradigmatic shifts in the story as it was transformed to the screen. In simultaneously reproducing and refuting the established ethics and positivism of Victorian society, Marigny argues, *Dracula* foreshadows postmodern literature, epitomized in Coppola's faithful and liberal adaptation of *Dracula* with intertextual references to older "horror" films, particularly Cocteau's *La Belle et la Bête*. As Marigny maintains, "Coppola's rather unusual treatment of *Dracula* can be considered as postmodern in the sense that it is a deconstruction not only of the novel but more generally of traditional horror films."

In "Postmodern Verbal Discourse in Coppola's *Bram Stoker's Dracula*," Jean-Marie Lecomte argues that Coppola integrates voice-over narration, off-screen voices, and invisible narrators with the aesthetics of the Hollywood horror film in an attempt not only to reproduce the various levels of discourse found in Stoker's novel but also to thematize the power struggle fought on the plurivocal screen. Examining the canon of Dracula films over the last century, Lecomte studies how their filmic discourse and "soundscape," or "visual sound," works (or does not) to transmit the necessary "overtones of abstract thought that visual codes cannot express." One of Coppola's achievements in his film is his ability to convince the hearer-viewer that he or she is not merely listening in on cinematic conversations between fictional characters but is in fact at the center of several narrative and discursive stances and, as a result, feels immersed in a visual polyphony. This "verbal allegory," as Lecomte puts it, allows Coppola to create a "postmodern Dracula" who is not merely "reducible to a mixture of figures past" but who, in conjunction with the other filmic Draculas of the last century, is in fact "culture-bound," that is, he reveals "how a community faces death at a given point in time."

While Lecomte concentrates on the film's verbal discourse, Jacques Coulardeau explores its visual discourse, namely the numerous religious symbols that Coppola imports which underscore or contradict the novel's underlying message. "The Vision of Religion in Francis Ford Coppola's *Dracula*; or, Religion in the Postmodern Age" opens with the claim that visually religion is reduced in the film to obvious symbols like crosses and crucifixes, but that cognitively there is a complex undercurrent of religious iconography, numerology, and semiotics at work on the viewer. In fact, the religious dimension to the film works on the level of innuendo, understood meaning, or ideological and cultural allusions present in the audience's collective historical conscience. Coppola inverts Stoker's horror story and turns it into a love story in order to establish his central theme that universal love, not hate, is what will ultimately save humanity from evil. "Assessing the film's Christian dimension reveals its postmodern nature," Coulardeau writes, where "Coppola's desire to push limits but refusal to choose sides in the holy wars" demonstrates his deft ability to reach commercial audiences while challenging religious and ethnic questions that are at the heart of the human divide represented so well in the novel.

I have divided the term "post/modern" in this book's title for various reasons. The most obvious one is that, while postmodern theory may be at the heart of each essay, not all could be classified as "postmodern" per se; that is, not all reproduce the methodology of certain types of essays found in some of the leading postmodern journals of today. If they are postmodern at all, it is because they are founded on the basic principles of postmodern theory as they are revealed to us through *Dracula* (both Stoker's novel and Coppola's film) and through Dracula (the myth and the industry built around it), including:

- Simulacrum from Jean Baudrillard and the "disappearance of the real" (there are so many versions of Dracula in the films that we have strayed far from Stoker's original novel).
- Intertextuality (as theorized by Gérard Genette, for example), with an emphasis on Fredric Jameson's concept of the pastiche and on Jean-François Lyotard's "incredulity" toward metanarratives (or *grands récits*), of which Dracula has become one.
- A foregrounding of irony, not so much to destroy the past in a modernist sense but to revisit it with ironic distance (as Coppola does, not only with respect to the novel but also with reverences to the film industry in general).
- Self-consciousness and self-reflectivity in art (art that is aware of itself as art in a very narcissistic way that de-naturalizes its own content).
- A challenge to the distinction between high and popular art, of which *Dracula* is one of the best examples.
- Fragmentation (not in the modernist sense of lost unity but rather in the postmodern one that celebrates our liberation from a controlling form and exhilarates in eclecticism, randomness, and incompletion).
- "Bricolage" (that patchwork of disparate materials which serves to unify a text), and the blending of literary genres (the diary, the ship's log, etc. in the novel, and the Western, the silent film era, etc. in the film).[9]

These "touchstones" that leave their mark on each essay in this collection are postmodern in spirit, if not in praxis, not because the authors represented here value them more than other aesthetics, but rather because postmodernism can explain more holistically the changes made in the Dracula myth since the dawn of modernism in Stoker's late nineteenth century. Joseph Valente, in *Dracula's Crypt: Bram Stoker, Irishness, and the Question of Blood*, notes that among the future scholarship destined for *Dracula*, postmodernism will figure prominently:

> Far from an underlying motive in Stoker's writing, as has been generally supposed, racialist ideology increasingly forms an object of suspicion, one that anticipates later critiques, post-structural, post-modern, and postcolonial.[10]

Dracula, as this book will collectively argue, defies time entirely and thus promises to undermine any critical study of it that precisely tries to situate it within a given epoch, including a postmodernist one. Given its relationship to late-capitalist economy, to post-Marxist politics, and to commodity culture, and given its universal appeal to human fears and anxieties, fetishes and fantasies, lusts and desires, Stoker's novel will forever seem *modern*—or at least contemporary, as its various transformations in the media, culminating with Coppola's film, have proven. In that sense, *Dracula* is post/modern—always haunting our future, as it has repeatedly done so our past.

No author, or editor for that matter, can claim sole possession of a book's content. As such, I would like to thank Nancy-Université's Department of English, and its research group I.D.E.A. (*Interdisciplinarité dans les études anglophones*), for having provided the funds necessary for the 2006 conference, from which the essays collected here were taken. I would also like to acknowledge the help of the following people: William Hughes, editor of *Gothic Studies* and renowned *Dracula* scholar, for his invaluable advice and keen eye; Jean-Marie Lecomte, for his efficiency in documenting the citations taken from Coppola's film; Thomas J. Schafer, Chief of Communications (IDPH), for his efforts in unearthing the Dracula-related fliers, press releases, and campaign posters that the IDPH used in its 1993 AIDS campaign; and all of my contributors, for the pains they took in recalibrating their conference papers to reflect the book's revised focus. I would also like to thank my editors at Cambridge Scholars Publishing, in particular Andy Nercessian, Amanda Millar, and Carol Koulikourdi. Finally, I would like to thank my wife Nathalie for her love, her patience, and her unwavering support in all my endeavors, academic or otherwise.

To facilitate this book's reading, all references to Bram Stoker's *Dracula* (Norton, 1997) and Francis Ford Coppola's *Bram Stoker's Dracula* (Newmarket, 1992) have been incorporated into the text, with the abbreviations *D* or *BSD* preceding page numbers. All variations between the film's spoken dialogue and its written script have been placed in the notes.

JSB,
Nancy, France
28 February 2007

Notes

1 The criminal trial involving the New Jersey-based Armour Pharmaceutical Company, Dr. Roger Perrault (former medical director of the Canadian Red Cross), two Canadian physicians, and one American physician for failing to properly screen blood that resulted in thousands of Canadians being infected with HIV and hepatitis during the 1980s and 1990s has, by the time of this preface's drafting in February 2007, still to be concluded.

2 Brian Wilson Aldiss, *Dracula Unbound* (New York: HarperCollins, 1991). See also Alexander Renault, "Queer Vampires: Suicide by Sodomy: The Last Quarter of the Twentieth Century and AIDS," available at http://www.queerhorror.com/Qvamp/articles/sodomy_renault.html (1 Oct. 2006), and Antonio Ballesteros-Gonzáles, "Count Dracula's Bloody Inheritors: The Postmodern Vampire," *Dracula: Insémination. Dissémination*, ed. Dominique Sipière (Amiens: Sterne, 1996), 107-19.

3 "If I Can Control Myself, So Can You," Campaign Poster, Illinois Department of Public Services (Springfield: State of Illinois, 1993), P.O. X25898 1750. The campaign, appropriately launched on Halloween at a seasonal "haunted house" at an abandoned hospital in Chicago, included television public service announcements, posters, brochures, transit cards, and billboards. In his press release, dated 30 October 1992, IDPH Director Dr. John R. Lumpkin writes:

> The Illinois Department of Public Health has enlisted Dracula as its new AIDS spokesperson [spooksperson?] to urge Illinois teenagers to "see the light" and learn how to protect themselves against HIV, the virus that causes AIDS.
>
> The message from Dracula: "Stop living in the dark—get the facts about AIDS. When I learned about AIDS, I changed my ways. If I can control myself, so can you! Beware of fly-by-night relationships." (1)

In a January 1993 letter addressed to Public Service Directors, Lumpkin adds:

> We made the unusual choice in selecting Dracula as our new spokesperson, but he isn't the type of Dracula you see in "Bram Stoker's Dracula" [Coppola's then recently released film]. He's a much more benevolent and enlightened Dracula who knows a lot about HIV/AIDS and how to prevent HIV transmission. (1)

See John R. Lumpkin, "AIDS: Facts for Life," Illinois Department of Public Health Press Release, 30 Oct. 1992: 1-2; and John R. Lumpkin, "AIDS: Facts for Life," Illinois Department of Public Health letter, Jan. 1993: 1.

4 See David J. Skal, *Hollywood Gothic: The Tangled Web of Dracula from Novel to Stage to Screen*, rev. ed. (1990; New York: Faber and Faber, 2004).

5 See Carlen Lavigne, "Sex, Blood and (Un)Death: The Queer Vampire and HIV," *Journal of Dracula Studies* 6 (2004), available at http://blooferland.com/drc/images/06 Carlen.rtf (2 Feb. 2007).

6 Daniel Farson, *The Man Who Wrote Dracula* (London: Michael Joseph, 1975). See Audrey Latman, who argues in her essay, "Spilled Blood: AIDS in Francis Ford Coppola's *Bram Stoker's Dracula*," *Latent Image* 10 (Winter 1993), that Coppola "intertwines the 1897 tale with cinematic expressions of 1992's societal horror, AIDS" (n. pag.). See also *Latent Image*, available at http://pages.emerson.edu/organizations/fas/latent_image/index.htm (15 Oct. 2006).

---

7 See, for instance, Carol Corbin and Robert A. Campbell, "Postmodern Iconography and Perspective in Coppola's *Bram Stoker's Dracula*," *Journal of Popular Film and Television* 27.2 (Summer 1999): 40-48.

8 See, for example, Ronald R. Thomas, "Specters of the Novel: Dracula and the Cinematic Afterlife of the Victorian Novel," *Victorian Afterlife: Postmodern Culture Rewrites the Nineteenth Century*, eds. John Kucich and Dianne F. Sadoff (Minneapolis: University of Minnesota Press, 2000), 288-310.

9 Jean Baudrillard, *Simulacra and Simulation*, trans. Sheila Faria Glaser (Ann Arbor: University of Michigan Press, 1994); Gérard Genette, *Palimpsestes: La littérature au second degré* (Paris: Éditions du Seuil, 1982); Fredric Jameson, *Postmodernism, or, The Cultural Logic of Late Capitalism* (Durham: Duke University Press, 1991); and Jean-François Lyotard, *The Postmodern Condition: A Report on Knowledge*, trans. Geoff Bennington and Brian Massumi (1979; Minneapolis: University of Minnesota Press, 1984). See also Linda Hutcheon, *The Politics of Postmodernism*, 2nd ed. (1989; London and New York: Routledge, 2002).

10 Joseph Valente, *Dracula's Crypt: Bram Stoker, Irishness, and the Question of Blood* (Urbana and Chicago: University of Illinois Press, 2006), 25.

Part I: (Post)Modernism in *Dracula*

CHAPTER ONE

ON THE SANGUINE NATURE OF LIFE: BLOOD, IDENTITY, AND THE VAMPIRE

WILLIAM HUGHES, BATH SPA UNIVERSITY

Dracula, as Ken Gelder suggests, is "a highly productive piece of writing." Indeed, "it has become productive *through its consumption*," so that the act of reading embodies not merely the ingestion of the text but the engendering of what Gelder calls "new knowledges, interpretations, different *Draculas*."[1] This academic act of reading, an act which is both complicated and paralleled by the novel's status in popular culture as a text which is predominantly known or seen rather than actually read, underpins *Dracula*'s tense location in the fulcrum-balance between Victorian theme and postmodern praxis. A product of its age as much as of its assumed Gothic genre, *Dracula* is, as critical consensus would have it, shot through with characteristic late-Victorian themes both explicit and encoded. Gelder's words, though, must be borne in mind here. It is arguably impossible to read these themes, selective and spectacular as they are, with any orientation other than that which is given to the reader by postmodern praxis. These themes, and their relative emphasis, are integral to a process of production not wholly located in the nineteenth century. Hence, the continually productive nature of *Dracula* studies ought further to remind the critic that *praxis* is a term which embraces both the existence of an accepted practice or custom *and* the actual practising of an art or skill. Thus, if *Dracula* is as productive of meaning as Gelder suggests it is, then, logically, so is the criticism and commentary, written or cinematic, that surrounds it.

What might superficially be considered Victorian theme is thus absorbed into postmodern praxis, and the practice of criticism is productive in consequence of a customary viewpoint, a consensus that the novel *means* something in terms of, variously, cultural commentary, psychological expression, or symbolic exposure. Indeed, Victorian theme might arguably be said to be nothing more than a projection of postmodern praxis, given that the reviewers of Stoker's own day exhibit little interest in what academic critics have depicted as its quintessentially fin-de-siècle themes of race, disease, and gender, to name but three. Clearly, to these public commentators, the novel was first and foremost a tale of horror, rather than a narrative of the present. Its occult script carries none of the rhetorical charge, apparently, of the conventional invasion narratives cast in the manner of George Chesney's 1871 novel *The Battle of Dorking*, nor indeed that of H. G. Wells's more speculative *The War of the Worlds* (1898). Thus, a reviewer for the *Manchester Guardian* notes that even though "the region for horrors has shifted its ground," Stoker's novel "is often more grotesque than terrible." In common with others, that reviewer regards such anachronisms as the vampire as being "limp and sickly in the glare of a later day," an emphasis which would seem to suggest that the reviewing establishment of 1897 saw no substantive commentary on contemporary issues in Stoker's allegedly topical novel.[2] Similarly, though the superstitious and gruesome content of the work was often derided by British reviewers, no commentator appears to have been outraged enough to comment explicitly upon the sexual parallels in both the symbolism of blood and the seductive invitations issued by the hungry female vampires of both Transylvania and London. This was no Hill-Top or Problem Novel, it seems.

The inappropriateness of the theme of superstition, it appears, preoccupied Stoker's reviewers, the vampire and his sanguine diet arguably being bound up more with that anachronism rather than with the expression of a present crisis. Yet, for all this, as David Punter suggests, "At the heart of *Dracula* (if the pun may be forgiven) is blood."[3] That such themes and equations may signify contextually in the work is beyond doubt. Quincey's concern that Arthur's sexual *jus primae noctis* has been pre-empted by the transfusion of blood in Chapter 12 is as explicit an equation as can be in a mainstream novel. For all this, blood, other than in its status as a gruesome detail rather than a symbolic substance, remains strikingly absent from the reviews of 1897. It becomes, though, once brought into pre-eminence in postmodernity, the emblem of a praxis, a preoccupation of the twentieth-century practice of criticism, rather than a theme that is discretely Victorian. At the heart of *Dracula* criticism, as it were, is blood—blood overdetermined as a psychoanalytical substitute for semen, or as Foucault would have it, a marker in "the order of signs," so that one consciously might in family, nation, or race "be of the same blood."[4] Stoker, arguably, recognises the latter, for in *Personal Reminiscences of Henry Irving* he celebrates the racial connections between the British and the Americans through the phrase "Blood is thicker than water"[5]—though it is seemingly too trite, or too inappropriately deployed, to be commented upon by his contemporaries. The universal fluid, "a reality with a symbolic function," seems curiously unreferenced as a fable in its own time. Even more curious, though, is its uneven deployment as a symbol within *Dracula*—its uneven, as it were, applicability and accessibility in "the order of signs." If blood means something to those who merely appreciate or defend it, the vampire hunters and the modern critics, then it has quite another set of associations to those who physically consume it.

At this point, it is worth turning briefly to a surprisingly neglected 1980 critical reading of *Dracula* by Charles S. Blinderman. Blinderman's reading of the novel considers an evocative substance, "a reality with a symbolic function," as it were, and develops how Victorian culture manages its signification of secular functionality and spiritual imposition. Here, science and religion conventionally oppose each other, though the novelty which Blinderman exposes is the way in which an authoritative scientist, T. H. Huxley, concludes his overtly secular reading of the substance with the suggestion that the application of materialism to such phenomena need not exclude the presence of those less tangible influences conventionally termed "spirit."[6] Indeed, "matter and spirit," Huxley suggests, "are but names for the imaginary substrata of groups of natural phenomena," so that an equation may be forced between the two interpretations, even where the former is preferred over the latter for its precision of examination and terminology.[7] The evocative substance in this case, though, is not blood, but protoplasm, a microbial entity celebrated by Huxley and others as the common denominator of all organic life on earth. Blinderman and Huxley, though, do throw down an implicit challenge for those who read blood far more towards its symbolic than its functional aspect. Though that challenge has been taken up in recent readings of the physiology of the novel, there is still more to be said regarding the relationship between the speculative metaphysics behind the science of Huxley and his contemporaries and the manner in which blood functions as a disputed complex of meanings in the perception of the characters depicted in *Dracula*.

Though Blinderman does not acknowledge it, Huxley is explicit in identifying protoplasm as a basic component, protean in shape and highly active, of human blood ("PBL" 133). This protoplasm merely "differs in detail, rather than in principle" ("PBL" 133) from that contained in plants, though one major distinction separates flora and fauna in the economy which Huxley proposes: "plants can manufacture fresh protoplasm out of mineral compounds, whereas animals are obliged to procure it ready made" ("PBL" 132, 133). The human may thus harvest plant and animal alike for his own sustenance. Echoing the rites of Roman Catholicism for what is presumably a Scottish Protestant audience, Huxley describes his own assimilation of protoplasm:

> A singular inward laboratory, which I possess, will dissolve a certain proportion of the modified protoplasm, the solution so formed will pass into my veins; and the subtle influences to which it will then be subjected will convert the dead protoplasm into living protoplasm, and transubstantiate [food] into man. ("PBL" 137)[8]

Thus arises a circularity of nutrition which Huxley develops somewhat graphically in a flippant reference to his own culinary regime:

> If digestion were a thing to be trifled with, I might sup upon lobster, and the matter of life of the crustacean would undergo the same wonderful metamorphosis into humanity. And were I to return to my own place by sea, and undergo shipwreck, the crustacean might, and probably would, return the complement, and demonstrate our common nature by turning my protoplasm into living lobster. ("PBL" 137)

It is tempting, at this juncture, to recall Stoker's apparently frivolous ascription of the genesis of *Dracula* to a nightmare following on a surfeit of dressed crab.[9] How much might be different, indeed, if that crab had been documented as a lobster, and that any substantive record existed that linked Stoker explicitly either to Huxley or his published lecture.

Things, though, are seldom that convenient, and the only substantial connection between the well-read and culturally aware author and the scientist would appear to be their separate contributions to James Knowles's journal, *The Nineteenth Century*. But if Stoker was not aware of this particular published lecture, he was surely cognizant with the broad debate between secularity and spirituality in which Huxley and many others played a part, and which indeed is mobilised not merely in *Dracula* but in Stoker's later fictional study of death and resurrection, *The Jewel of Seven Stars* (1903). Huxley, teasing the reader with his agnosticism, proposes "a union of materialistic terminology with the repudiation of materialistic philosophy" ("PBL" 141), and this lies, arguably, as much behind the ritual resurrection which Stoker styles as "The Great Experiment" in *The Jewel of Seven Stars* as it underpins Van Helsing's adjustment of conventional clinical hypnotism to a blood-based occult telepathy in *Dracula*. For Huxley— and, in many respects for Stoker also—it is not materialism that is the problem, but rather the utilitarian progress of that doctrine to a point where "matter and law" become "co-extensive with knowledge, with feeling, and with action" ("PBL" 143). Huxley, again, notes the fear of his contemporaries of all persuasions:

> The advancing tide of matter threatens to drown their souls; the tightening grasp of law impedes their freedom; they are alarmed lest man's moral nature be debased by the increase of his wisdom. ("PBL" 143)

This despair anticipates Stoker's somewhat forceful 1909 essay on the censorship of fiction, but its tone of alarm has its parallels in the characterisations of *Dracula* too, and, indeed, in how the characters respond to, and mobilise, the variant values of blood, material and spiritual, within the novel.[10] An excessive materialism, it might be suggested, singularises meaning to the merely utilitarian:

blood is necessary for life, either as a restorative within the bodily economy, or as a supplement from outside. Its symbolism is a secondary, if not irrelevant, consideration.

The portrayed clash of material and spiritual in *Dracula*, though, is far from straightforward. On the one hand, there is a protracted (though at first admittedly reluctant) spiritual commitment where one might least expect it in Victorian modernity—in those who defend the letter of the law, and those committed to the prosaic processes of the physiological body in medicine.[11] Harker seems scarcely aware of the non-biological consequences of spilling blood until his wife is attacked; Seward reads only the physically debilitative effects of blood loss until he perceives the resurrected and hungry Lucy in the churchyard. On the other hand, there is an absolute and all-consuming materialism in the very place where it really ought not to be—in those whose association is with the body mobilised by life after conventional death, a life whose very sentience and mobility raise uneasy questions with regard to the immortality of the soul and the integrity of personality and identity to flesh. Those questions, it would seem, do not spring readily to the singular minds of those who consume blood merely as a nutritive substance.

Between these two extremes, of vampire-hunter and vampire, lies the lunatic Renfield, whose cumulative economic approach to the body aligns him somewhat with Huxley's flippancy. Like Huxley, who eats the lobster whose descendents might well eat him, Renfield will eventually die and, in an age where burial remains the norm even for the indigent and the institutionalised, will decompose, producing grubs and maggots which will in turn feed the spiders and sparrows which a lunatic might eventually eat.[12] The lunatic's programme of consumption is systematic, as Seward learns from the notebook which tabulates the cumulative value of each creature in terms of what it has ingested.[13] When Renfield is taxed by Seward as to what will happen to the souls of the creatures he has eaten, however, the lunatic becomes utterly confused:

> "Oh, it is a soul you are after now, is it?" His madness foiled his reason, and a puzzled look spread over his face as, shaking his head with a decision which I had but seldom seen in him, he said:—
> "Oh, no, oh no! I want no souls. Life is all I want." (*D* 235-36)

Indeed, it is arguable that Renfield's confusion arises from his failure to acknowledge the possibility of a soul, not on theological grounds, but because such an intangible thing cannot be consumed, has no nutritive value, no status in the cumulative life (*D* 236-38). As he says,

> "I don't want any souls, indeed, indeed! I don't. I couldn't use them if I had them! They would be no manner of use to me. I couldn't eat them, or—" (*D* 236)

The soul, if it exists, is the point at which decomposition and reabsorption must stop. Seward is, by his own admission, trying to provoke the lunatic (*D* 235, cf. 61), but it is significant that he uses *this* issue, rather than a more materialistic question of contaminated or diluted blood. The soul is a troubling accompaniment to the otherwise secular disposal of both life and the body. It is, indeed, the same issue of the soul's uncertain destination, translated into the "paths of flame" wherein the immortality associated with the drained cadaver of Lucy might tread, through which Van Helsing enforces the compliance of the reluctant vampire hunters in the mutilation of a familiar body (*D* 184). It is Renfield's perplexity which recalls his humanity, so that he may later pray to an intangible God (*D* 207), and even when rendered unable to speak by the Count's glamour proclaim himself "a sane man fighting for his soul" (*D* 218). This is not a religious conversion, but an epistemological shift.

Count Dracula, however, is quite another matter in that he perplexingly represents both the logical continuation of, and a singular break with, the materialistic philosophy of Huxley and Renfield. Like his opponents, the Count is an animal in the sense of Huxley's lecture, in that he must ingest the secretions of others in order to maintain his longevity—a process testified by his periodically darkening hair and leech-like engorgement (*D* 53). He is a true apex to the food chain, however, in that he does not become in turn consumed. At his demise, his elemental dust is scattered but not absorbed (*D* 325). His flesh nourishes no other creature.

Blood, though, does not have the same meaning for Count Dracula as it does for Renfield. His "special pabulum," as Van Helsing calls it, is "special" only in that "he eat not as others" (*D* 211). Arguably, for him it can be regarded only as food, a secular substance, as it is first for Renfield—though the Count never finds his opinions swayed either by troubling speculations about, or residual memories of, spirituality. For all the spiritual emphases of the novel, its juxtaposition of Continental Roman Catholic superstition with Anglo-American Protestant rationality, the Count never avails himself of the spiritual meanings invested in blood, whether these be the sexual symbols of Quincey Morris or the spiritual ones of Van Helsing. He has been a pupil at the Scholomance or School of the Devil (*D* 212, 263), yet seems to be unaware of his own proselytising activities as detailed by Van Helsing (*D* 273; cf. 278), or indeed of the very existence of the hell to which he has apparently driven Lucy (*D* 193; cf. 183). Though the Count respects the Host, as a biological virus might abhor the presence of bleach, he utters no blasphemies, denies or defies no deities. We have only Van Helsing's word that Lucy has been damned, and only the enshrouding discourse of Christian redemption that colours Mina's gaze to convey meaning to the look which crosses the vampire's face at his dissolution (*D* 325). It is debatable how much meaning, therefore, is invested in blood within the revenant lifestyle itself.

Even when the Count boasts of his conquests in the very face of his opponents, his words might be said to reflect consumption as much as ownership. Significantly, he sees his auditors primarily as food, "like sheep in a butcher's," and the "girls" who "are mine already" have been absorbed into his body, making them not explicitly damned but merely secondary predators in a pecking order with himself at the head: they are already "my creatures, to do my bidding and to be my jackals when I want to feed" (*D* 267).[14] The vampire blood which Mina ingests prior to this does not feed her, nor does it damn her, but it does establish that contact which makes her the Count's jackal and his earpiece. His intoned words, "flesh of my flesh, blood of my blood, kin of my kin" (*D* 252) do suggest a marriage ritual, but the first two remain firmly anchored in the incorporation of substance, an appetite further underscored by his reference to her as "my bountiful wine-press" (*D* 252). Van Helsing, too, seems to evade the sexual improprieties that may be symbolised in such an act by depicting the event as a baptism rather than a marriage or seduction (*D* 280). The Count's boast is, in any case, somewhat shallow and premature. Of the two girls he mentions, one is dead, even to him, the other very much alive, and still motivated by a spirituality vested in blood which is as potent as his own secular reading of it in terms of hunger and fulfilment.

Because the Count loses what is effectively a conflict between two different ways of viewing the body, the materialistic meaning of blood becomes secondary in the novel to that of its status as a signifier of spiritual import. Though other significations, particularly those of race and family, are present, the spiritual would seem to predominate—not always theologically, but certainly in consistent opposition to the secular. Life becomes again finite—the body rots, but the spirit lives on. That persistence is something to be celebrated, for it recalls that humanity is again perceptible as being more than simply food, more than protoplasm that may decompose and be reabsorbed as minerals for plants, as blood for vampires. This inscription of a broadly spiritual value to blood in the novel initiates a principle of signification whereby criticism is enabled to accrete further meanings to the substance, meanings which have often eclipsed the debate upon materialism within the script with the cultural symbolisms current in a society of sanguinity paradoxically located within that with sexuality. That much is as true of the revision of the novel in film as it is in criticism, though *Bram Stoker's Dracula*, Francis Ford Coppola's 1992 adaptation does, because of its historicised preface to the narrative, re-engage the issue of blood and the Count's appreciation of that substance.

Because of the presence of Elisabeta, the name a teasing pointer, of course, to the Hungarian Countess who commodified blood as a cosmetic, the cinematic Count loses his blind materialism, and gains a direction of purpose not present in the novel.[15] Though his initial awareness of the apparently re-incarnated wife of Jonathan Harker would appear to be the result of an accident, it lends specificity to his invasion far beyond the mere satisfaction of an appetite for blood among the nameless "teeming millions" of London (*D* 53). Though the blood which flows from the abused cross on the occasion of Elisabeta's suicide advances an obvious religious symbolism, the Count's renunciation of Christianity and presumed alliance with the Devil are somewhat less stressed across the length of the film than they are, for example, in Alan Gibson's *The Satanic Rites of Dracula* (1974). Indeed, in Coppola's film, the Count's novelistic child-brain and bovine appetite are discarded in favour of a reticence and discrimination which stops him drinking from a prone Mina at the cinematograph. This is a reticence, in other words, that lies within the self, and which betrays the notion that the cinema character has an awareness of what that bite might actually lead to, what that exchange of bloods might actually achieve. Again, it is worth emphasising that it is the bite, rather than the visual presence of blood, which underscores the relationship between the cinematic Count and his nineteenth-century victims. The blood, notably, flows copiously in the Count's presence only at the religiously explicit Dark-Age outset of the film. Later incidents of predation are characteristically marked by more modest stains and spillages upon the body of the individual, even where an act of mutual ingestion has taken place. Contemporary sexuality apparently demands a far more direct signifier than blood, the latter being too easily associated with disease. The bite, it would seem, is that signifier.

The praxis that is criticism, drawing as it does upon the preoccupations of a secular world in which blood has attained new meanings and sexuality an enhanced predominance, appears to have thus shifted the Count's late Victorian materialism. In Coppola's adaptation, he is seemingly as aware of the symbolisms vested both in blood and in the bite as his opponents have been historically—though those meanings betray the expansion of signification that has been brought to blood by the practice of criticism. Though the Count still stands outside of the food chain, consuming though not decaying, he has gained similar qualities to those who oppose him, qualities, namely, of insight, of the marital symbolism of the vampire relationship, and of the value of the human as integrated body and soul rather than nutritive substance. The Count and his opponents have never been so close, even though his desire for Mina/Elisabeta is possibly more selfish and exclusive than the original defence of Harker's wife as scripted in Stoker's novel (*D* 210).

Blood, as David Punter suggests, continues to lie at the heart of *Dracula*, and, indeed, at the heart of its criticism also, though it has to be said that Coppola has given that heart a somewhat romantic palpitation. What needs to be emphasised, though, is that the complex of meanings that circulate within blood is even more complex than it might first appear, its status as a reality with a symbolic function demanding, more than ever, a recognition of the reality as much as the function. If a vampire is outside of society, then surely, the argument runs, he will not, or cannot, appreciate blood as a cultural signifier in any sophisticated way. If the vampire were given a voice to express the meaning of blood, that meaning may well differ significantly from that held by those who oppose, or who celebrate, his mission of ingestion and consequent colonisation. Stoker's Count is denied access to the surface of the text, being represented only by a fragment of writing and the observations of his mortal opponents. He cannot speak of blood, but is spoken for, and in language that is contaminated by the human perspective on his diet. Coppola's Count, though revisionist and vocal, does not speak blood in the manner in which Stoker's own Dracula would have it.

Notes

1 Ken Gelder, *Reading the Vampire* (London: Routledge, 1994), 65, original italics.
2 *"Dracula*, by Bram Stoker," *Manchester Guardian*, 15 June 1897, 9. Elsewhere, the *Pall Mall Gazette* celebrates the contextual commonplaces that locate the novel in modernity, but reads it primarily as horror fiction, as does the *Glasgow Herald* and *The Bookman*. The latter two celebrate the resemblance to Wilkie Collins's writings, though neither recalls the "mission" so easily associated with that novelist's epistolary fiction. See "For Midnight Reading," *Pall Mall Gazette*, 1 June 1897, 11; *"Dracula*, by Bram Stoker," *Glasgow Herald*, 10 June 1897, 10; *"Dracula*, by Bram Stoker," *The Bookman*, 12 August 1897, 129.
3 David Punter, *The Literature of Terror: A History of Gothic Fictions from 1765 to the Present Day* (London: Longman, 1980), 256.
4 Michel Foucault, *The History of Sexuality*, vol. 1: *An Introduction*, trans. Robert Hurley (London: Penguin, 1984), 147.
5 Bram Stoker, *Personal Reminiscences of Henry Irving*, 2 vols. (London: William Heinemann, 1906), 1:327.
6 Charles S. Blinderman, "Vampurella: Darwin & Count Dracula," *Massachusetts Review* 21 (1980): 411-28.
7 T. H. Huxley, "On the Physical Basis of Life," *The Fortnightly Revie*, 1 February 1869, 143, 145. All subsequent references are taken from this edition and appear parenthetically in the body of the text abbreviated "PBL."
8 Huxley's article is the text of a lecture delivered in Edinburgh on Sunday, 8 November 1868, and organised by the Rev. J. Cranbrook.
9 This story was first popularised in Harry Ludlam's *A Biography of Dracula* (1962). Paul Murray has recently uncovered the original source of Ludlam's ascription in a 1957 letter from the author's son to his biographer. See Paul Murray, *From the Shadow of Dracula: A Life of Bram Stoker* (London: Jonathan Cape, 2004), 171.

10 Compare, for example, Huxley's comments on the value of volition in human enterprise ("PBL" 145), with those advanced by Stoker in his 1908 essay for *The Nineteenth Century*, "The Censorship of Fiction," reprinted in Bram Stoker, *A Glimpse of America and Other Lectures, Interviews and Essays*, ed. Richard Dalby (Westcliff-on-Sea: Desert Island Books, 2002), 159-60.

11 Mental health in *Dracula* is, incidentally, largely premised on the physiological medicine of W. B. Carpenter and others. See William Hughes, *Beyond Dracula: Bram Stoker's Fiction and its Cultural Context* (Basingstoke: Macmillan, 2000), 139-51.

12 James Stephens Curl notes that burial as a practice began to decline in England from the 1880s, though the choice of cremation or urn burial was still regarded as somewhat eccentric until well into the twentieth century. See *The Victorian Celebration of Death* (Stroud: Sutton, 2001), 107.

13 "Whole pages of it are filled up with masses of figures, generally single numbers added up in batches, and then the totals added in batches again, as though he were 'focussing' some account, as the auditors put it" (*D* 69).

14 Cf. (*D* 252), where Mina is depicted in a future life both as "companion" and "*helper*" (my italics).

15 See Tony Thorne, *Countess Dracula: The Life and Times of Elisabeth Báthory, The Blood Countess* (London: Bloomsbury, 1997), passim.

CHAPTER TWO

STRAINING THE LIMITS OF INTERPRETATION: BRAM STOKER'S *DRACULA* AND ITS EASTERN EUROPEAN CONTEXTS

LUDMILLA KOSTOVA, UNIVERSITY OF VELIKO TURNOVO

As the indisputably "canonical" text of late Victorian (and later) vampire fiction, Bram Stoker's novel *Dracula* has decidedly benefited from the collapse of traditional standards of "literariness" and the opening up of literary criticism to wider domains of critical writing. The novel, as a consequence, has generated a phenomenal number of readings. This has been attributed to, among other things, "the uncanny ability of its central figure to call forth a diverse and even mutually contradictory set of symbolic associations."[1] Behind Dracula's "uncanny" versatility, we can detect the "aggregate" nature of his monstrosity, which thriftily "condense[s] many [negative] traits into one [Gothic] body."[2] On the whole, the book's interpreters have tended to "consume" that monstrosity through hermeneutic models evoking wide and symbolically resonant areas such as sexuality. Writing in the early 1990s, Ken Gelder singled out the sexual theme as the central topic of the novel's critical readings.[3]

Significantly, during the twentieth century's closing decade, politics became a prominent element in interpretations of *Dracula*, without, however, completely replacing sexuality. By and large, political "concretizations" of Stoker's text tend to engage with three major themes: Ireland, the British Empire, and Eastern Europe as perceived by the western gaze. Needless to say, there are numerous thematic overlaps in/between individual critical readings. This essay will examine some interpretations belonging to the third category before presenting a reading that similarly foregrounds the text's engagement with Eastern Europe.

Recent critical gazes on *Dracula*: from reading to re-writing

Interpretations highlighting Dracula's Eastern European identity and the significance of the novel's Transylvanian setting exemplify a well-established tendency in postmodern critical writing to problematize the legitimacy and "naturalness" of traditional conceptual frameworks by recovering forgotten or repressed contexts, (re)discovering intertextual links, and thus accounting for the cultural work that texts do. The majority of those readings are likewise linked, in varying degrees, to the tremendous political changes that occurred in Eastern and Central Europe in 1989 and in the 1990s: the collapse of repressive communist regimes, the dismantlement of the "Eastern bloc," and the disintegration of Yugoslavia. One of the consequences of the political shifts has been the re-invention of the cultural-symbolic map of Europe through the revival of pre-WWII patterns of perception of the "old" continent's regions. Thus, military conflicts in Yugoslavia and general economic instability in post-communist South Eastern Europe led to the re-emergence of the Balkans as a geopolitical metaphor for backwardness, barbarism, and tribalism.[4] In the process, Bram Stoker's *Dracula* was repeatedly invoked both in western commentaries on the region and in work by local intellectuals. It is my intention here to examine some of the key aspects of the Gothic text's extensive application to South Eastern Europe and its discontents.[5] To my mind, this critical practice poses methodological questions about the limits (and limitations) of the interpretation of literary *oeuvres* and of their contextualization in historical and geographical terms. Things are further complicated by the symptomatic presence of factual errors and inaccurate statements in some of the readings under consideration, which later interpreters have carelessly reproduced in their own work.

My examination starts with Stephen Arata's 1990 essay "The Occidental Tourist: *Dracula* and the Anxiety of Reverse Colonization."[6] This text does not explicitly identify the novel's setting as Balkan, but it may be said to have paved the way for later *Balkanizing* readings. I also look at Vesna Goldsworthy's section on *Dracula* in *Inventing Ruritania: The Imperialism of the Imagination* (1998), two articles from the journal *Connotations* (1999–2001) by Eleni Condouriotis and Carol A. Senf respectively, and Tomislav Z. Longinović's highly symptomatic application of the book to the Balkan condition.

Stephen D. Arata's essay exemplifies the thematic overlap I mentioned earlier. It is as much concerned with issues of Empire and imperialism as with the novel's Eastern European (anti)hero and setting. The author begins by stressing the importance of situating late nineteenth-century Gothic narratives such as *Dracula* in "the historical context in which these works were written and originally read."[7] Stoker's text, in his opinion, "enacts the period's most important and pervasive narrative of decline, a narrative of reverse colonization."[8] He distinguishes between stories of "reverse colonization," which involve infiltration by "'primitive' forces [. . .] originat[ing] outside the civilized world," such as in H. Rider Haggard's *She* (1887), and "invasion scare" or "'dynamite' novels" premised on the rivalry between Britain and other "Great Powers" or on "articulat[ing] a middle-class fear [. . .] of foreign revolutionaries [. . .] and of [the] industrial underclass."[9] In both cases, privileged imperial space is threatened and/or polluted by the plans and/or actual presence of undesirable aliens.

The critic perceptively links Stoker's novel to the genre of travel writing, itself a vehicle for cultural and political commentary. However, he does not, I feel, base his interpretation of the text's Transylvanian setting on sound historical research. For example, Arata claims that the setting was "part of the vexed 'Eastern Question' that so obsessed British foreign policy in the 1880s and '90s"[10] but fails to explain how Transylvania as an eastern province of the Habsburg Empire is related to a series of events that primarily had to do with the political destiny of Ottoman Turkey and its successor states.[11] As it happens, there *was* a connection: the Habsburg government feared that the disintegration of the Ottoman Empire and its replacement by smaller nation states might provide a stimulus for nationalism in its own multiethnic provinces and thus bring about the demise of Austria-Hungary. Transylvania was one of those provinces, and its "polyracial character"[12] is foregrounded in Stoker's novel, as is the fact that German, the Empire's official language, is the main vehicle of communication between the local people and Jonathan Harker.[13] There is no indication in *Dracula*, though, that any particular ethnic group in the province is contemplating secession from Austria-Hungary. To be sure, Arata's vague reference to the "Eastern Question" only serves to stress Transylvania's vaguely *Oriental* location, and this is a point to which I will return in my commentary on Senf's article.

Moreover, Arata's argument that Transylvania is an appropriate setting for Stoker's vampiric fantasy because of its multiethnic diversity is supported by a passage from Charles Boner's 1865 travelogue *Transylvania; Its Products and Its People*, which refers to the Habsburg capital of Vienna rather than to the Empire's eastern province.[14] While the point about the lack of ethnic uniformity in the region is valid, and Stoker's text certainly verifies the connection between vampiric transgression and "polyracial" chaos, Arata's questionable accuracy and his offhand treatment of a source, which he himself identifies as "the standard Victorian work on [Transylvania],"[15] are serious flaws that detract from the value of his arguments. Significantly, in his 1994 commentary on the cultural symbolism of vampiric fiction and film, Ken Gelder negligently reproduced Arata's misreading of Boner's *Transylvania*.[16]

Notwithstanding its inaccuracies, "The Occidental Tourist" is full of insights, such as Arata's observation on Dracula's Occidentalism, which is of paramount importance as a hermeneutic element that alerts us to the Count's cultural hybridity.[17] Most of the author's critical apparatus comes from postcolonial theory, which he successfully applies to a *part* of the ambiguous terrain of South Eastern Europe. As was remarked above, Arata does not attempt to extend his reasoning to the rest of the region. Vesna Goldsworthy, however, has aptly reminded us that South Eastern Europe did not experience "conventional" colonial domination by the West but was nonetheless subjected to "the imperialism of [its] imagination," which turned parts of it into "exotic backdrop[s] in travelogues and tales of romance, adventure and political intrigue."[18] The 1990s witnessed the trend to theorize South Eastern Europe via postcolonial studies. In the process, Dracula turned into a "crucial Balkan metaphor"[19] epitomizing western exclusion of the region and its denizens from Europe "proper."

Goldsworthy's reading, which reiterates Arata's emphasis on the Count's Occidentalism, has greatly contributed to the establishment of this tendency. In all fairness, however, it should be stressed that she herself meticulously qualifies Dracula's (and *Dracula*'s) "Balkanness" in her *Inventing Ruritania*. Goldsworthy relates Stoker's novel to "a gradual [. . .] move [within European Gothic writing] towards a Balkan setting" as "places in Italy and Spain [became] too familiar to function as successful Gothic locales."[20] The critic emphasizes the "imaginary" quality of *Dracula*'s Transylvanian setting[21] and its author's syncretistic labor in "piec[ing] together an exotic historical amalgam" of a variety of textual sources.[22] Goldsworthy admits that not all of Stoker's sources "deal[t] with the Balkans."[23] On the basis of this, one may well ask if the novel's setting really stands in a relation of symbolic synonymy to the Balkans, as is suggested by the title of Goldsworthy's chapter, "*The Balkans* in Popular Fiction" (my emphasis). In the manner of the *Ruritania* of her book's title, *Dracula*'s setting appears to fit other, notably *Central European*, localities as well.[24]

Events in former Yugoslavia led to a deepening of the sense of crisis in Europe. What was at stake was the conventional sense of *Europeanness* itself. As violence escalated, references were repeatedly made to the Ottoman past of Yugoslavia and, indeed, the whole of South Eastern Europe, thus problematizing the myth of the "old" continent's tradition of dominant Christianity. Bram Stoker's text was drawn into the ongoing debates, and scholars from South Eastern Europe especially tended to equate its resident demon with the historical figure of Vlad Ţepeş.[25] Eleni Condouriotis's "*Dracula* and the Idea of Europe" exemplifies this problematic historicizing. She draws attention to a "preoccupation in the novel with [the] repressing [of] historical discourse" and goes on to argue that the repression is "selective" and "target[s] the Ottoman history of Eastern Europe."[26] Moreover, in her view, the "delegitimation" of that area of European history happened at a time "when the nations newly emerging from Ottoman rule challenged the idea of Europe that had been defined through the Concert of Europe"[27] in the early nineteenth century. Condouriotis's reading is thus closely linked to the Eastern Question. She does not merely mention this tangled network of historical events but attempts to examine its political implications for the British Empire and the "old" continent as a whole.

Condouriotis is at her most perceptive when she alerts us to the absence from Stoker's novel of specific references to what must have been recent European history for the author and his contemporaries, such as the 1876 Bosnian and Bulgarian atrocities and the Russo-Turkish War of 1877–78 and its political aftermath. In this respect, *Dracula* markedly differs from Stoker's later Balkan fantasy, *The Lady of the Shroud* (1908), which is by far more sensitive to current history and politics. However, it is difficult to accept Condouriotis's claim that "Stoker's reinvention of the historical figure [of Vlad Ţepeş] [was] driven by his desire to disclaim [. . .] medieval, Christian Europe, reemerging into modernity, monstrously out of date."[28] Further on, she maintains that since it had become "politically untenable" for Eastern Europe to be left to "linger behind the 'Iron Curtain' of the Ottoman Empire," it had to be "refigured" and "brought under the cultural influence of Western Europe [. . .] without the traces of Ottomanization."[29] While such a scenario may appear plausible within the context of late nineteenth- and early twentieth-century Balkan cultural history, there is little in Stoker's novel to support it.[30] Dracula does refer to his epic battles with the Turks but mostly represents them as evidence of his superior strength and courage. He does not portray himself as a champion of Christianity so much, despite a brief reference to "the shame of Cassova" (*D* 34), i.e. Kosovo, but rather as a powerful warrior matching his might against that of the Turks (*D* 34-35). For Condouriotis, he is "an Ottomanized European" and "a blasphemous Christian hero."[31] Indeed, both South Eastern European history and folklore preserve the memory of such "impure" figures, and the historical Vlad Ţepeş may well have been one of them.[32] Bram Stoker's *Dracula*, though, is not cast in such a role. Nor is there any ground for linking him to the Ottoman reformer Abdul Aziz, who was the Empire's 32nd *Sultan* (not its *Grand Vizier*, as Condouriotis claims[33]) and ruled between 1861 and 1876.[34]

Condouriotis's thoughts on *Dracula* (and Dracula) are characterized by ingenuity and originality. All the same, one wonders whether what she presents is not, after all, a *re-writing* of the novel to fit the standards of latter-day historiography of the Balkans rather than a critical *reading* of it. Bram Stoker's text does relate to "the idea of Europe" in significant ways, but to uncover some of those, we need to adopt a more precise historicizing approach to it and its literary contexts, as well as to take into account Dracula's "aggregate" monstrosity. As was pointed out above, the text's monster calls up a wide range of associations, and anchoring him firmly in a particular historical area invariably produces an impoverishing effect.

In her response to "Dracula and the Idea of Europe," Carol A. Senf commends Condouriotis for drawing attention to "the East" as "a *region* [sic] that the West continues to ignore at its peril."[35] She identifies Arata as the first critic to refer to the Eastern Question but offers no comment on the absence of proper historical contextualization in his reading. Senf is right in stressing the "mysteriousness" of the Eastern Europe that Stoker presents in *Dracula* and the fact that it is "more mythic than real."[36] What she fails to take into account, however, is that the mythologizing that went into producing the novel's Transylvania is meaningful and needs to be analyzed further. In fact, "the Idea of Europe" of Condouriotis's title has a lot to do with that transformation of observed and represented reality into myth.

Senf does not accept the parallel Condouriotis makes between Dracula and Abdul Aziz but is not bothered by the historical figure's faulty identification as *Grand Vizier*.[37] I find this transference of unverified references troubling (cf. Gelder's reproduction of Arata's mistake). In my view, it indicates that despite the enduring critical favor for (new) historicism, learned commentators do not always pay sufficient attention to sources and facts. Moreover, Senf's elision of differences between Transylvania and the larger geographical terrain of Eastern Europe (or "the East," as she terms it) implies that such differences for her are negligible. The implication may not be intentional, but that *is* likewise culturally meaningful.

Tomislav Longinović's "Vampires Like Us: Gothic Imaginary and 'the serbs' [sic]" identifies *Dracula* as a "narrative elaboration of past European traumas."[38] Like Condouriotis, the author assumes that the novel's vampire is identical with "Vlad Dracul Tzepesh [sic]" and that Stoker's text is part of an attempt to "erase" the area of Europe's past marked by "the arbitrariness of Islamic rule."[39] Overall, the article is an extended meditation on South Eastern Europe's historically determined victimization, by the West no less than by the Ottoman Orient. In the process, Longinović transforms memorable episodes from *Dracula* into allegories of the West's incomprehension of the Balkan condition or of Balkan intellectuals' willful suppression of ultra-nationalism and other morally unacceptable aspects of their native legacy. The allegorizing strategy is illustrated by passages such as the following:

Not unlike the vampire, the West cannot see its own reflection in the mirror of Balkan temporality, and it buries its fears of intrusion from the East in the dark chambers of Dracula's castle. Intellectuals in "Other" Europe, meanwhile, were always torn between the mirror of the West and their own "nativist" tendencies. Also like the reflection of the Transylvanian count, the "nativist" drives of the nationalist elites were better obscured and buried deep in the cellars of medieval castles.[40]

Longinović thus re-writes Bram Stoker's text to make it accommodate his own ideas on global (in)justice. Significantly, he tries to wring compassion for "the unfortunate count, who is formed by the colonial gaze of the West which senses the presence of its own bloodthirsty past reflected in [. . .] the vampiric imagination."[41] This interpretive maneuver brings the author fairly close to Prince Vlad's representation in Coppola's 1992 film, which similarly stresses the Eastern European (anti)hero's victimization and aims at invoking empathy—if not sympathy—for him.[42] From Longinović's perspective, empathy for the Count should help the international critical audience, for whom his essay is intended, to gain a historically informed understanding of the Balkan situation and the ideological uses of vampirism and thus overcome its media-induced anti-Serb prejudices.

"Balkanizing" re-writings of Bram Stoker's novel and its central character, such as Longinović's, tend to repeat a conflationist interpretive maneuver, which is to be found in some of the region's western representations as well. The maneuver in question has to do with "the issue of adjacency by which the neighboring lands of [South] Eastern Europe [are] associated" and which is "dramatized to suggest a sort of [shared] geographical destiny."[43] As a result, territories in the region are assumed to be largely interchangeable and turn into "Balkan 'everycountries.'"[44] While later popular fiction and film were to make use of Dracula (and of *Dracula*) in just this way, Bram Stoker did not. Therefore, critical representations of "the king vampire" as an all-Balkan (anti)hero do not so much as unmask western denigration of the region as they do perpetuate the tendency to erase distinctions and facilitate over-generalizations about its different parts.

On the other hand, "Balkanizing" interpretations attempt to fill in certain "gaps" in Stoker's text. Thus, a representation of Dracula as a champion of the Christian cause might well explain his desire to "satiate his lust for blood" among London's "teeming millions" (*D* 53) as a reaction to Britain's betrayal of that cause at, for instance, the 1878 Congress of Berlin.[45] The British delegation at the Congress favored the continued Ottoman presence in Europe and thwarted Russia's plans for the establishment of a larger Bulgarian state in the Balkans. However, it is also possible to account for Dracula's apparently unmotivated desire for "revenge" (*D* 267) on his western opponents by concentrating on his literary antecedents as a Gothic villain of extraordinary malignancy. Apart from being based on presumptions about political views that Bram Stoker never expressed, interpretations that seek to read specific historical references into a text that is reticent about recent history and politics in South Eastern Europe invariably limit its suggestiveness.

Overall, *Dracula* focuses on the diagnosis and eradication of a highly objectionable form of Eastern European monstrosity by a group of westerners ironically identified by Christopher Craft (and employed throughout this book) as "the Crew of Light."[46] As we saw, contextualizing the clash between the Crew and their supernatural opponent can be a tricky proposition insofar as some of the frameworks provided by recovered/uncovered contexts can reduce the text's ideological complexity to a cluster of privileged meanings congruent with the critic's own political and/or ethical agenda. Despite those and other perils of interpretation, I propose to recover yet another Eastern European context for Stoker's novel.

Viewing *Dracula* through terrorist spectacles

The context in question is provided by what may be termed late nineteenth-century British and American *terrorist fiction*. The term was not used at the time but seems nonetheless an appropriate descriptor for a popular literary subgenre, which represented transgressive figures from Eastern Europe that successfully infiltrated key areas of western life.[47] The three novels I have selected for comparison with *Dracula* are Joseph Hatton's *By Order of the Czar. The Tragic Story of Anna Klostock, Queen of the Ghetto* (1890), Richard Henry Savage's *My Official Wife* (1891), and L. T. Meade's *The Siren* (1898). In singling them out for discussion, I am following Arata's advice of situating *Dracula* in "the historical context in which it was written and originally read." Unlike the text's "Balkanizing" interpreters, I am positioning my reading within a predominantly *literary* context, albeit one with distinct *political* implications.

The political implications in question are closely bound up with "a distinct constellation of [. . .] fears"[48] and anxieties in the fin-de-siècle Anglo-American public sphere.[49] Despite British and U.S. traditions of isolationism, readers on both sides of the Atlantic could no longer feel safe from political violence that appeared to be ubiquitous. The British directly experienced the Fenian bombing campaign of 1884–85 that was known to have been planned and financed in America. More to the point, both Britons and Americans were aware of acts of terrorism taking place in continental Europe, such as the 1880 assassination of the Russian Tsar Alexander II. Moreover, fears and anxieties were fueled by the rapidity with which political violence was covered by the international media. Throughout the nineteenth century, communications had developed at an amazing speed. Apart from the "wide network of railways, steamers and telegraph lines"[50] binding all Europe together, the "old" and "new" worlds were finally joined in 1866 via a telegraph cable that was laid across the bottom of the Atlantic Ocean. The existing state of affairs tended to produce an incipient *global consciousness* as traditional contrasts between *home* and *abroad*, relative safety and unavoidable danger, were increasingly problematized.

Both Stoker's novel and these three works of terrorist fiction are preoccupied with boundaries and their transgression. This may be related, *inter alia*, to what was perceived, in the 1880s and 1890s, as *an influx* of Eastern Europeans into the West and, specifically, into the industrial cities of Great Britain and of the United States. A considerable number of those immigrants were Jewish, who had to leave the Russian Empire on account of pogroms and discriminationist legislation following the assassination of Alexander II. However, there was also an exodus of Jews from Romania and Austria-Hungary.[51] Not all immigrants were politically committed enemies of tsarism or any of the other repressive political regimes in continental Europe. One suspects that economic motives played a major role in the process of migration. While the press and popular fiction writers tended to be above all resentful of the crowds of economic migrants to Britain and the United States, they were fascinated by educated, upper-class political émigrés from Eastern Europe. Even a cursory look at the *Brooklyn Times, Harper's New Monthly Magazine, The North American Review, The Atlantic Monthly*, and *The New Englander and Yale Review* reveals a focus on Russian Nihilism and "Cosmopolitan Anarchism,"[52] as well as on the role played in them by upper-crust rebels. Some of the articles that appeared in those American editions had previously been printed in the British press or were intended for a mixed Anglo-American readership.[53]

Anxieties over the destiny of upper-class political émigrés and, generally speaking, the destiny of a world in which tyrannical foreign empires persecuted well-educated, cultured, and enlightened individuals found expression in fin-de-siècle works of terrorist fiction such as the three novels listed above. *By Order of the Czar* was inspired by an article that appeared in the *Brooklyn Times* in 1887 (see note 52), whereas *My Official Wife* was produced by a best-selling American author, but enjoyed considerable success in Europe.[54] *The Siren* was published a year after *Dracula*, thus proving that the preoccupation with the Eastern European presence in the West did not wane as the 1890s drew to a close.

All three novels focus on glamorous female terrorists who issue out of Eastern Europe, are filled with strong hatred of Russian autocracy and other forms of political repression, and introduce elements of chaos into the otherwise orderly lives of the westerners that they come into contact with. These politically committed *femmes fatales* are made particularly dangerous by the exceptional qualities they are portrayed as possessing: they are "excellent linguists,"[55] are quite above average in intelligence, and manage to exercise self-control in the most stressful situations. The worldly American narrator of Richard Henry Savage's *My Official Wife* envies the poise of "the Nihilist who could write philosophy while handling a dynamite bomb."[56] Like the Occidentalist Count, the female "revolutionists" are represented as culturally hybrid figures insofar as they come from European regions assumed to be backward and primitive and are related "by blood" to their indigenes but have acquired the superior knowledge and accomplishments of the West. They are thus borderline characters positioned between Eastern Europe and the West. A major part of their power lies in their "mirroring back" of some of the West's key cultural and political practices.[57]

Whether or not Stoker was familiar with terrorist fiction remains conjecture. However, he could not have avoided the numerous articles about Eastern European émigrés and immigrants that the press poured out. That he disapproved of Nihilism and anarchism is borne out by the negative references to them in *The Lady of the Shroud*, whose Nordic superhero Rupert Sent Leger places them, together with the New Woman, among the incurable ills of modern civilization.[58] While I do not intend to impose a purely "revolutionist" identity on Dracula, I believe that there are meaningful parallels between him and the central figures of terrorist fiction. As I pointed out above, the novels' terrorist (anti)heroines embodied anxieties about the destiny of the modern world. Physically attractive, highly talented, and well educated (though victimized by a tyrannical system), the female "revolutionists" invoked sympathy in the West, which, however, did not completely occlude their potential for sexual trouble and manipulation. These glamorous women were portrayed as both victims and victimizers insofar as they ruthlessly exploited the western men who fell under their spell. Western attitudes to them were therefore marked by strong ambivalence. Viewed within this context, Bram Stoker's vampiric Count represents the dark side of those attitudes. He stands for the dangers posed by Eastern Europeans without any of the fascinating characteristics of the terrorist *femmes fatales*. A comparison between Dracula and the (anti)heroines of the novels listed above, along the lines of gender, sexuality and power, should bear out my inferences.

Commenting on ideologically determined social and racial hierarchies, William Ian Miller recognizes the facile tendency, in critical writing, to equate states of subordination with feminization.[59] He claims that this "gender model is better at explaining certain styles of hierarchy than others" and draws attention to the "threatening style[s] of masculinity" characteristic of some traditionally "low" groups whose "manner [. . .] reveal[s] the *feminization* of the *men above them*."[60] Miller's reasoning is partially relevant to the representations of gender relations in the four novels under discussion. However, those representations have little to do with some "threatening" form of masculinity but are instead characterized by a disruption of the conventional masculine/feminine binary. One of the consequences of the disruption is the effective humiliation of the novels' upper-class western male characters. In some cases, their degradation takes the form of feminization but, as will be shown, in *Dracula*, it even goes beyond that, as the pillars of patriarchy are first likened to dead animals and then threatened with the imposition of a menial, animal-like identity in the future.

The central female characters of the three terrorist novels problematize conventional distinctions between femininity and masculinity. Anna Klostock of the eponymous novel, Helene Marie (*My Official Wife*) and Vera Nugent (*The Siren*) are all portrayed as glamorously beautiful women, whose femininity is irreparably flawed. Anna starts her career as a Nihilist by killing the Russian general who raped her and had her brutally flogged. The traces of the flogging are literally *written* on her body, which is disfigured by "deep ridges and welts, [. . .] angry patches of red, and weird daubs of gray."[61] Helene Marie, who is motivated by both hatred of Russian autocracy and a desire to revenge her Jewish mother's humiliation and death at the hands of the Russians, always carries a "little bulldog revolver" which she threatens to use even upon the American narrator.[62] Vera Nugent is exhorted by her Nihilist mentor, Countess Fedora, to follow the example of historically renowned "phallic" women such as Joan of Arc and Charlotte Corday.[63] Besides, as a "siren" she appeals sexually to both men and women.[64] An attractiveness that cuts across masculine/feminine gender lines is also characteristic of Helene Marie.[65]

The gender indeterminacy of the three terrorists is represented as a function of their political involvement. They are contrasted with a number of "ordinary" British, American, and Russian women, whose femininity is not in any way problematic. What makes the terrorists particularly dangerous is the *feminizing* effect they have on the western men with whom they come into contact. As a result, the westerners either perform acts that are conventionally gendered "feminine" or fail to assert their masculinity in situations that call for such an assertion. Thus, Anna Klostock's British admirer, Philip Forsyth, faints when she reveals her disfigured back to him and to her fellow-conspirators.[66] Colonel Lenox, the American narrator of *My Official Wife*, is incapable of making love to Helene Marie when she offers herself to him.[67] His impotence is glossed over as a sign of his unswerving adherence to the gentlemanly code.[68] Vera Nugent openly admits that she possesses a fatal "power of fascination" which causes "victims to fall along the way."[69] Her British cousin Frank, an officer in the elite Coldstream Guards, is one of the "victims" that she reduces to a state of quasi-feminine passivity. It is important to bear in mind that the three (anti)heroines do not merely embody the male fear of the feminine on which psychologists and psychoanalysts have so often commented.[70] Rather, they have an enervating, *feminizing* effect on upper-class western men because of their own gender indeterminacy, that is, because they are definitely not *feminine* women in the conventional sense.

Stoker's vampire defies traditional cultural oppositions and hierarchies, but critics have been particularly attentive to his disruption of the masculine/feminine dichotomy. Despite the assumption that the novel's villain is of the masculine gender, there are traits that link him to femininity and female power. His name, as Christopher Craft has reminded us, is as seductively misleading as Honoré de Balzac's (and Roland Barthes's) Sarrasine.[71] It has been suggested that Dracula shares some of the attributes of Kali, the blood-drinking Mother Goddess of the Hindu pantheon.[72] Anne Williams has further linked the monster to other terrible feminine figures, such as Circe and Hecate.[73] His resemblance to the savage goddesses of classical paganism should also account for his fear of garlic, a phallic, "spear-leek" plant that was considered to be displeasing to them.[74] However, an identification of the monster as a Terrible Mother is bound to be almost as problematic as his identification as a Terrible Father who must be killed by his sons (in this case, his western opponents led by Van Helsing) in accordance with the Freudian model of tribal survival. It should be noted that Dracula is demonic precisely because the gender polarities through which human civilization (really or supposedly) operates cannot be used to describe his "personality." This lack of fixity is also signaled by his sexuality, which is non-phallic but penetrative, and thus definitely goes beyond the masculine/feminine binary.

Moreover, the Count possesses seemingly irrepressible barbaric vigor, which manifests itself in his ability to reproduce his monstrous self through the bodies of countless number of women. Significantly, his vampiric progeny inherits his gender indeterminacy, as is borne out by his three Transylvanian daughters/brides whose soft, red lips conceal sharp, penetrating teeth. In the context of the novel, Dracula's unholy fecundity contrasts with the sexual lassitude of his western opponents. Only one of them, the Briton Jonathan Harker, proves capable of fathering a child. The other members of the "Crew of Light" are portrayed as childless.

Despite his paternity, Harker's conduct is marked by numerous signs of feminization. Thus, in the course of his encounter with Dracula's "voracious harem,"[75] he assumes an attitude of passive expectancy, which is conventionally stereotyped as "feminine." After Harker's return from Transylvania, Mina finds that "the very essence of [his] strength is gone" (*D* 143) and remarks upon his "nervous fit[s]" and "lapse[s] into forgetfulness" (*D* 155, 156). She comments also on his reaction to the rejuvenated Count in the following "emasculating" terms: "[t]he *poor dear* was evidently terrified at something—very greatly terrified; I do believe that if he had not had me to lean on and to support him he would have *sunk down*" (*D* 155, my emphasis). To an age obsessed with "race," degeneration, and the fall of empires to the extent that the late Victorian period was, such "emasculation" could appear very disconcerting. While Dracula's ability to prey upon British women is an oblique comment on the growth of degenerative tendencies in Britain, Harker's feminization directly signals the decline of the nineteenth century's most powerful empire.

By contrast, Dracula's sexual voracity is closely bound up with his ambition for absolute conquest. The ambition is expressed in a speech addressed to the "Crew of Light" in which he taunts his opponents with their weakness:

> "You think to baffle me, you—with your pale faces all in a row, like sheep in a butcher's. You shall be sorry yet, each one of you! [. . .] My revenge is just begun! I spread it over centuries, and time is on my side. Your girls that you love so much are mine already; and through them you and others shall yet be mine— my creatures, to do my bidding and to be my jackals when I want to feed." (*D* 267)

The Count first humiliates the "Crew of Light" by denying them a human status. He claims that they are "like sheep at a butcher's" (*D* 267), that is, not even live animals but slaughtered ones hanging from the meat hooks and therefore reduced to mere "thingness." The comparison implies that Dracula himself is in a position of power: he is active, whereas the pale-faced westerners are passive and helpless. Through his superior sexual power, the Count has already deprived them of their "girls," but this is only the beginning of his domination over their world. Dracula does not aim at merely appropriating their territory or material wealth. He is determined on transforming everyone, irrespective of his/her gender, into a subservient "jackal" that would do his "bidding" and provide "food" for his boundless appetite(s). The vampire's "jackal" is the absolute antithesis of the sovereign individual of the liberal tradition. Whereas the self, envisioned by the liberal imagination, operates through free choice, Dracula's creatures would be incapable of proper action.[76] Their chief "virtue" would be absolute obedience. Their existence would be a function of the master's will. This is a terrifying vision of absolute unfreedom, which clearly anticipates Orwell's dystopias.

The manipulative *femmes fatales* of the terrorist novels already live in a world of unfreedom. They are opposed to Russian autocracy and its corrupt menials, on the one hand, but, on the other, together with their associates, enact scenarios that emphatically deny the value of human life and free choice. Helene Marie proclaims that her "life is [her] country's" and so is her "honor if need be."[77] When Vera Nugent questions the tasks that her Nihilist cell imposes upon her, she is cynically told that she is completely dispensable and her life is worthless: "[w]hat is one girl's life when we consider the millions who suffer?"[78] Total dedication to the cause motivates the female "revolutionists" in everything they do. Their condition is marked by a paradox: on the one hand, they appear to be "liberated" from the constraints of conventional femininity while, on the other, they enjoy fairly little freedom insofar as they are under the total control of the secret societies they belong to. These societies compel them to restrict the freedom of others through sexual seduction and manipulation, thus hoping to extend their own power over governments, empires, and the world at large. As a result, the female terrorists are fully comparable to Dracula's "jackals." They are the agents of a future dystopian state.

Both the vampiric Count and the female "revolutionists" pose grave dangers to western society's political and moral foundations. The four novels carry an unequivocally conservative message: to ward off further trouble, the Supermonster and the unruly women are to be incapacitated. Curiously, their incapacitation takes the form of gender fixing. Dracula is submitted to what Christopher Craft has ironically called "corrective penetration,"[79] which involves the puncturing of the monster's heart with a sharp object such as a stake. The sexual implication of the act is obvious: it aims at fixing the vampire's gender as *feminine* and thus resolving the category crisis caused by his dangerous bending of the masculine/feminine binary. This is also a way for the members of the "Crew of Light" to reassert their repeatedly problematized masculinity and proclaim their dominant position.

The terrorist women are not staked though the heart, but they, too, are reduced to passivity or inaction, which are symbolically synonymous with "proper" femininity. Anna Klostock is arrested by the tsarist police and permanently exiled to Siberia. Helene Marie is drugged into unconsciousness to prevent her from shooting the Tsar. Vera Nugent commits suicide as she finds it impossible to murder her own father and assassinate the Tsar with bouquets of poisoned roses. Through the incapacitation of the female terrorists, patriarchal society re-establishes the masculine/feminine binary as the norm and, to all intents and purposes, precludes its further disruption.

Conclusion

The similarity in conflict resolution in all four novels does not signal transference of narrative elements from one text to another. Rather, it is indicative of "the constellation of fears" and anxieties I mentioned earlier. It does not matter much whether those fears and anxieties were caused by an exaggerated image of "reverse colonization" or by an equally exaggerated impression of the influx of Eastern Europeans into Great Britain and America.

As Horkheimer and Adorno have demonstrated for anti-Semitism, hatred and resentment of the Other (unfortunately) provide fuel for the "ritual[s] of civilization."[80] However, texts such as *Dracula* and the three terrorist novels discussed here do not simply enact civilizational rituals of hate and resentment, nor separate "native" from "foreign" once and for all. As Judith Halberstam has demonstrated, such texts are also concerned with their unavoidable proximity and with the consequent disappearance of the "purity of [national] heritage and lineage."[81] The disturbing Other may be removed or destroyed, but the trace of his/her presence remains. It is tempting to judge critical readings by the number of traces they have managed to recover/uncover by situating texts in different contexts and straining the limits of interpretation.

Notes

1 Michael Valdez Moses, "The Irish Vampire: *Dracula*, Parnell, and the Troubled Dreams of Nationhood," *Journal x* 2.1 (1997): 68.
2 Judith Halberstam, "Technologies of Monstrosity: Bram Stoker's *Dracula*," *Victorian Studies* 36.3 (Spring 1993): 334. I owe the idea of the novel's "consumption" by its critics to Halberstam's article.
3 Ken Gelder, *Reading the Vampire* (London: Routledge, 1994), 66.
4 On the "disappearance" of the Balkans from Europe's mental map during the Cold War era, see Michael Haynes, "The Rhetoric of Economics: Cold War Representation of Development in the Balkans," *The Balkans and the West: Constructing the European Other, 1945–2003*, ed. Andrew Hammond (Aldershot, England and Burlington, VT: Ashgate, 2004), 26-30.
5 There is an ongoing controversy over the use of the terms "South Eastern Europe" and "Balkans." For a lucid commentary on the terms and some of their contextual implications, see Maria Todorova, *Imagining the Balkans* (London and New York: Oxford University Press, 1997). In this chapter, I am going to use both terms interchangeably.
6 Stephen D. Arata, "The Occidental Tourist: *Dracula* and the Anxiety of Reverse Colonization," *Victorian Studies* 33 (1990): 621-45. The essay was subsequently included in Arata's book *Fictions of Loss in the Victorian Fin de Siècle* (Cambridge: Cambridge University Press, 1996). All my references are to the earlier version of the text.
7 Stephen Arata 621.
8 Stephen Arata 623.
9 Stephen Arata 623-24.
10 Stephen Arata 627.
11 For commentary on the "Eastern Question," see Barbara Jelavich, *History of the Balkans*, 2 vols. (New York: Cambridge University Press, 1983). By the 1890s, the "Eastern Question" had gained new complexity as the Ottoman Empire's successor states

laid claims to territories that either remained under Turkish rule or were governed by Austria-Hungary.

12 Stephen Arata 628.

13 Cf. "I found my smattering of German very useful here; indeed, I don't know how I should be able to get on without it" (*D* 9).

14 Charles Boner, *Transylvania; Its Products and Its Peoples* (London: Longman, 1865), 1.

15 Stephen Arata 629.

16 See Ken Gelder 14.

17 Stephen Arata 637.

18 Vesna Goldsworthy, *Inventing Ruritania: The Imperialism of the Imagination* (New Haven: Yale University Press, 1998), x.

19 Misha Glenny, "Only in the Balkans," *London Review of Books*, 29April 1999, 9.

20 Vesna Goldsworthy 76.

21 Vesna Goldsworthy 80.

22 Vesna Goldsworthy 81.

23 Vesna Goldsworthy 81.

24 For commentary on the relationship between Hope's Ruritania and the Balkans, see Ludmilla Kostova, "Theorising Europe's 'Wild East': *Imagining the Balkans* and *Inventing Ruritania*," *The European English Messenger* 10.1 (Spring 2001): 71-73.

25 The classic statement of the equation is provided by Radu R. Florescu's and Raymond T. McNally's *Dracula, Prince of Many Faces: His Life and His Times* (Boston, Toronto, and London: Little, Brown, 1989). For a critical perspective upon it, see Elizabeth Miller, *Dracula: Sense and Nonsense* (Westcliff-on-Sea: Desert Island Books, 2000), as well as Andrew Smith's review article, "Bringing Bram Stoker Back From the Margins," *Irish Studies* 9.2 (2001): 241-46.

26 Eleni Condouriotis, "Dracula and the Idea of Europe," *Connotations* 9.2 (1999–2000): 143-44.

27 Eleni Condouriotis 144.

28 Eleni Condouriotis 153.

29 Eleni Condouriotis 153.

30 For commentary and a bibliography on South Eastern European scenarios of de-orientalization, see Ludmilla Kostova, "Claiming a 'Great Briton' for Bulgaria: Reflections on Byron's Bulgarian Reception (1880s–1920s)," *Byron: Heritage and Legacy*, ed. Cheryl Wilson (New York: Palgrave, forthcoming).

31 Eleni Condouriotis 153.

32 On the use of "villains" in the Balkan cultural imaginary, see Keith Brown, "Villains and Symbolic Pollution in the Narratives of Nations," *Balkan Identities: Nation and Memory*, ed. Maria Todorova (London: Hurst, 2004), 233-52.

33 Eleni Condouriotis 154.

34 On Abdul Aziz, see the *Encyclopaedia Britannica*, 11th Edition, now a publication in the public domain.

35 Carol A. Senf, "A Response to 'Dracula and the Idea of Europe,'" *Connotations* 10.1 (2000–2001): 48, my emphasis. Senf's discourse is occasionally marked by a cavalier usage of symbolic-geographical terms such as "East" and "West," which, in my view,

denotes dubious knowledge of geography. Nor is this tendency restricted to her writing only. Thus, in his *Reading the Vampire*, Ken Gelder situates Transylvania between "Western Europe and the Far East" (1).

36 Carol Senf 51.

37 Carol Senf 49.

38 Tomislav Z. Longinović, "Vampires Like Us: Gothic Imaginary and 'the serbs,'" *Balkan as Metaphor: Between Globalization and Fragmentation*, ed. Dušan Belić and Obrad Savić (Cambridge, MA and London: The MIT Press, 2002), 39.

39 Tomislav Longinović 39, 40.

40 Tomislav Longinović 45.

41 Tomislav Longinović 45.

42 For a clarification of that aspect of the film, see Christopher McGunnigle, "My Own Vampire: The Metamorphosis of the Queer Monster in Francis Ford Coppola's *Bram Stoker's Dracula*," *Gothic Studies* 7.2 (Nov. 2005): 172-84.

43 Larry Wolff, *Inventing Eastern Europe: The Map of Civilization on the Mind of the Enlightenment* (Stanford: Stanford University Press, 1994), 185.

44 K. E. Fleming, "*Orientalism*, the Balkans, and Balkan Historiography," *American Historical Review* 105.4 (2000): 1218.

45 Matthew Gibson makes such a claim in yet another "Balkanizing" reading. See his "Bram Stoker and the Treaty of Berlin," *Gothic Studies* 6.2 (Nov. 2004): 236-51. It may be argued, however, that the Congress of Berlin was not the only occasion on which Britain supported the Ottoman Empire and thwarted Russian plans favoring the Balkan Christians.

46 Christopher Craft, "'Kiss Me with Those Red Lips': Gender and Inversion in Bram Stoker's *Dracula*," *Speaking of Gender*, ed. Elaine Showalter (New York and London: Routledge, 1989), 226. Though the expression does not appear in Stoker's novel, it has become a stock expression to describe Dracula's pursuers, perhaps because Coppola used it in his film.

47 On the use of "terrorist fiction" in a similar context, see David Trotter, "The Politics of Adventure in the Early British Spy Novel," *Spy Fiction, Spy Films and Real Intelligence*, ed. Wesley K. Wark (London: Frank Cass, 1991), 33-38.

48 Daniel Pick, "'Terrors of the Night': *Dracula* and Degeneration in the Late Nineteenth Century," *Critical Inquiry* 30 (1988): 71.

49 On the conception of a shared Anglo-American public sphere in the 19th century, see Michelle Hawley, "Harriet Beecher Stowe and Lord Byron: A Case of Celebrity Justice in the Victorian Public Sphere," *Journal of Victorian Culture* 10.2 (Winter 2005): 233.

50 David Trotter 33.

51 See Jules Zanger, "A Sympathetic Vibration: Dracula and the Jews," *English Literature in Transition* 34.1 (1991): 34, and Carol Margaret Davison, *Anti-Semitism and British Gothic Literature* (Houndmills, Basingstoke, and New York: Palgrave, 2004), 120-27.

52 My reference is to an article in the *Brooklyn Times*, which describes a group of "Russian Nihilists, Polish Liberators, French Communards, German Socialists, and *Cosmopolitan Anarchists* [my emphasis]" (Hatton 271), who were forced to leave their native countries and re-settle to New York. The article provided inspiration for British

journalist Joseph Hatton's novel, *By Order of the Czar. The Tragic Story of Anna Klostock, Queen of the Ghetto* (London: Hutchinson and Co., 1890).

53 A good example is provided by the work of Henry Norman (1858–1939), who was on the staff of the *Daily Chronicle* but also contributed to American publications.

54 American novelist Richard Henry Savage (1846–1903) enjoyed an international reputation, and his books were circulated throughout Europe by the Leipzig-based publisher Tauchnitz. For further details, see Ludmilla Kostova, "Love and Death Across Cultures: Richard Henry Savage's *In the Old Chateau, a Story of Russian Poland* and Late Nineteenth-Century American Images of Eastern Europe," *Dialogues: American Studies in an International Context*, ed. Milena Katzarska (Plovdiv: Zombori, 2002), 199-206.

55 Joseph Hatton 271.

56 Richard Henry Savage, *My Official Wife* (Leipzig: Bernard Tauchnitz, 1891), 127.

57 On the use of "projection theory" in critical readings of *Dracula*, see Carol Margaret Davison 142-44.

58 Bram Stoker, *The Lady of the Shroud* (1908; London: Alan Sutton, 1994), 330.

59 William Ian Miller, *The Anatomy of Disgust* (Cambridge, MA and London: Harvard University Press), 253.

60 William Ian Miller 253, my emphasis.

61 Joseph Hatton 357.

62 Richard Henry Savage 160.

63 L. T. Meade [Elizabeth Thomasina Smith], *The Siren* (London: F. V. White & Co., 1898), 75-76.

64 L. T. Meade 110, 129, 145, 276, 277.

65 Richard Henry Savage 138, 140, 142.

66 Joseph Hatton 357.

67 Richard Henry Savage 109.

68 Richard Henry Savage 109.

69 L. T. Meade 129.

70 See, for instance, William Ian Miller, 100-5.

71 Christopher Craft 227.

72 Anne Williams, *Art of Darkness: A Poetics of Gothic* (Chicago and London: The University of Chicago Press, 1995), 123.

73 Anne Williams 131.

74 Anne Williams 131.

75 Carol Margaret Davison 137.

76 On Stoker and liberalism, see David Glover, *Vampires, Mummies, and Liberals: Bram Stoker and the Politics of Popular Fiction* (Durham and London: Duke University Press, 1996).

77 Richard Henry Savage 109.

78 L. T. Meade 73.

79 Christopher Craft 230.

80 Qtd. in Carol Margaret Davison 165.

81 Judith Halberstam 349-50.

CHAPTER THREE

BRAM STOKER'S *DRACULA*: TRADITION, TECHNOLOGY, MODERNITY

DAVID PUNTER, UNIVERSITY OF BRISTOL

In this essay, I want to examine some ways in which *Dracula*, perhaps somewhat surprisingly, can be considered not as a text of the Gothic (although of course it is that) but as a text of what has sometimes been considered to be Gothic's opposite: namely, modernity. In doing so, I shall not address very many moments in the text itself, a text with which readers are all very familiar; I shall instead circle round the text, offering some perspectives which might throw the text under a slightly different light.

I shall begin with five hypotheses about modernity. I am considering modernity here not in the limited sense implied by, for example, the twentieth-century movement of modernism but rather as a phenomenon which occurs in all ages and indeed in all cultures, and which is therefore as relevant to the "moment" of the late nineteenth century as it might be to, for example, a consideration of D. H. Lawrence, T. S. Eliot or Ezra Pound.

1. Modernity signifies a difference or escape from the past; but also, more crucially, it is not the same as "the present." It is therefore always different from "what is"; it comes to challenge stasis and to point up the ways in which even the present is passing away under the tides of the new. In most cases, indeed, it would be fair to say that modernity is also "different from itself"; we cannot point to a particular age and identify exactly what is, or what was, "modern" in that age because since the modern is the essence of what is resistant to canonisation and codification it will always produce itself in the form of a plethora of projects and programmes, linked in part by their ability to shock and challenge the established order. *Dracula*, I would say, was such a work of "shock"; despite its recuperative features, it lays down a challenge, a challenge, we might say, to the limits of the human.

2. Modernity has a particular relation to culture, including the literary. This is because culture is always striated by the past and the future; where the world of labour may thrive on stasis and the need for stability in order to assess and fulfil economic need, the world of culture exists in part as a testing-ground of possibilities. Some of those possibilities, as it were, "take," as the Dracula "myth" appears to have "taken" and developed over the centuries; the moment of modernity will, again, be marked by a resistance to being confined by pre-existing notions of the limits of the human, just as *Dracula* tests what human forces may be necessary in order to rebut the forces which continually threaten it.

3. Modernity will very often have a complex relation with the "foreign." At the most obvious level, this is because cultures evolve at different rates in different places; thus "imports" of foreign artefacts (even if as strange as Dracula's coffin), whether these are from other cultures perceived as "civilised" or from ones perceived as "primitive," will often be crucial as a way of voicing that within the host culture which might otherwise appear unable to be voiced. In this respect, there will always be something uncanny about modernity, some sense that it is in opposition to the *heimlich*, that with which we feel "at home"; modernity challenges us, as it were, in our own homes, it reminds us of other, frequently more disturbing possibilities of perception, and, as in *Dracula*, it decentres and destabilises our everyday domestic assumptions.

4. The modern takes its place variously as an opposition to the "ancient," the "archaic," the "classical," but it cannot live without a certain encounter with these forms. This encounter can take many paths: it may involve an absorption of the past, as in the case, for example, of Henry Moore's sculptures; it may involve a recasting of past symbols, as in the emblematic case of the series of Francis Bacon's paintings known as the "Screaming Popes"; it may at least *appear* to reject the "representationalism" of the past altogether, as in much abstract painting. But an encounter with the past there will always be, even if only, in T. S. Eliot, with the fragments and remnants of that past, shards which, like the undead, have been stripped of their original meanings but which will nevertheless not "go away," will never leave a cleared cultural site on which the modern can make a truly new beginning. We might say that this has been the fate of *Dracula*; even though the text asserts supremacy over the forces of the undead, it has of course mainly been the figure of the vanquished Count which has lived on.

5. Modernity always and everywhere has a political dimension; it is consequently also inseparable from economic and technological conditions and developments. Walter Benjamin in his crucial essay "The Work of Art in the Age of Mechanical Reproduction" (1936) suggests that the moment of modernity is the moment at which the work of art loses its "aura," its uniqueness, becomes reproducible, but we may say that the history of western culture is striated by many such moments, from the invention of the printing-press through to the

current possibilities for representation offered by the graphics of cyberspace. Modernity will, however, according to Benjamin also participate in a more general condition of culture, namely the obliteration of the grounds of its own production; there will be something phantomatic to it, something which is, like the ghost or the vampire, both haunted and haunting, progressive and nostalgic. Thus even a text like *Dracula* is not free from commentary on the means of literary production; indeed, as I shall suggest, this is a theme with which it engages with astonishing persistence.

One of the most critical moments in the history of modernity in the West is, as Jean-François Lyotard points out in *The Postmodern Condition,* the "enlightenment" of the eighteenth century; but although obviously the enlightenment dealt ostensibly in the rule of reason and order, the banishing of ghosts and demons, the relegation of belief and prejudice to an older anthropological realm, nonetheless it would be fair to say that the mutual involvement of enlightenment and the trace of the ancient reaches a kind of apotheosis in Mary Shelley's *Frankenstein* (1818). *Frankenstein* is usually, of course, taken to be a novel emblematic of the fate of an overreaching technology, of a use of science so quasi-divine in its attitude that it inevitably produces its own disastrous fate. The actual scenario of the novel, however, is more complex than that. For one thing, it is framed within the narrative of one Walton, who is a kind of romantic explorer of previously unknown regions and hardly an archetype of cool reason. For another, the sort of overweening, Promethean search for knowledge which Mary Shelley apparently criticises is probably represented as much by her husband, the arch-romantic poet Percy Shelley, as by any particular scientist, and so the question of enlightenment becomes less than clear. And for a third, although it appears that in the person of Victor Frankenstein, the author may be wishing to criticise science and technology, such—inevitably for a young woman in the early nineteenth century—was her lack of knowledge of scientific discourse and practice that the actual processes in which Victor engages in the construction of his monster owe—as he himself says—as much to the archaic world of alchemy as they do to more "modern" regimes such as galvanism. What is "constructed" in *Frankenstein* is, in one sense, "new"; but it is simultaneously a threading together of the remnants of the past, of the charnel-house.

Frankenstein's take on modernity, then, is curiously oblique, and reflects some of the paradoxes and contradictions to be encountered in Enlightenment thinking in general. These tensions continue throughout the nineteenth century—in, for example, Tennyson's premonitions of a technologised future[1]—but here we need to turn to a specific moment towards the end of that century when, in a variety of forms, modernity again comes to the forefront of the public imagination. Here in the 1880s and 1890s, for example, we come upon a plethora of fictional scientists engaged in dubious modernising processes. One of the best-known of them, of course, is the central figure in H. G. Wells's novel, *The Island of Doctor Moreau* (1896), who is an arch-moderniser, a new kind of scientist who strives to bring modern discoveries to bear on age-old problems; his ambition is nothing less than to force the animal kingdom into some kind of semblance of human shape. In this sense, the arguments in *The Island of Doctor Moreau* about modernity have strong and continuing connections with the present day, with the critical exception, perhaps, that Moreau is—more or less—a lone scientist, whereas more contemporary arguments about genetics and embryo cloning would focus more on the role of, for example, the giant corporation and its ability to defy both law and "natural" morality.

The end of the nineteenth century also, of course, saw another modernising challenge. It took most obviously the form of the "New Woman," by which we may signify the emergence of a debate about gender equality which, again, has ramifications down to (and no doubt beyond) the present day, and which forms another of the keystones of the complex edifice which is *Dracula*. Here again, *Dracula* forms a kind of "test-bed" for competing arguments and sensibilities, between modernity and tradition, between an order which might be perceived as emerging towards the future and one which remains firmly embedded in the past.

Frankenstein, as is well-known, is subtitled "The Modern Prometheus"; here, at the other end of the nineteenth century, we might see its natural counterpart *Dracula* as also, and perhaps more startlingly, addressing issues about modernity. We might consider, for example, the issue of degeneration in *Dracula*, the fear often expressed in the text that the danger awaiting modern man is of returning down the evolutionary spiral. It would be difficult to overestimate how pressing a fear, in the wake of Darwinian revelations about human kinship with the apes, this was towards the close of the nineteenth century. One of the major figures in this debate was Max Nordau, whose book *Degeneration* was translated into English in 1895 and contains passages such as the following:

> One epoch of history is unmistakably in its decline, and another is announcing its approach. There is a sound of rending in every tradition, and it is as though the morrow would not link itself with to-day. Things as they are totter and plunge, and they are suffered to reel and fall, because man is weary, and there is no faith that it is worth an effort to uphold them. Views that have hitherto governed minds are dead or driven hence like disenthroned kings, and for their inheritance they that hold the titles and they that would usurp are locked in struggle. Meanwhile interregnum in all its terrors prevails; there is confusion among the powers that be; the million, robbed of its leaders, knows not where to turn; the

strong work their will; false prophets arise, and dominion is divided amongst those whose rod is the heavier because their time is short.[2]

It is of course easy to see in this rhetoric echoes of biblical apocalypticism, but there are other traces here which relate, as they also do so often in Bram Stoker, to a fear of modernity. For the "morrow" not to link itself with today it would, presumably, have to be *totally* different; the anxiety here is of a future emerging for which we are not prepared, which will catch us by surprise; a realm of the future, perhaps, even what we might now call a realm of science fiction, for which we have no maps, in which we shall not know where to turn for guidance. The apparent battle, again, between the divinely sanctioned—"enthroned"—forces of the past and the "usurpers" who may come to challenge this "divine right" can be represented as a battle between those forces which resist the challenge of modernity and those, unexplained and inexplicable as they may be, who represent this dangerous path into an uncertain future. What is particularly interesting about *Dracula* is the way in which this struggle is enacted within the text; of course in one sense, Van Helsing and his team represent the modern, while the Count stands for the unremitting pull of the past; yet we might also say that the pull towards the future and the modern equally represents a return to safe domesticity, while it is Dracula himself who suggests the possibility of exploring hitherto unknown realms.

What we may deduce from this, then, is another significant paradox about modernity. On the one hand, modernity asserts the dominance of— scientific or rational—knowledge; it promises to banish the dark places of the mind, to lay the ghosts to rest and to exterminate the monsters. But on the other, it beckons us towards an unknown future, where old certainties will no longer hold and old writs will no longer run. Modernity is thus deeply imbricated in what we might fairly call an uncanny struggle between knowing and unknowing, between a notion of restrictive certainty and one of libertarian doubt. It is certainly this "libertarian doubt" which afflicts Nordau:

> Men look with longing for whatever new things are at hand, without presage whence they will come or what they will be. They have hope that in the chaos of thought, art may yield revelations of the order that is to follow on this tangled web. The poet, the musician, is to announce, or divine, or at least suggest in what forms civilisation will further be evolved.[3]

What Nordau is in part calling attention to here is the value assigned to sheer— or mere—novelty; he is predicting, with perhaps uncanny accuracy, a condition of society in which the "new" has credibility in and of itself, and in which the business of looking into its credentials, its provenance, is short-circuited by a kind of overarching glamour. What is at least as interesting here, however, is the role he ascribes—with, of course, the utmost suspicion—to the artist as the avatar of modernity. It is for the artist to "announce, or divine, or at least suggest" the future—even though, of course, these three verbs carry very different freights of meaning on a spectrum of presumed creative authority.

To return to *Dracula*, the next point to make is that *Dracula*, perhaps as a matter of surprise to the first-time reader, is replete with references to technological advancements. In her edition of the text, Glennis Byron quotes Jonathan Harker, referring to his shorthand diary: "It is nineteenth century up-to-date with a vengeance."[4] She goes on to say:

> The claim could equally be made of *Dracula* itself. From telegraphs, typewriters, and telephones, to shorthand, phonographs, and kodaks, Bram Stoker's *Dracula* flaunts its modernity: it is concretely embedded in the ever-growing late Victorian world of information technology. [. . .] Newspaper cuttings, telegraphs, ships' logs, journal entries, letters, interviews—all come together in the typescript Mina produces in triplicate. Even Dracula is aware of the need to collect data and avidly seeks the power it confers.[5]

One of the interesting features of this list is that many of its elements are technologies which are used for communication *at a distance*, as the Greek root "tele-" indicates. The modernity of *Dracula* thus consists, at one rather formal level, of the representation of a stage of evolution or progress which allows for an escape from the domestic or national confines of the traditional novel; and I would add, although Byron does not quite say this, that this element of progress stands in stark contrast to the figure of Dracula himself, who signifies a clinging to older roots of power. Seen in this light, the novel ends by demonstrating the superiority of modern technology over older ways of life: the replacement of an order of power based on the "ancient house," in all senses of that word, by a different order; and the replacement of a surviving aristocracy by a technocracy, the "Crew of Light," focused on the scientist figure of Van Helsing but also, and importantly, including a representative of America, symbol of a new age, in the calm, reasonable form of Quincey Morris. Behind this there also lies the notion of a power based on extreme individualism—the Count, despite his absorption in his own familial history, is in one sense the last of his race—being supplanted by a power based on modern, quasi-democratic concepts of teamwork and cooperation: no one individual is strong enough to withstand Dracula, but the kind of working together permitted by new technologies permits a flow of information which eventually proves successful in the quasi-epic struggle.

It is, however, worth noticing that the flow of modernity runs in two directions in the text, and this moves us on to gender issues. As has often been said, the role of women in *Dracula* is deeply ambiguous. To an extent, they are portrayed as passive victims, even as the weak spot in the team's armour; on the other, there is a sense in the novel that one reason why they need to be rigidly controlled is precisely because of a fear that they might become, indeed, "out of control," and this reflects contemporary anxieties about the "New Woman," the emergence in the late nineteenth century of a significant set of demands for gender equality, which also signifies a version of modernity, but one which Stoker himself, and the novel, are evidently reluctant to accept. However, this also indicates a kind of ideological reversal; just as the female vampires are subject to Dracula's authority, so are the "new women" eventually subject to the authority of their male counterparts, so that the putative move towards the future becomes circular, ends by repeating a past from which we might be supposed to have escaped.

And behind this again, there lies the fear of degeneration, an anxiety about the continuing pull, signified in the vampires, back to a more archaic form of life. If the modernising elements of *Dracula* beckon the reader forward into the future, then vampirism signifies a countervailing beckoning back into the past. Similarly, the conquest of Dracula clearly requires an effort, a harnessing, of will; to succumb to the vampire involves a relinquishing of this strenuousness, a return to a somnambulistic world which might appear menacing before it is entered but is afterwards restful, trancelike, standing for a dream of history from which we might never need to awake.

And this, we might further say, is both the general fear and the lure of decadence in its late nineteenth-century form. Climbing upwards towards the modern is difficult, engaging all the faculties of the intellect; it might be easier, the novel reflects—while ending by sternly repudiating this thought—to relapse into the past, to let the vampire—which, in this sense, represents the past itself—do his work and allow for a certain forgetfulness in the face of the difficulty of handling the ever-increasing flow of information.

And this connects onto one of the most interesting features of recent theories of modernity, which is the extraordinary emphasis they have placed on the ways in which the modern, despite its protestations, remains "haunted" by its own past. This emerges in diverse areas; it emerges, for example, constantly in postcolonial writing and theory; it emerges in Jacques Derrida's notion of "hauntology"[6] (by which he intends a pun on "ontology," since they are homophones in French); it emerges also in the whole repertoire of hauntings, crypts, and phantoms which characterise recent advances in psychoanalytic theory and technique.

To take the latter instance, we might consider, for example, this ghostly paragraph from Nicolas Abraham and Maria Torok's psychoanalytic work, *The Shell and the Kernel* (1994):

The phantom is a formation of the unconscious that has never been conscious—for good reason. It passes—in a way yet to be determined—from the parent's

unconscious into the child's. [. . .] The phantom's periodic and compulsive
return lies beyond the scope of symptom-formation in the sense of a return of the
repressed; it works like a ventriloquist, like a stranger within the subject's own
mental topography.[7]

What they are describing here is an area of the mind which lies even below the
unconscious. According to this view, we might say that the very enterprise of
the modern in shifting the vampiric weight of tradition, in breaking free from
the trace of the past, is itself in some sense "phantomatic"; just as the child
remains at all times the "product" of the parent, so new cultural movements
serve to contain within themselves, albeit in "unknown," or at least in unthought
form, the relics of a past which cannot be buried, or re-buried, because the
corpse itself is unavailable on any specific topography. Thus we might see
Dracula as an attempt to bury the past, to find a new, safer kind of coffin; but
the very longevity and survival of the myth marks the continuing of this
enterprise, the impossibility of a "clean break" with the past.

It would then be the case that we can say that modernity—and in our
case, the modernity which inhabits and forms the text of *Dracula*—is haunted
by its Other; but perhaps what is more important is the series of ways, including
Derrida's analysis of "hauntology," in which modernity has tried precisely to
come to grips with this Other, with this constant seepage whereby the distinctly
modernistic gesture towards rational precision seems to end up contaminated by
its own "imprecise" past. It is true, however, that the kind of self-reflective
modernity represented by these contemporary theorists moves a decisive step
beyond the motifs of severance and experimentation which characterised
modernity's earlier avatars; it recognises, following one of the suppressed
textual movements within *Dracula*, the "impossibility of banishment."
According to this line of thinking, we might say that here is always a ghost. That
ghost might be Hamlet's emblematic ghost, the ghost of the undead father; or it
might be the ghostly lines on the map of postcolonial countries (or even the
ghostliness of Transylvania); or it might be the ghost that is continually present
in the evolution of new technologies, from typewriting to the postmodern
"writing" of an e-mail message. But the ghost cannot be banished, any more
than *Dracula* can be "written out" of cultural history.

But perhaps one of the principal scenarios of modernity is captured in
Dr Seward's diary when he recounts Van Helsing's own speculations on Lucy's
"case":

[. . .] there are things old and new [he recalls of Van Helsing's words] which
must not be contemplate [sic] by men's eyes, because they know—or think they
know—some things which other men have told them. Ah, it is the fault of our
science that it wants to explain all; and if it explain not, then it says there is
nothing to explain. But yet we see around us every day the growth of new

beliefs, which think themselves new; and which are yet but the old, which
pretend to be young [. . .]. (*D* 171)

So the question posed here, as it is throughout *Dracula*, would be: what is truly
old, what is truly new? Do modern discoveries remove us from ancient roots, or
do they, in some uncanny fashion, return us to an unwelcome proximity with
precisely those roots? Van Helsing offers Seward a list of things in which he,
Van Helsing, presumes he, Seward, does not believe: "corporeal transference,"
"materialisation," "astral bodies," "the reading of thought," "hypnotism"—but
at the mention of hypnotism Seward, of course, pulls him up short, saying
"Charcot has proved that pretty well." Van Helsing, as usual, is cannier, asking
Seward how it is that Seward can "accept the hypnotism and reject the thought-
reading," for "there are things done today in electrical science which would
have been deemed unholy by the very man who discovered electricity" (*D* 171).

So what is truly modern? Indeed, is there any such thing? Are we here
in the presence of a late Hegelian notion of history as a series of continual
returns, a set, or spiral, of recapitulations of the past within which there is
nothing truly new? Here modernity would seem to turn on itself. As I mentioned
earlier, there is a sense in which the modern figures in the host body as a
continual dealing with foreignness, with the "foreign body." In *Dracula*, there
are any number of "foreign bodies," but clearly the main opposition, the main
structure, concerns the opposition—which is linguistic as much as anything
else—between the foreigner Dracula and the foreigner Van Helsing. Here, of
course, the old Gothic plot is maintained: the Protestant Northern European is a
bastion of light against the threat of darkness which comes, variably, from the
south or from the east. There may be other reasons for the choice of Whitby as
Dracula's landing-place, but among them surely there is the perception that it is
undeniably north—at least in terms of Stoker's largely metropolitan audience.

So modernity in *Dracula* is always and everywhere under siege, but it
will win out in the end: the forces of the dark, of the unenlightened, will be
banished, sent back to where they came from. It of course marks one of
Dracula's enduring holds on the western imagination that this image is further
complicated or troubled by the stated fact that Dracula's family of *boyars* have
been, down the ages, in the forefront of the defence of Christendom; but I
suggest that what is being enacted here is the perennial fear of empire, which is
that its furthest outposts will turn out, when the imperial centre can be bothered
to send supplies, to fail to operate the corroded lines of communication, to have
"gone native"—like W. H. Auden's archetypal Tungrian soldier, servant of the
empire yet lost and alone on that last outpost, Hadrian's Wall.[8]

One needs also to think how brilliantly the lines of communication
operate in the pursuit of Dracula. Here is Van Helsing again, now as recounted
in Mina's journal:

As I knew that he wanted to get back to Transylvania, I felt sure that he must go
by the Danube mouth; or by somewhere in the Black Sea, since by that way he
come. [. . .] He was in sailing ship, since Madam Mina tells of sails being set.
These not so important as to go in your list of shipping in the *Times*, and so we
go, by suggestion of my Lord Godalming, to your Lloyd's, where are note of all
ships that sail, however so small. (*D* 275)

And so we have the traces here—and we also find them, interestingly enough, in
Arthur Conan Doyle's stories—of a postmodern worldwide web, of an all-
embracing information service which, naturally enough, operates best from
London and from its position not only as supreme maritime power but as
modern regulator of the potential anarchy of the high seas.

Yet again, there is a continual lock, a continuing duplicity, on these
modern methods in *Dracula*. Virtually at the end, in Jonathan Harker's final
"Note," we find this memorable reminder:

I took the papers from the safe where they had been ever since our return so long
ago. We were struck with the fact, that in all the mass of material of which the
record is composed, there is hardly one authentic document; nothing but a mass
of type-writing, except the later notebooks of Mina and Seward and myself, and
Van Helsing's memorandum. We could hardly ask anyone, even did we wish to,
to accept these as proofs of so wild a story. (*D* 326-27)

One might say that there is a certain bathos in this conclusion. What has seemed
indeed to be "so wild a story" turns out to have been—again, as so often in
Conan Doyle—something entirely different: namely, the "writing up of an
account." We may have experienced dealings with the ancient, the antique, even
the antediluvian, but in the end the question is whether modern means of
representation and reproduction have proved adequate in the transmission of this
story.

Stoker, we might say, is more than aware of the potential scepticism of
a modern audience; he knows that old tales around the camp-fire will no longer
do. He needs verification, or at least a certain reflexive irony about verification.
And if we look back through the history of the Gothic, with its plethora of half-
forgotten manuscripts, its half-told tales which will never be completed, we can
see that it is true that this dealing with scepticism, this awareness of a modern
audience which prides itself on not being fooled or taken in, is there from the
start, from Horace Walpole, Ann Radcliffe, Charles Maturin, indeed Mary
Shelley: the Gothic, seen in this light—which is by now a gaslight—can be seen
as a mechanism for transmitting the archaic into the modern, and it has therefore
always to stand guard over its own provenance, its own verification.

Yet the question remains: if a story is validated by typewriter, by
telegraph or, as we now might have it, by e-mail and the internet, does this

amount to a support for the story or are we plunged into a world which we would now refer to as a world of virtual reality where the proliferation of the modern means that we read every story in the awareness that there is really no story at all, no compelling master-narrative (or even metanarrative, to borrow Lyotard's term)?

I return to my five original hypotheses about modernity. *Dracula* is a text about the difficulty of escape from the past. It has recapitulated its own difficulty constantly through its main avatars, including, crucially, filmic ones. It has to do, surprisingly literally, with the problematic terrain of foreignness on "English soil." It takes its place on the terrain of an encounter with the ancient, which cannot be accommodated but which cannot be truly banished either. It is a fundamentally political text in the sense that it is haunted in its potentially progressive ideas by that which drags those ideas back towards a deeper past, while at the same time it stages a debate between those two sides of the argument, the dangerous pull back to the old and the equally dangerous—or at least menacing—pull forward towards a newly difficult future.

Notes

1 See Alfred Lord Tennyson, "Locksley Hall Sixty Years After," *Selected Poems*, ed. Aiden Day (London: Penguin, 1991), 332-44.

2 Max Nordau, *Degeneration* (1895; Lincoln and London: University of Nebraska Press, 1993), 6. See Bram Stoker, *Dracula*, ed. Glennis Byron (Peterborough, Ontario: Broadview Press, 1998), 470.

3 Max Nordau 6.

4 Glennis Byron 12.

5 Glennis Byron 12.

6 See, for example, Jacques Derrida, *Spectres of Marx: The State of the Debt, the Work of Mourning, and the New International*, trans. Peggy Kamuf (London and New York: Routledge, 1994), 10.

7 Nicolas Abraham and Maria Torok, *The Shell and the Kernel: Renewals of Psychoanalysis*, vol. 1, trans. Nicholas T. Rand (Chicago and London: University of Chicago Press, 1994), 173.

8 See W[ystan]. H[ugh]. Auden, "Roman Wall Blues," *Collected Shorter Poems 1927–1957* (London: Faber, 1966), 93-94.

Part II: Post/Modernism in Stoker's *Dracula*

CHAPTER FOUR

"EVERY SPECK OF DUST […] A DEVOURING MONSTER IN EMBRYO": THE VAMPIRE'S EFFLUVIA IN *DRACULA* BY BRAM STOKER

NATHALIE SAUDO, UNIVERSITÉ DE PICARDIE

In his *Dissertation sur les revenants en corps, les excommuniés, les oupires ou vampires, brucolaques* (1751), Dom Augustin Calmet tells such a vast number of improbable stories that his ability to suspend his disbelief seems boundless. However, on several occasions, like Seward, he stops believing and draws the line. He cannot accept the fact that vampires have the potential to circulate:

> That bodies which have died of a violent disease or were killed while in perfect health, or which have simply fainted, should vegetate under ground and in their graves; that their beards, their hair and their nails should grow; that they should give out blood; that they should remain soft and supple; that they should not smell; that they should produce excrements or things of that sort: it is not this which we find hard to believe. The vegetation of human bodies can indeed result in such effects; that they should even eat or devour what is around them. It is only natural that a man buried alive should be mad with rage when he emerges from his torpor and fly into an excess of violence. The main difficulty, however, is to explain how vampires get out of their graves to haunt the living, and how they get back into them; for all the accounts we have read take this for granted without ever telling us how and in what circumstances it is done, although this would be the most interesting part of the tale.[1]

In other words, while the existence of vampires is beyond doubt for Calmet, their comings and goings are questionable. It is precisely one of the specificities of *Dracula* to take an aesthetic, and sometimes almost scientific interest in the modalities of vampiric circulation and to provide ample evidence of the forms this circulation takes. In his novel, Stoker exploits the full range of what could be called dissolutions; be it as a smell, dust, particles, or molecules, Dracula travels fast and unobtrusively.

I have chosen the generic term "effluvia" to connect the different modalities of vampiric circulation and to analyse the various signifiers denoting dispersion in the text. My inquiry will in part remain on the surface of the text, in quest of the dissemination and mutations of those effluvia from dust (*D* 40) to fog, flecks (*D* 131), specks (*D* 48, 307), mist (*D* 226-27, 276), snow-flurries (*D* 309, 316-18), atoms (*D* 320), molecules (*D* 238), pillar of smoke (*D* 131), various smells and stenches, and magnetism. Why use a word that is absent from the book? The word "effluvium" is etymologically related to the idea of flow, which is central to *Dracula*, through the theme of liquidity. Although it is tinted with a quasi-spiritual dimension, this technical term was used in the nineteenth century to describe phenomena of uncertain origin (for instance, the particles emitted by magnetic or electrified bodies). It is thus frequently found in texts that describe various sources of air pollution, as in certain late nineteenth-century law texts.[2] As a twenty-first-century equivalent to the word "effluvium," I would offer "vampour," a portmanteau that echoes the novel's interplay of signifiers to its postmodern readers who participate in what Jean-François Lyotard calls the "pragmatics of language particles."[3] Reading *Dracula*, then, requires the hunting for words that, in connoting infectious circulation, emulate the vampire's own volatility. The vampire's capacity to break into a multiplicity of particles or metamorphose to avoid detection or capture—much like a virus's ability to mutate to avoid eradication—is what may ultimately have defeated the "Crew of Light"; yet it is precisely his mutability, which has intrigued twentieth-century readers and viewers alike, that has enabled Dracula to return in different media.

Dracula has evolved into a myth and a metanarrative of its own, but it subverts some of its rules and constraints: there are several narrators, whose truthfulness is open to doubt, since they even question their own reliability. The purpose of the great crusade is defeated by the enemy's diffuseness. The power of the tale lies not so much in the crusaders' great conquest as in the creation of a multiform, voracious, and agile Dracula, which postmodern readers have tended to identify with more readily than with his upright, steadfast opponents. Francis Ford Coppola's film adaptation of Stoker's novel is a good case in point. This paper's aim, then, is to explain why. In studying the various modes of the vampire's circulation in *Dracula* and in providing a context for them, I shall try to show that although these effluvia originate in a particular context, they take part in the stylistic game of dispersion. I contend that Stoker's fascination for vampiric circulation and the form it takes are determined historically and betray a universal fear of indifferentiation, which goes beyond its time-period to reach the very heart of human anxieties. Yet indeterminacy can also prove greatly stimulating: Dracula's dissolutions and dispersals are the ideal playground for the postmodern reader.

Vampours

Mists and vapours are the traditional signifiers of the Gothic landscape. They contribute to the gloom, terror, and ruggedness of sublime landscapes, with their suggestion of "natural power." They also contribute to the dramatising of events by creating light effects and by veiling and unveiling the scene thanks to curtain-like clouds. Vampours are composed of a mass of particles, such as dust, fireflies, or snow, each connoting dispersion and proliferation. During Jonathan's first trip to Castle Dracula, "fine" and "powdery" snow starts falling (*D* 19), and it comforts Jonathan like a soft blanket. His second trip takes place during a snowstorm where "snow flurries [...] come and go as warnings" (*D* 309), and release and absorb ghosts (*D* 318). Dracula blends into this Gothic landscape, which has become alive with mysterious natural powers. Such a mimetic relation to nature could already be found in Varney's dramatic entrance during a great hail-storm in *Varney the Vampyre* (1847). The pattering of the hail merged with the beating of Varney's nails on the glass: "It is its finger-nails upon the glass that produces the sound so like the hail, now that the hail has ceased."[4] In Dracula's case, however, the air is literally alive, and while the snow is falling, "there is a strange excitement in the air" (*D* 318). The general excitement that pervades the male and female characters in *Dracula* is afloat in the atmosphere. What is more, Dracula himself turns into a magical landscape, releasing supernatural emanations. Van Helsing's description of Romania is an appropriate portrait of the Count. The wounds and orifices in his body can be compared to "deep caverns and fissures that reach none know whither"; his mouth, to a volcano, "some of whose openings still send out waters of strange properties, and gases that kill and make to vivify" (*D* 278). Van Helsing's conclusion to his portrait epitomises Dracula's occult physical and psychic powers: "Doubtless, there is something magnetic or electric in these combinations of occult forces which work for physical life in strange way" (*D* 278). These are the powers I shall now analyse, from his infectious stench to his electrifying influence or magnetism.

Smell

It is not well known that vampires smell, yet Stoker's "malodorous" vampire (*D* 221) has "rank" breath (*D* 24), and "reeking lips" (*D* 251), all of which nauseate his neighbours. This can easily be explained by the fact that the vampire is rotten to the core and smells like the disintegrating, rotting corpse he really is. But smelly discharges may hide more than that. A smell becomes particularly unpleasant when its origin or its nature cannot be identified. The smelling subject makes guesses, while the smelled object remains elusive. Once the source of the smell has been identified, its power diminishes. In other words, all smells have the capacity to defamiliarise surroundings, and some smells may even be domesticated. Apart from suggesting the pungency of blood and emanations from the earth, Dracula's smell is not a physical, recognisable odour: it is described rather in moral terms as corruption itself becoming corrupt or as "ills of mortality" (D 221). But there is something disturbing in any bodily smell. In one of his studies in the history of sense perception, Alain Corbin writes that the unease generated by bad smells is related to the fact that a smell is the first stage of an individual's dissolution. To smell is to map out an area where the smelling subject and the object smelled mix and blend into one another:

> Olfactory sensitivity to putrefaction betrays the anxiety of a being that is unable to *fix itself*—this is the main idea—to retain the elements it is composed of, which have come from preceding beings, and which will go on to combine in new beings. Putrefaction works like a clock, and studies devoted to it are stories. It follows that olfactory vigilance does not only aim at detecting threats or risks of infection. The sense of smell is not only on guard. Its vigilance is the permanent awareness of the dissolution of beings, and of oneself. For Oscar Wilde's Dorian Gray, as for us, destruction is represented primarily in visual terms; for Professor Hallé's contemporaries, it was done in olfactory terms as well. It is not easy for us to understand this attitude; when *we* encounter a noisome smell, we are tempted to laugh, betraying our embarrassment and incomprehension.[5]

The standards of sensitivity of Stoker's characters and contemporaries are undoubtedly olfactory: their fight against Dracula requires their smell to be so mobilised as to be able to push back the stench of the vampire, "as though that loathsome place were a garden of roses" (D 221). The vampire-killers take refuge in an English rose-garden in an attempt to dissipate the uncertainty and hesitations generated by the vampire's "nauseous whiffs" (D 221).

There is something about a smell that reaches the essence of being with others or other things, constituting a form of participation. It exposes the uncertainty of the subject and the ambivalence of the object. Smells betray the continuous dissolution of human bodies and point out each individual's tendency to degeneration. Bad smells foreshadow putrefaction and death; neutral odours imply the conformity of an individual to his surroundings; pleasant smells simultaneously beckon and permeate the others' bodies. Corbin's conclusion bears light upon the study of *Dracula*: "Smell is the sense of transitions, thresholds and margins; it reveals the processes of transformation at work in beings and things."[6] Transitions, thresholds, and margins are central to *Dracula*. As a story, it tells of the crossing of various frontiers and limits (East and West, the two atmospheres) and encourages crossovers (nutrition and sexuality). As a novel, it plays with boundaries (human and animal, madman and scientist, etc.) so that Dracula's readiness to dissolve into vampours is a reminder of the fact that the "fortress of identity"[7] itself is unstable. In this, as in other matters, such as the dislike of the smell of garlic, the vampire is normal to an extreme, for all bodies undergo permanent dissolution, which in turn creates unease. Yet, the most frightening dissolution of all lies in the continuity between man and beast, where the vampire's effluvia can be read in the light of evolutionary discourse.

Dissolution

Evolutionism ascribed a regressive quality to dissolution or disintegration. Evolution meant the gradual integration of matter as opposed to the permanent threat of its dissipation. This was accompanied by the creation of more integrated complex structures and the greater specialisation and differentiation of functions. Yet, the process of evolution was inseparable from the correlative process of degeneration. The relevant technical term, "dissolution," was used by social Darwinists, such as Herbert Spencer, and period psychiatrists alike, including the father of English neurology, Hughlings Jackson. Victorian psychiatrist Henry Maudsley described degeneration as "a process of *dissolution*, the opposite of that process of *involution* which is pre-essential to evolution."[8] This technical word is used twice in *Dracula*, each time in the expression "final dissolution" (*D* 320, 325), which describes those who die of vampirism. Becoming a vampire, then, is a process of dissolution, both in the sense of regression on the evolutionary scale, and of dissemination, which prefigures the ultimate dispersion into dust or ashes. In the context of the end of the nineteenth century, the "devouring monsters in embryo" that are released by the "specks of dust" (*D* 307) represent various infectious germs. By associating the embryo with the corpse, this description conjures up the vision of an aged cannibalistic foetus. The widespread use of this motif in fin-de-siècle culture reflects the fascination for a form of life that was tiny, and yet heir to a long line of descent; young and fresh, and yet wrinkled and monkeyish; full of potential, and yet potentially monstrous.[9] A good case in point is Aubrey Beardsley's gentlemen-foetuses, who look so old and so worn out that they indeed threaten to crumble into dust.[10]

The vampire thus embodies another great scientific scare of the late nineteenth-century: indifferentiation. Used by evolutionists and social Darwinists to describe the last stage of a degenerating organism, the term equally evokes the state when such debilitating organisms are no longer differentiated from live, primitive organisms. The ultimate peril was to regress to the stage of protoplasm or nondescript molluscs such as ascidians, creatures that greatly fascinated nineteenth-century scientists given their status as the smallest form of organised life. Nineteenth-century scientists and doctors were acutely aware that man's fate was potentially similar since he was a synthesis of these various organic life forms, a combination process that was both continuous and fragile. By perfecting this combination process, man played a part in his own development. In *Dracula*, the power of combination is denied to the vampire (*D* 210) because he is thought to be lower than civilised man on the evolutionary scale, and closer to Lombroso's criminal, or to the savage. In H. Rider Haggard's *Allan Quatermain* (1887), a novel which also presents many "good specimens of manhood or humanity," the expression "faculty of combination" is used to draw a comparison between the savage and the white man: "I say that, as the savage is, so is the white man, only the latter is more inventive, and possesses the faculty of combination."[11] However civilised man may be, from a scientific viewpoint, he is nothing more than a combination of atoms predisposed to return to their molecular state. In this respect, evolution could be described as an unremitting fight against dispersion.

T. S. Wells and F. W. Lowndes, the authors of the article "Disposal of the Dead" in the second volume of Stevenson and Murphy's *Treatise on Hygiene and Public Health* (1893–96) start by reminding their readers that man is nothing but

> a tenant at will of a variable proportion of organisable matter; in death, he ought to render it back into the common stock for the use of others, without in any way barring the succession. If he interferes artificially with the natural course of events among the elements of his mortal covering, either retarding development or impending dispersion, it is an act of vicious perversity.[12]

In other words, from a biological perspective, human bodies are meant to circulate in atomic form; no man actually owns his own body. God and hygienists dispose. For the authors, who are guided by hygienic considerations, bodies to be disposed of necessarily belong to a natural cycle and their functions should not be perverted. Heredity must be understood within the history of the race:

> All organised beings are in a state of perpetual transformation. It has been so from the beginning, and will go on so to the end. The atoms only, of which they are composed, are unchangeable. They alone never lose their identity, and as there is neither annihilation nor new creation of them, each in turn, "plays many parts". These atoms which make up the existing generation have been part and parcels of the generations that have gone before, and will, in future, take their places in similar evolutions of formation and destruction. One generation is not only the successor of another, but is as well its material inheritor.[13]

The vampire's consumption of the living and, conversely, production of dust and other airborne particles lay bare the continuity between life and death expressed here. If the biblical expression "The Blood is the Life" in its subverted form reduces life to the circulation of material corpuscles, eternal life is symbolised by the immutable transmission of physical matter.

Interestingly enough, such a conception of the human body naturally leads one to consider the many micro-organisms at work in living creatures, and the subsequent infections and contagions to which they may be exposed. Among these atoms and molecules, germs and microbes hide. Even the dead body contains life. T. S. Wells and F. W. Lowndes add: "Now a body to be buried is not simply dead organic matter. Under ordinary circumstances, it is the abode of myriads of living organisms."[14] The hygienists thus maintained that "[t]here [was] life in death."[15] This statement should be read in light of an earlier scientific discovery that radically transformed Victorian Europe: Louis Pasteur's germ theory. Fermentation and diseases in general were no longer considered as forms of chemical decomposition (a form of death) but rather as the work of millions of living microorganisms. "Life in death" had been proved to be a reality, and the face of Gothic fiction suddenly changed. Many fin-de-siècle Gothic novels provided a characteristic analysis of the human body, where its disintegration allows for a positive inquiry into the human psyche. The vampire's effluvia constitute one such analysis. They demonstrate that there is both morbid life in death, and death in life, since evolution is inseparable from its corollary, degeneration.

"[D]isease-breeding gases"

In *Dracula*, the use of religious discourse interspersed with technical terms transforms vampirism into a metaphor for infection. This infection can be variously interpreted as the plague (the rats and stench), as phthisis, the pulmonary version of tuberculosis (the stertorous breathing of the vampire's victims), or as syphilis (the association of circulation, pollution, and shame).[16] It even evokes non-infectious diseases of uncertain origin, such as neurasthenia.[17]

The nebulous nature of vampirism is reflected in the ill-defined medical terminology of hygienists and doctors of the era. Towns resemble paludal swamps in that they release stray morbid bodies. In his famous pamphlet, *The Bitter Cry of Outcast London* (1886), Andrew Mearns complained that "[t]he air [was] laden with disease-breeding gases."[18] James Cantlie even declared in his lecture on degeneration (1885): "I want to find out if there is such a thing as '*urbomorbus*' or 'city disease,' independently of trade disease; hence I chose to study London."[19] A few pages later, this hazy *urbomorbus* had become a palpable reality that allowed him to detect signs of degeneration. In the first part of *In Darkest England and the Way Out* (1890), William Booth spoke more openly of malaria in London, given that the title of his book was inspired by Sir Henry Morton Stanley's *In Darkest Africa* published the same year. Cities, swamps, and the tropics discharge similar effluvia: "Darkest England, like Darkest Africa, reeks with malaria. The foul and fetid breath of our slums is almost as poisonous as that of the African swamp. Fever is almost as chronic there as on the Equator."[20] Even legal documents used the expression "effluvia, vapours or gases" to provide an all-inclusive description of possible airborne sources of infection.[21] Whether in the form of monstrous concatenation or that of accumulation, the rhetoric used in the previous examples illustrates how the air itself could become an intense source of fear, and how language could turn it into a monstrous entity.

One last example, borrowed from Antony Wohl's book on public health in Victorian Britain, should confirm this. His book presents an impressive sample of committees and pressure groups for cleaner air who complained about smog and industrial grime: the 1862 Select Committee on Injury from Noxious Vapours, the 1878 Royal Commission on Noxious Vapours, the 1884 National Smoke Abatement Society, the 1887 Select Committee on the Smoke Nuisances Bill, and others, such as the Lancashire and Cheshire Association for Controlling the Escape of Noxious Vapours and Fluids, and the Manchester Association for the Prevention of Smoke.[22] These evocative names, which today would merely bear the label "pollution," constitute a good sampling of all the infectious, ethereal forms that the vampire can take, in both a material and a linguistic way.

Because Pasteurian medicine proved that germs were needed for an infection to develop, the air was no longer suspected of being alive with infectious germs and fragments of living and dead bodies but proved to be so.[23] At the same time, the general public and hygienists remained strongly influenced by miasmatic conceptions of disease, which attributed an infectious quality to smells and miasma in general.[24] In a small column of the *British Medical Journal* (1887), under the title "Infection and Disinfection," the appreciative summary of an article that appeared in the February issue of *The Fortnightly Review* reads:

> [Dr Roose] points out that deodorization and disinfection have nothing in common. [...] The mere creation of an odour which overpowers some other odour, or the use of a material which only retards decomposition, has no claim to be trusted to destroy or modify the virus of infective diseases.[25]

Antony Wohl provides an anecdote which illustrates how deeply rooted miasmatic conceptions of disease were then, and how much preventive hygiene remained an issue of language and style:

one of the [Ladies' Sanitary Association] foremost propagandists, Miss Rayney, pointed out that "NASTY AIR" was an anagram of "SANITARY"—"who'd have thought it?", she mused, "And yet, after all, that nasty air is the breeze that has kindled the Sanitary Association into life."[26]

In France, doctors were having a difficult time convincing the general public that "tout ce qui pue ne tue pas, tout ce qui tue ne pue pas." When it comes to effluvia, words, like letters, transpose until form resembles content.

Some decadent novels developed an aesthetic of mysterious diseases, by making poetical use of a wide range of sonorous terms, thus weaving poisonous words into the very fabric of the text. In the most famous of them, *The Picture of Dorian Gray*, written three years before *Dracula*, moral and physical diseases coexist, and poisonous bodies expand into "influences." Once again, language encourages such associations: the infectious disease influenza, a word borrowed from the Italian for "epidemic," spread throughout London in 1890.

From influenza to influence

The generic word "influence" occurs eight times in *Dracula*, and all of these occurrences have aroused my curiosity, as they are so varied and so vague. The word is sometimes used in its original meaning of astral sympathies: the "malign influence of the sun" (*D* 110) or the "weather influences" (*D* 281). In its purest form, influence denotes incorporeal movement or pure circulation: "It would almost seem as if there was some influence which came and went" (*D* 102). The word is so elusive that it takes on multiple connotations, as for example in the following passage where hypersensitivity to germs, magnetism, or moral ideas can be inferred: "Lucy is so sweet and sensitive that she feels influences more acutely than other people do" (*D* 85). However, at the end of the nineteenth century, influences evoked theories of electromagnetism, where they accounted for the mysterious movement of invisible magnetic particles. In physics, influence was a synonym for induction. The influence machine was a device that created electricity through the use of several brass balls acting as inductors and was said to be "capable of imitating the effects of a thunder-storm upon a small scale, giving sparks several feet in length and following in rapid succession."[27] When Dracula orchestrates the movement of the wolves, controlling the circulation of invisible particles, he is compared to a conductor, a profession that appeared in the nineteenth century.[28] The etymology of the word bears out the belief in a connection between orchestration, mesmerism, and electricity. The word "influence" encapsulates the all-powerful exhalations that travel through the air and create interactions between physical and moral bodies;

the novel is inhabited by influences of multiple and sometimes unknown origin.[29]

Among the many vampours afloat in *Dracula*, there are magnetic bodies that account for Mina's pity towards Dracula and for her telepathic and hypnotic relationship with him. In the novel, which contains discussions on hypnotism and a reference to Charcot, the full range of corpuscles is exploited. In their most abstract and mysterious form, powerful influences are described as a kind of "fascination" (*D* 227, 319), a word equally dear to Wilde in *The Picture of Dorian Gray*.

Pursuing the vampire's effluvia, then, has revealed a fear of dispersion and of indifferentiation, although both are at work in the book itself. Since vampirism appears as a form of fascinating attraction or captivation, this phenomenon was most likely to happen in the human aggregate, a milieu congenial to Dracula: the crowd.

The captivation of the crowd

Dracula, who occasionally speaks in the first person plural (*D* 33), dreams of dissolving into London's "teeming millions" (*D* 53): "I long to go through the crowded streets of your mighty London, to be in the midst of the whirl and rush of humanity, to share its life, its change, its death, and all that makes it what it is" (*D* 26). Although Dracula is a great consumer who tries to absorb others, he is also eager to integrate and melt into the crowd.

Passing from particles to crowds might seem to be a change of scale. In fact, the description of the crowd as a text and as a social phenomenon is not much different from that of vampirism. In Stoker's time, the standard reference book and best seller on the psychology of crowds was *La Psychologie des foules*, written by sociologist Gustave Le Bon in 1895 and translated into English as early as 1896 under the title, *The Crowd: A Study of the Popular Mind*. In fact, Le Bon's depiction of the dangers of the crowd has much in common with the anxieties generated by vampirism. Why should one want to learn about crowd psychology? So as not to be "devoured" by crowds. Le Bon's metaphors and comparisons are particularly revealing, especially as, in Robert Nye's introduction to the 1995 re-edition of the English translation, "Le Bon does not use these terms […] as simple metaphors; he is giving expression to a conviction of the biological science of his day that the qualities of rationality and will are relatively recent evolutionary acquisitions built up on a substratum of primordial instincts."[30] The destructive nature of the crowd makes it akin to a gathering of microbes responsible for the decay of corpses, or the obscure forces that cause the ruin of old buildings: "In consequence of the purely destructive nature of their power, crowds act like those microbes which hasten the dissolution of enfeebled or dead bodies. When the structure of a civilisation is rotten, it is always the masses that bring about its downfall."[31] The crowd is comparable to a new chemical element, where the bodies are stray particles waiting to be attracted by the magnetism of the crowd. It releases captivating effluvia and emanations that fascinate and hypnotise:

> the most careful observations seem to prove that an individual immerged for some length of time in a crowd in action soon finds himself—either in consequence of the magnetic influence given out by the crowd, or from some other cause of which we are ignorant—in a special state, which much resembles the state of fascination in which the hypnotised individual finds himself in the hands of the hypnotiser.[32]

The mesmerised subject who loses all self-control "descends several rungs on the ladder of civilisation"[33] and evolution, and becomes a mere automaton controlled by the all-powerful crowd. Although the composite crowd is composed of innumerable components, it still has its own psychology comparable to that of children, barbarians, or savages.[34] Dracula's composite body predisposes him to melt into the crowd, which was perceived as attracting and aggregating the stray influences and bodies.

The issues I have engaged with seem to bring out a form of coherence in the universe and character of Dracula, but such coherence is in fact based on the principle of fragmentation and indeterminacy. This has an unsettling effect on the narrative as a whole and on its ending. Jonathan's son, Quincey, is indeed the only being who truly compares with Dracula's regressive and composite nature: he bears a collective name; his blood is tainted with Dracula's; and he has some of Quincey Morris's spirit pass "into him" (*D* 326). This throws a dark light on the last pages of the novel: it might well be that baby Quincey is the monster in embryo, which a close reading of the novel leads us to expect and imagine with unease. The hero of my own postmodern sequel to *Dracula* is Quincey Harker.

Conclusion

The themes presented here—smells, hypnosis, influence and fascination—all feature the terrifying permeability of "bodies," recalling the idea of transfusions and vampirism itself. More generally, they represent the critical moment of indifferentiation, when ego and non-ego mix to such an extent that it becomes impossible to distinguish between the nature and species of a body and its limits. The same phenomenon occurs on a linguistic level, since the comprehensiveness and vagueness of the terms that describe the vampire's effluvia maximise their threat by stimulating the imagination and evading any precise definition, while also creating a perfect correspondence between form and content. Viewed from another angle, effluvia also betray the inter-relation of historically-bound fears linked with the separation of the genders, of man from animal, or, more generally, the self from the Other. Do the vampire's opponents release effluvia to counter these vampours? The word "sympathy" and its compounds, which appear some fifteen times in the novel, have been left out of the network of terms I have analysed here even though these words share the same connotations of mysterious correspondences and affinities. This strongly moral term belongs to the universe of reaction, and like the expression "sweet pity," it belongs to a linguistic domain that is strictly moral.

Understanding Dracula's effluvia helps reveal the many social fears and scientific questionings of the end of the nineteenth century and synthesise the many scientific terms scattered throughout the novel. They hold the remains of a miasmatic theory of disease, or the late nineteenth-century fascination with supernatural forms of communication, such as magnetic phenomena and mesmerism. They also help uncover the influence of evolutionary discourse on nascent sociology. Effluvia create an area where belief and reason, science and superstition conjoin. As such, *Dracula* is a striking example of Lyotard's scientific discourse *qua* narrative (even though no specific scientific theory is presented in the novel, or presentable for that matter because it consists of a combination of fragments from theories, some of which are pseudo-scientific), for while scientific discourse (like religious discourse) may lend authority to the narrative, its scientific or pseudo-scientific "theories" also work to undermine it. Scientific narration is thus left unstable, narrative cohesion thus defeated by linguistic indeterminacy, and the novel's "meaning" is found solely in the reader's response to its language games.

Notes

1 Dom Augustin Calmet, *Dissertation sur les revenants en corps, les excommuniés, les oupires ou vampires, brucolaques* (Paris: Jérôme Million, 1986), 238, my translation. The original French reads:

Que les corps qui sont morts de maladie violente ou qui ont été exécutés pleins de santé, ou qui sont simplement évanouis, végètent sous la terre et dans leurs tombeaux ; que leurs barbes, leurs cheveux et leurs ongles croissent ; qu'ils rendent du sang ; qu'ils soient souples et maniables ; qu'ils ne sentent point mauvais ; qu'ils rendent des excréments ou choses semblables, ce n'est pas ce qui nous embarrasse. La végétation du corps humain peut produire tous ces effets ; qu'ils mangent même et qu'ils dévorent ce qui est autour d'eux. La rage dont un homme enterré tout vivant est transporté, lorsqu'il se réveille de son engourdissement et de sa syncope, doit naturellement le porter à ces excès de violence. Mais la grande difficulté est d'expliquer comment les vampires sortent de leurs tombeaux pour venir les infester, et comment ils y rentrent ; car toutes les relations que nous voyons supposent la chose comme certaine, sans nous en raconter ni la manière ni les circonstances, qui seraient pourtant ce qu'il y a de plus intéressant dans ce récit.

2 Thomas Stevenson and Shirley Murphy, eds., *A Treatise on Hygiene and Public Health*, 3 vols. (London: Churchill, 1893-96), 3:113. In handbooks on hygiene from the last decades of the nineteenth century, the word "effluvia" is generally associated with the word "organic."

3 Jean-François Lyotard, *The Postmodern Condition: A Report on Knowledge*, trans. Geoff Bennington and Brian Massumi (1979; Minneapolis: University of Minneapolis Press, 1988), xxiv.

4 James Malcolm Rymer, *Varney the Vampyre; or The Feast of Blood*, volume one, chapter one. Available at http://etext.lib.virginia.edu/toc/modeng/public/Pre Var1.html (8 Oct. 2006).

5 Alain Corbin, *Le Miasme et la Jonquille: L'Odorat et l'Imaginaire social, XVIIIe–XIXe siècles* (Paris: Flammarion, Champs, 1986), 22-23, my translation. The original French reads:

L'attention olfactive au putride traduit l'angoisse de l'être qui ne peut se *fixer*—et c'est là le maître-mot—, retenir les éléments qui le composent, qu'il tient d'êtres précédents et qui permettront la combinaison d'êtres nouveaux. La putréfaction est horloge et les études qui lui sont consacrées se font histoires. Dès lors, la vigilance olfactive n'a pas seulement pour but de détecter la menace, le risque d'infection. L'odorat-sentinelle se révèle ici un concept trop étroit. Cette vigilance est écoute permanente d'une dissolution des êtres et de soi. Pour le Dorian Gray d'Oscar Wilde—comme pour nous—le repère de destruction est visuel ; pour les contemporains du Pr Hallé, il est aussi d'ordre olfactif. Il nous est difficile de comprendre une telle attitude ; et l'hilarité, signe de l'incompréhension, nous tente devant l'affolement provoqué par le miasme nauséabond.

6 Alain Corbin, *Le Temps, le désir et l'horreur: Essais sur le XIXe siècle* (Paris: Flammarion, Champs, 1998), 229, my translation. The original French reads: "L'odorat est [...] le sens des transitions, des seuils et des marges, qui révèle les processus de transformation des êtres et des choses."

7 Robert Louis Stevenson, *The Strange Case of Dr Jekyll and Mr Hyde* (1886; London: Penguin, 2002), 57.

8 Henry Maudsley, *Body and Will: Being an Essay Concerning Will in Its Metaphysical, Physiological & Pathological Aspects* (London: Kegan Paul, Trench, 1883), 240.

9 Evanghélia Stead, *Le Monstre, le Singe et le Fœtus: Tératogonie et décadence dans l'Europe fin-de-siècle* (Paris: Droz, 2004), 419-510.

10 Brian Reade, *Aubrey Beardsley* (Woodbridge: Antique Collectors' Club, 1998), plates 173, 190, 211, 212, 235, 246, 273, and 285.

11 H. Rider Haggard, *Allan Quatermain* (1887; Oxford: Oxford University Press, 1995), 10.

12 Thomas Stevenson and Shirley Murphy, 2:674.

13 Thomas Stevenson and Shirley Murphy, 2:673.

14 Thomas Stevenson and Shirley Murphy, 2:710.

15 Thomas Stevenson and Shirley Murphy, 2:700.

16 Vampirism, which occurred as an epidemic, was often thought to be the cause of epidemics, such as the plague. "The stench of the vampire [. . .] is one aspect of the nexus between vampirism and the plague. In European folklore, vampires 'cause' epidemics (even in the movies, vampirism is catching). Now, foul smells were commonly associated with disease, also as a cause, perhaps because people reasoned that, since corpses smelled bad, bad smells must be a cause of disease and death. Typically, by way of combating such spells, people introduced good-smelling (or strong-smelling) substances [. . .]." Paul Barber, *Vampires, Burial, and Death: Folklore and Reality* (New Haven and London: Yale University Press, 1988), 8.

17 The fact that some anaemic patients were made to drink fresh blood from slaughterhouses is a matter of folklore (Joseph-Ferdinand Gueldry, "The Blood-Drinkers," 1898) rather than reality. See Bram Dijkstra, *Idols of Perversity: Fantasies of Feminine Evil in Fin-de-Siècle Culture* (New York: Oxford University Press, 1988), 338. Slaughterhouses are always described in textbooks on hygiene as a source of urban filth and a great risk to public health.

18 Andrew Mearns, *The Bitter Cry of Outcast London* (London: Clarke, 1883), 19.

19 James Cantlie, *Degeneration amongst Londoners: A Lecture Delivered at the Parkes Museum of Hygiene, January 27, 1885* (London: Field & Tuer, 1885), 24-25.

20 William Booth, *In Darkest England and the Way Out* (London: International Headquarters of the Salvation Army, 1890), 14.

21 See the following extract from a by-law framed by the London County Council, under the Slaughterhouses &c. Act (1874): "Every blood drier shall cause every process of his business in which any offensive effluvia, vapours, or gases are generated, to be carried on in such manner that no offensive effluvia, vapours, or gases shall escape into the external atmosphere; and he shall cause all such offensive effluvia, vapours, or gases to be effectually destroyed" (Stevenson and Murphy, 1:906). The first chapter of this volume is concerned with air, and the book includes a chapter on "Offensive and Noxious Businesses," the beginning of which deals with the utilisation of blood.

22 Antony S. Wohl, *Endangered Lives: Public Health in Victorian Britain* (London: Dent, 1983), passim.

23 "The organic suspended matters consist principally of grains of pollen, algae, fragments of hair, wood, straw, stable manure, débris of insects, &c." (Stevenson and Murphy, 1:5).

24 One doctor observed that "[i]t is important to be able to ascertain the quality of the air in enclosed spaces. There are various methods of doing this, of which not the least useful is the information furnished by the *sense of smell*, on entering a room from the external air." Arthur Newsholme, *Hygiene: A Manual of Personal and Public Health* (London: George Gill & Sons, 1892), 167.

25 *British Medical Journal* 1 (1887): 344.

26 Antony S. Wohl 68.

27 G. W. de Tunzelmann, *Electricity in Modern Life* (New York: Collier, 1902), 48.

28 Alison Winter, *Mesmerized: Powers of Mind in Victorian Britain* (Chicago: University of Chicago Press, 1998).
29 See, for example, the following references: "the disturbing influence" (*D* 62), "into the very soul of the patient that he [Charcot] influence" (*D* 171), and "Mrs Harker yielded to the hypnotic influence even less readily than this morning" (*D* 299).
30 Robert Nye, Introduction, *The Crowd: A Study of the Popular Mind*, by Gustave Le Bon (New Brunswick and London: Transaction, 1997), 14.
31 Gustave Le Bon 38.
32 Gustave Le Bon 51.
33 Gustave Le Bon 52.
34 Gustave Le Bon 56.

CHAPTER FIVE

FRAGMENTED, INVISIBLE, AND GROTESQUE BODIES IN *DRACULA*

FRANÇOISE DUPEYRON-LAFAY, UNIVERSITÉ PARIS 12

The body is a central feature and a major theme in *Dracula*. It is the locus of territorial power struggles as the vampires strive to absorb and appropriate bodies but also to multiply and spread. Like a disease or an epidemic, vampiric colonisation affects or contaminates both bodies and spaces. Besides, in the narrative, thematic, and symbolic fields, the body is a focus of multiple contradictions. Indeed, it is both a taboo that is nevertheless pervasive, ubiquitous, and inescapable, and an object of repulsion and attraction in the same way that the grotesque, as defined by Geoffrey Galt Harpham, is "a civil war of attraction/repulsion."[1]

 Dracula is a quintessentially late Victorian text. Its theme and ideological concerns fully testify to many fin-de-siècle fears and obsessions. Structurally, however, with its fragmented narratives and the absence of an omniscient point of view—narrative techniques that were already present in Wilkie Collins's *The Woman in White* (1860) or *The Moonstone* (1868)—*Dracula* holds the seeds of post/modernism. Both thematically and structurally, then, *Dracula* can be viewed as grotesque, understood in Wolfgang Kayser's,[2] and not Bakhtin's, perspective. We could even argue that the vampire's hybrid and grotesque body contaminates and shapes the narrative body itself. As Dominique Iehl lucidly argues in *Le Grotesque*:

> In all the text he studies, Kayser identifies the same grotesque structure. But what he terms grotesque no longer has anything in common with the dynamic expansion and the joyful proliferation of the Rabelaisian world. Its sense of dilation and lusty enjoyment is taken over by a sense of frustration and constriction. For Bakhtin, the grotesque means an appropriation of the world. For Kayser, the grotesque looms up with the frightening sense that we are losing our grasp on reality which is becoming an alien presence.

[. . .] Kayser here depicts a process of gradual destruction and our growing awareness that order, coherence, meaning are being abolished. It starts with a sense of the uncanny, a sense of exclusion from a rationally organized world, and ends with an experience of emptiness and nothingness. [. . .] The foundations of the real are being undermined or are collapsing.[3]

In Stoker's, as in Collins's, works, narrative decentralisation prevails, unlike what we find in many other Victorian novels, such as Dickens's or George Eliot's, for instance. A defamiliarising, *unheimlich* text, *Dracula* explodes boundaries and erodes familiar narrative landmarks, and its reader is forced to work his or her way through a fragmented, generically hybrid novel (replete with fantastic, Gothic, sensational, and detective elements) without any single unified focaliser. This no doubt owes to that fact that the reader is left with a very vague impression of the characters' physical appearances. Whereas typical Victorian works feature protagonists that are described physically in minute detail, which contributes to their realistic depth and three-dimensional, or "round," natures, *Dracula* barely offers a clue as to what its characters look like—the colour of their hair or eyes, how tall they are, their general aspect, the clothes they wear, etc.—despite the fact that the body and its integrity are the main issues at stake. This concerns both male characters (Jonathan Harker, Dr Seward, Quincey Morris or Arthur Holmwood) and female ones (Lucy or Mina).

In Lucy's letters to Mina (Chapter 5), for instance, the reader gleans but a few details about Seward: "[h]e is an excellent *parti*, being handsome, well-off, and of good birth. He is a doctor and really clever. [. . .] I think he is one of the most resolute men I ever saw, and yet the most calm. He seems absolutely imperturbable. I can fancy what a wonderful power he must have over his patients" (*D* 56-57); or Quincey Morris: "He is such a nice fellow, an American from Texas, and he looks so young and so fresh [. . .]. I suppose that we women are such cowards that we think a man will save us from fears, and we marry him" (*D* 58-59). Holmwood, however, remains a shadowy figure; Lucy does not provide any indication as to what he looks like, and we have to be content with his role as lover and fiancé. We know nothing about Jonathan or Mina, either. As for Lucy herself, the few physical features associated to her are quite general and vague, although fraught with symbolic value: seen by Mina, Lucy appears as the typical angelic figure a young Victorian woman was supposed to be: "Lucy met me at the station, looking sweeter and lovelier than ever" (*D* 63) and "Lucy was looking sweetly pretty in her white lawn frock [. . .] She is so sweet with old people; I think they all fell in love with her on the spot" (*D* 65). The two female characters, particularly Lucy, only begin to be described—in a most fragmented and incomplete way, however—when they begin to transform themselves after their contact with the vampire.

This quasi-generalised absence of physical data cannot but puzzle the reader as the various narrators are usually quite observant and perceptive, and pay particular attention to detail. Lucy, for instance, tells Mina in one of her letters that when she looks at herself in a mirror, she endeavours to "read her own face" (D 57). The "heroes" themselves (Seward, Morris, Holmwood) are but briefly evoked in Lucy's letters to Mina. What details she does proffer either remain vague or mean little beyond basic psychological or moral markers, as with Seward, whom Lucy sums up as "the lunatic-asylum man, with the strong jaw and the good forehead" (D 58), an echo of contemporary phrenological theories. The young male characters in Dracula embody a late Victorian virile ideal that is strongly reminiscent of the tenets of Muscular Christianity.[4] They also stand for the Anglo-Saxon racial purity perceived as under threat in this fin-de-siècle that was haunted by the fear of degeneracy and contamination by pathogenic agents, both national and foreign. These young men are true, genuine men, as the transfusion scenes amply demonstrate. Van Helsing's reaction to Holmwood's proposal to "give the last drop of blood" in his body is telling: "Van Helsing slapped him [Holmwood] on the shoulder. 'Come!' he said. 'You are a man, and it is what we want'" (D 113). Likewise, Quincey Morris appears as the very embodiment of true masculinity: "'A brave man's blood is the best thing on this earth when a woman is in trouble. You're a man, and no mistake. [. . .] God sends us men when we want them'" (D 136).[5]

After all, Lucy could have married any one of these three young men, and the three of them propose to her almost simultaneously: "Just fancy! THREE proposals in one day! Isn't it awful!" (D 57). It is therefore sufficient to draw a general portrait of these almost interchangeable male characters, one that primarily stresses their energy and power. Quite significantly, the brave, fearless scion of a pure Anglo-Saxon stock, the American Quincey Morris, is referred to by Seward as a "moral Viking"[6] for his fortitude at Lucy's funeral: "What a fine fellow is Quincey! I believe in my heart of hearts that he suffered as much about Lucy's death as any of us; but he bore himself through it like a moral Viking. If America can go on breeding men like that, she will be a power in the world indeed" (D 156). This image of a warrior's courage points to the stereotype of the primacy and superiority of Northern peoples and races and confirms the glorification of masculine values in Dracula. The same type of vision (with the reference to Scandinavian mythology) controls the scene of Lucy's exorcism: "But Arthur never faltered. He looked like a figure of Thor as his untrembling arm rose and fell, driving deeper and deeper the mercy-bearing stake [. . .] His face was set, and high duty seemed to shine through it; the sight of it gave us courage [. . .]" (D 192). Jonathan's hand carries similar heroic connotations for Mina: "[. . .] Jonathan had taken my hand. [. . .] it was life to feel its touch—so strong, so self-reliant, so resolute. A brave man's hand can speak for itself; it does not even need a woman's love to hear its music" (*D* 210).

The only two characters spared this representational haziness are Dracula and Van Helsing, both described in detail, respectively by Harker in Chapter 2 and by Mina in Chapter 14. This makes sense as both are patriarchal figures that offer an inverted or negative image of each other and represent polar archetypes engaged in a Manichean struggle. As such, they deserve a full portrait, unlike the other masculine characters who merely embody types or dramatic functions, as in Greimas's "*schéma actantiel.*"

What predominates in the portrait of Dracula is animalism, hairiness, abnormality, and the suggestion of the cruelty and violence of a predator:

> By this time I had finished my supper, and by my host's desire had drawn up a chair by the fire and begun to smoke a cigar which he offered me, at the same time excusing himself that he did not smoke. I had now an opportunity of observing him, and found him of a very marked physiognomy.
>
> His face was a strong—a very strong—aquiline, with high bridge of the thin nose and peculiarly *arched nostrils*, with *lofty domed forehead*, and hair growing scantily round the temples but profusely elsewhere. His *eyebrows were very massive, almost meeting over the nose*, and with bushy hair that seemed to curl in its own profusion. The mouth, so far as I could see it under the heavy moustache, was fixed and rather cruel-looking, with peculiarly sharp white teeth. These protruded over the lips, whose remarkable ruddiness showed astonishing vitality in a man of his years. For the rest, his ears were pale, and at the tops extremely pointed. The *chin was broad and strong*, and the cheeks firm though thin. The general effect was one of extraordinary pallor.
>
> Hitherto I had noticed the backs of his hands as they lay on his knees in the firelight, and they had seemed rather white and fine. But seeing them now close to me, I could not but notice that they were rather coarse, broad, with squat fingers. Strange to say, there were hairs in the centre of the palm. The nails were long and fine, and cut to a sharp point. As the Count leaned over me and his hands touched me, I could not repress a shudder. It may have been that his breath was rank, but a horrible feeling of nausea came over me, which, do what I would, I could not conceal. (*D* 23-24, emphasis added)

As for Van Helsing, we notice the presence of phrenological stereotypes, particularly in the equating of the breadth and shape of the forehead with intelligence. However, radically different though he may look at first sight, since he is clean-shaven, he shares multiple common points with the vampire: bushy eyebrows, strong chin, sensitive nostrils, powerful forehead, all of which confirms their status as doubles or "enemy brothers":

> I rose and bowed, and he came towards me, a man of medium weight, strongly built, with his shoulders set back over a broad, deep chest and a neck well balanced on the trunk as the head is on the neck. The poise of the head strikes me

at once as indicative of thought and power. The *head is noble, well-sized, broad,* and large behind the ears. The face, clean-shaven, shows a *hard, square chin,* a large resolute, mobile mouth, a good-sized nose, rather straight, but with *quick, sensitive nostrils,* that seem to broaden as the *big bushy brows* come down and the mouth tightens. The *forehead is broad* and fine, rising at first almost straight and then sloping back above two bumps or ridges wide apart, such a forehead that the reddish hair cannot possibly tumble over it, but falls naturally back and to the sides. Big, dark blue eyes are set widely apart, and are quick and tender or stern with the man's moods. (*D* 163, emphasis added)

In addition to the fact that most of these characters are types, there exists another reason for the general reluctance to describe bodies in *Dracula.* The Judeo-Christian vision, that was still prevalent in the Victorian period, regarded the body as subservient, if not as radically impure, because of its animal drives. Of course, the impact of evolutionist theses on Victorian mores had not helped much either. Their unpalatable conclusion that man's ancestry and inheritance was ineradicably animalistic sparked contemporary fears of human regression and degeneration, evident in fin-de-siècle literature from Stevenson's *The Strange Case of Dr Jekyll and Mr Hyde* (1886), with the "troglodytic," ape-like Hyde, to Machen's *The Great God Pan* (1894) or Wells's *The Island of Doctor Moreau* (1896), to name but a few. The portrait of Dracula is obviously refracted through this evolutionist prism and testifies to the contemporary anxiety about the latent bestiality in man.

In *The Gothic Body: Sexuality, Materialism and Degeneration at the Fin de Siècle* (1996), Kelly Hurley emphasises the role deviant sexuality played in late Victorian literature: "Deviant sexuality could be classed as 'degenerate' in four senses: its recapitulation of the less evolved sexuality of so-called primitives, its hereditability, its deteriorative effect on mind and body, and its general corrupting influence on public morals."[7] Deviant sexuality was of course an all-encompassing notion that included any sexual activity outside matrimony. Women were viewed as creatures branded by original sin, and Mina herself, obviously conditioned by contemporary gender stereotypes, evokes the Eve that lies dormant in any woman: "[. . .] I suppose it is some of the taste of the original apple that remains still in our mouths [. . .]" (*D* 164). Because of their innately corrupt nature, and their propensity to evil, women were seen as being prone to atavic regression. As Hurley points out, "The female body [. . .] was intrinsically pathological, and the subject inhabiting the body was erratic and unstable [. . .]."[8]

The fin-de-siècle intellectual context is clearly perceptible in the novel. In his criminological studies of the 1890s, Cesare Lombroso placed women at the bottom of the evolutionary ladder alongside savages (as less evolved races), criminals, and madmen.[9] Not surprisingly, then, we notice *Dracula* implicitly effects a sweeping negative association of three categories of "beasts" or "savages": images of bestiality affect lunatics (Renfield licking the blood on the floor like a dog, *D* 129), vampires (Dracula, his various metamorphoses into bats, birds, dogs, or wolves, and his bestiality: "the full lips of the blood-dripping mouth, champed together like those of a wild beast," *D* 247) and women. Lucy, drained of her blood, is reduced to the same status as Quincey Morris's vampirised mare: "I have not seen anything pulled down so quick since I was on the Pampas and had a mare that I was fond of go to grass in a night. One of those big bats that they call vampires had got at her in the night [. . .] and I had to put a bullet through her as she lay" (*D* 138). It should also be pointed out that the mare is an animal with potent sexual connotations. Of course, the sexuality of the three succubi in Dracula's castle is overtly bestial, as they are *both* women and vampires: "[. . .] as she arched her neck she actually licked her lips like an animal, till I could see in the moonlight the moisture shining on the scarlet lips and on the red tongue as it lapped the white sharp teeth" (*D* 42).

It is finally because of her ambiguous status that Mina, unlike Lucy, is spared from complete, definitive contamination. According to her admirer Van Helsing, she possesses a woman's heart but a man's brain (*D* 207), as well as other intellectual qualities usually ascribed to men: "'Ah, then you have a good memory for facts, for details? It is not always so with young ladies'" (*D* 164). Because of her maternal yearnings and instincts which Lucy, as a "bloofer lady" (*D* 187), and the three succubi lack (as seen, for instance, in the following explanations: "We women have something of the mother in us that makes us rise above small matters when the mother-spirit is invoked [. . .]" [*D* 203]; and "No one but a woman can help a man when he is in trouble of the heart [. . .]" [*D* 204]), Mina embodies another duality, one which also saves her: she is both a daughter of Eve and a Madonna, another strong Victorian polarity studied by Eric Trudgill in *Madonnas and Magdalens* (1976).[10]

Dracula is a novel of bodily metamorphoses: vampires disembody themselves and evaporate (e.g., the three sisters as luminous dust at Dracula's castle [*D* 48]; Dracula as a mist, [*D* 227]), which makes them more ubiquitous, dangerous, and *unheimlich* than in their solid bodily form. They turn into animals, become younger, but also transform their prey beyond all recognition, as we see with Lucy, who is irremediably defiled and turned into a "thing," that is, into a horrifying, grotesque caricature of her former self, according to her friends. "As a noun," Dominique Iehl suggests, the grotesque "implies that an object either occupies multiple categories or that it falls between categories [. . .]."[11] Lucy's death scene in *Dracula* presents "a condition of being beyond the reach of language":[12]

[. . .] we recognized the features of Lucy Westenra. Lucy Westenra, but yet how changed. The sweetness was turned into adamantine, heartless cruelty, and the purity to voluptuous wantonness. [. . .] When Lucy—I call the thing that was before us Lucy because it bore her shape—saw us she drew back with an angry snarl, such as a cat gives when taken unawares; then her eyes ranged over us. Lucy's eyes in form and colour; but Lucy's eyes unclean and full of hell-fire, instead of the pure, gentle orbs we knew. (*D* 187-88)

    Hurley considers that "[t]he female vampire in *Dracula* is a pathological version of womanhood [. . .]."[13] Besides, Lucy's teeth, with their connotations of aggressive, phallic sexuality, testify to a perversion of the model of "angelic" femininity, an unnatural inversion of the natural order, an offence against gender boundaries. As a vampire, that is, an active agent, and no longer a passive "angel in the house," Lucy becomes an example of Lyn Pykett's "improper feminine."[14] Lucy's violent sexuality makes of her a moral monster, as disturbing as prostitutes were in the eyes of some Victorians. As Eric Trudgill writes in *Madonnas and Magdalens*, "[r]evulsion at fallen women was in proportion to adoration of female purity," pointing out Hippolyte Taine's shocked reaction when he saw how prostitution was rife on his visit to London in the 1860s, a phenomenon the French philosopher and historian described as "a festering sore [. . .] on the body of English society."[15] Lucy's case confirms the reading of *Dracula* as a partly (un)conscious clinical study of the diseases— mainly imaginary—affecting Victorian society. The physical presence of the vampire, as an *unheimlich* alien, as both same and other, serves to expose the fin-de-siècle pathologies resulting from contamination by seditious agents— Jews and foreigners, decadent artists, hysterical and feminised men (writers), homosexuals, and fast or emancipated women subsumed under the term "The New Woman." Dracula is but a catalyst that lays bare the diseased Victorian body (and mind).

    However, the body is just as dangerous when it is absent or invisible. The empty coffins in Carfax, for example, suggest a diffuse and pervasive but untraceable danger. So too does Dracula's lack of a reflection in a mirror raise certain fears:

> I only slept a few hours when I went to bed, and feeling that I could not sleep any more, got up. I had hung my shaving glass by the window, and was just beginning to shave. Suddenly I felt a hand on my shoulder, and heard the Count's voice saying to me, "Good morning." I started, for it amazed me that I had not seen him, since the reflection of the glass covered the whole room behind me. In starting I had cut myself slightly, but did not notice it at the moment. Having answered the Count's salutation, I turned to the glass again to see how I had been mistaken. This time there could be no error, for the man was close to me, and I could see him over my shoulder. But there was no reflection of him in the mirror! The whole room behind me was displayed, but there was no sign of a man in it, except myself. [. . .]
>
> "Take care," he said, "take care how you cut yourself. It is more dangerous that you think in this country." Then seizing the shaving glass, he went on, "And

this is the wretched thing that has done the mischief. It is a foul bauble of man's
vanity. Away with it!" And opening the window with one wrench of his terrible
hand, he flung out the glass, which was shattered into a thousand pieces on the
stones of the courtyard far below. Then he withdrew without a word. It is very
annoying, for I do not see how I am to shave, unless in my watch-case or the
bottom of the shaving pot, which is fortunately of metal. (*D* 30-31)

Clément Rosset's analysis in Chapter 3 ("Le reflet") of *Impressions fugitives.
L'Ombre, le reflet, l'écho* (2004) proves particularly relevant here.[16] Rosset
points out the strong similarities between shadows and reflections, showing that
bodies deprived of either or both are perceived as monstrous and devilish. The
question Rosset poses is why mirrors are incapable of "reading" vampires:

How can we interpret the vampire's "impotence" in front of the mirror, his
inability to impress it? The oldest theory on this point, and the most common
one, even nowadays, is that the vampire being a dead creature whose appearance
subsists—at night—after his death, is necessarily a body without a soul, and that
only a body endowed with a soul, in other words an "animated" body, can have a
reflection. [. . .] [I]n the distant past [. . .] when a house was in mourning, mirrors
were turned back, with their faces to the walls, so that recently deceased bodies
could not be able to make out their fleeing souls in the glass and unite again with
them [. . .] but also so that the reflection of dead bodies could not contaminate
the reflection of living ones, and therefore, of living persons, through the strange
contamination of the mirror evoked by Cathos in *Les Précieuses ridicules*, when
he thus addresses the maidservant Marotte: "Bring us the mirror [. . .] and mind
you do not soil the glass by communicating your image to it." [. . .] The soulless
body of the vampire, deprived of the principle of animation that represents the
essence of living beings, has somehow become too weak to be able to impress
the mirror. [. . .] If living bodies cast shadows, the shadows of the dead, which
are already reflections in themselves, cannot be duplicated a second time by
being doubled again in the mirror [. . .] That's why the mirror, which is a kind of
device designed to register living bodies (or actual, existing objects), lets the
vampire go through it without registering him. Like a machine unable to
decipher the code of a magnetic card and rejecting it while telling its owner his
card is "unreadable," the mirror fails to identify the vampire. It is unable to
"read" it.[17]

Even when it is not whole, the body is just as dangerous, except in the
case of Lucy, whose decapitation is a mutilation which paradoxically aims at
restoring her spiritual integrity and her humanity. Representing a fragmented
body involves a process of cutting out and framing, which invests body parts
with terrifying emotional power. This is quite true of George Eliot's *Daniel
Deronda* (1876) where Grandcourt's delicate white hand haunts and obsesses
Gwendolen Harleth precisely because *it is* but a hand that concentrates tenfold
the whole evil power of its owner and precisely because what *she sees* is but a

hand, and the rest of the "picture" is left in the dark, its invisibility making it all the more frightening as there is a suggestion of its omnipotence and haunting ubiquity. Besides, the hand, because of the emotional grip it exerts on her, appears larger than life. This is the inevitable effect of metonymic representation in fantastic fiction as body parts are endowed with a disturbing life and power of their own, and shift from pure physical materiality to a fantastic and symbolic realm. Therefore, before she dies, Lucy has become nothing but a mouth with protruding teeth. Kayser's conception of the grotesque as an art form expressing an *unheimlich* sense of insecurity, of fragmentation, and of alienation should be evoked again here, especially in its modern dimension that, unlike the Bakhtinian grotesque, does not rest on a creative potential:

> Everything looks as if, for Kayser, the grotesque rested upon structures that reversed those studied by Bakhtin. Profusion is turned into dissolution, luxuriance into scarcity, expansion into constriction, creative hypertrophy into distortion, eccentricity into lunacy, organic development into automation, living amalgamation into mere hybridity. [. . .] Faced with such radical contrast, one may wonder whether it is not a question of two irreconcilable forms of the grotesque belonging to two radically distinct periods of the grotesque, an uplifting, euphoric grotesque culture with its heyday in the Renaissance and a dark, wry, solitary grotesque in existence between the 18th and 20th centuries.[18]

In *Dracula*, hands (e.g., Dracula's in the Transylvanian section and in the "baptism of blood" scene, *D* 247), mouths, lips, and teeth, or necks are literally obsessive presences. The references to Lucy's mouth and teeth constitute a leitmotif in the descriptions of her gradual metamorphosis: "Whist asleep she looked stronger, although more haggard [. . .] her open mouth showed the pale gums drawn back from the teeth, which thus looked positively longer and sharper than usual [. . .]" (*D* 139); "And then insensibly came the strange change which I had noticed in the night. [. . .] [T]he mouth opened, and the pale gums, drawn back, made the teeth look longer and sharper than ever" (*D* 146). Her bloody mouth and chin at the churchyard sum up all the horror of her transformation (*D* 187). Mina herself is gravely threatened as her altered appearance testifies to: "She was very, very pale—almost ghastly, and so thin that her lips were drawn away, showing her teeth somewhat prominently. [. . .] As yet there was no sign of the teeth growing sharper [. . .]" (*D* 257). The body even acquires a symptomatic value fraught with nameless terrors. The marks on Lucy's neck initially represent a hieroglyph for all, except for Van Helsing, who, unlike Seward, goes beyond a purely clinical approach in order to read those marks:

> [...] the narrow black velvet band which she seemed always to wear round her throat [...] was dragged a little up, and showed a red mark on the throat. Arthur did not notice it, but I could hear the deep hiss of indrawn breath which is one of Van Helsing's ways of betraying emotion. [...] Just over the external jugular vein there were two punctures, not large, but not wholesome-looking. There was no sign of disease, but the edges were white and worn-looking, as if by some trituration. (*D* 115)

Thus cut up and fetishised, body-parts become synecdoches—of evil, of the vampire, and of human impotence and loss of control, the widespread use of the grotesque indicating "that significant portions of experience are eluding satisfactory verbal formulation"[19]—mystic symbols, and signs to be read or deciphered, like Mina's forehead:

> There was a fearful scream which almost froze our hearts to hear. As he placed the wafer on Mina's forehead, it had seared it—had burned into the flesh as though it had been a piece of white-hot metal. [...] [A]nd she sank on her knees on the floor in an agony of abasement. Pulling her beautiful hair over her face, as the leper of old his mantle, she wailed out: —
> "Unclean! Unclean! Even the Almighty shuns my polluted flesh! I must bear this mark of shame upon my forehead until the Judgment Day." (*D* 258-59)

Like the fragmented text of *Dracula* that builds up gradually as characters slowly disintegrate, the fragmented body turns out to be far more eloquent and expressive than it would be if whole. Could not aberrant, fragmented bodies be a post/modern grotesque strategy remedying the inability of language to express a sense of the fin-de-siècle tragic?

Notes

1 Geoffrey Galt Harpham, *On the Grotesque: Strategies of Contradiction in Art and Literature* (Princeton: Princeton University Press, 1982), 9.
2 Wolfgang Kayser, *The Grotesque in Art and Literature*, trans. Ulrich Weisstein (Bloomington: Indiana University Press, 1963).
3 Dominique Iehl, *Le Grotesque* (Paris: PUF, 1997), 13, my translation. The original French reads:

> Dans toutes les oeuvres étudiées, Kayser retrouve une même structure grotesque. Mais ce qu'il appelle grotesque n'a plus rien de commun avec l'expansion dynamique, avec la prolifération joyeuse de l'univers rabelaisien. Ce qui était dilatation et jouissance devient frustration et réduction. Pour Bakhtine, le grotesque signifie une prise de possession du réel. Pour Kayser, il surgit dans le sentiment effrayant que toute la réalité se dérobe et nous devient étrangère.

[. . .] W. Kayser décrit ici un processus de destruction progressive, la prise de conscience de l'abolition de l'ordre, de la cohérence et du sens. Cela commence par un sentiment d'étrangeté, d'exclusion hors de l'univers organisé, pour s'achever dans une expérience du vide et du néant. [. . .] Les assises du réel s'effritent ou s'effondrent.

4 See Donald Hall, ed., *Muscular Christianity: Embodying the Victorian Age* (Cambridge: Cambridge University Press, 1994), where he notes that

Muscular Christianity was an important religious, literary, and social movement of the mid-nineteenth century. This volume draws on recent developments in culture and gender theory to reveal ideological links between Muscular Christianity and the work of novelists and essayists, including Kingsley, Emerson, Dickens, Hughes, MacDonald, and Pater, and to explore the use of images of hyper-masculinised male bodies to represent social as well as physical ideals. Muscular Christianity argues that the ideologies of the movement were extreme versions of common cultural conceptions, and that anxieties evident in Muscular Christian texts, often manifested through images of the body as a site of socio-political conflict, were pervasive throughout society. Throughout, Muscular Christianity is shown to be at the heart of issues of gender, class, and national identity in the Victorian age. (flap summary of the book)

5 Van Helsing momentarily falls from "grace" in Dr Seward's eyes after Lucy's funeral where his hysterical reaction makes him all of a sudden dangerously feminine, hence unmanageable and disturbing. The difference between men and women Seward alludes to is rather an explicit reference to woman's inferiority:

The moment we were alone in the carriage he gave way to a regular fit of hysterics. He laughed till he cried and I had to draw down the blinds lest anyone should see us [. . .] and then he cried till he laughed again; and laughed and cried together, just as a woman does. I tried to be stern with him, as one is to a woman under the circumstances; but it had no effect. Men and women are so different in manifestations of nervous strength or weakness! (*D* 157)

6 This image does not connote savage destruction or brutality, or a warlike streak, but rather carries positive overtones in this context, that of courage, and the purity of untainted blood, with all its consequences in the moral field.

7 Kelly Hurley, *The Gothic Body: Sexuality, Materialism and Degeneration at the Fin de Siècle* (Cambridge: Cambridge University Press, 1996), 71.

8 Kelly Hurley 120.

9 Lombroso's studies in criminology and his anthropometric methods were quite influential in the 1890s when many of his articles were published in British periodicals: "Illustrative Studies in Criminal Anthropology" (1891), "Atavism and Evolutionism" (1895), or "Criminal Anthropology: Its Origin and Application" (1895). *The Man of Genius* was translated into English in 1891 and *The Female Offender* in 1895 (see Hurley 182, 8n). The feminine is seen by Lombroso as intrinsically primitive, hence its potential for regression and criminal behaviour.

10 Eric Trudgill, *Madonnas and Magdalens: The Origins and Development of Victorian Sexual Attitudes* (London: Heinemann, 1976). Hurley insists on the same inescapable Victorian polarity:

> The nineteenth-century perception of woman as "the sex" [. . .] stands in sharp contradistinction to Victorian celebrations of woman as a domestic angel, an essentially disembodied creature. [. . .] Victorian representations of woman tend to polar extremes: women are saintly or demonic, spiritual or bodily, asexual or ravenously sexed, guardians of domestic happiness or unnatural monsters. These two incompatible perceptions of femininity (women as angels, women as beasts) are often found side by side within the same text [. . .]. (121)

11 Dominique Iehl 3.

12 Dominique Iehl 3.

13 Kelly Hurley 121.

14 Lyn Pykett, *The 'Improper Feminine': The Women's Sensational Novel and the New Woman Writing* (London: Routledge, 1992).

15 Eric Trudgill 105, 103n.

16 Clément Rosset, *Impressions fugitives. L'Ombre, le reflet, l'écho* (Paris: Les Éditions de Minuit, 2004).

17 Clément Rosset 52-53, my translation. The original French reads:

> Comment interpréter cette "impuissance" du vampire face au miroir, cette impossibilité où il est de l'impressionner ? La thèse la plus ancienne et toujours la plus courante sur ce point est que le vampire, étant un mort dont l'apparence survit,—de nuit—, à son décès, est nécessairement un corps sans âme, et que seul un corps doté d'une âme, c'est-à-dire un corps "animé," est susceptible de reflet. [. . .] [D]ans un lointain passé [. . .] lors des deuils, on retournait les miroirs vers les murs afin que les corps récemment décédés ne puissent y discerner dans le miroir leur âme fuyante et de nouveau s'unir à elle [. . .] afin aussi que le reflet des corps morts ne puisse contaminer le reflet des corps vivants, et par suite des vivants eux-mêmes, par une étrange contamination du miroir évoquée par Cathos, dans *Les Précieuses ridicules*, s'adressant à la servante Marotte: "Apportez-nous le miroir [. . .], et gardez-vous bien d'en salir la glace par la communication de votre image." [. . .] Le corps sans âme du vampire, dénué du principe d'animation qui fait l'essence de l'être vivant, n'a en quelque sorte plus la force d'aller impressionner le miroir. [. . .] Si les ombres des corps vivants se reflètent, les ombres des morts, qui sont déjà reflets en elles-mêmes, ne peuvent se dupliquer une seconde fois en allant se re-redoubler dans le miroir [. . .] C'est pourquoi le miroir, sorte d'appareil à enregistrer les corps vivants (ou les objets existants) laisse passer le vampire sans l'enregistrer. Telle une machine qui ne réussit pas à déchiffrer le code d'une carte magnétique et recrache celle-ci en déclarant à son propriétaire que sa carte est "muette," le miroir échoue à identifier le vampire. Il est incapable de le "lire."

18 Dominique Iehl 14-15, my translation. The original French reads:

> Tout se passe comme si, pour Kayser, le grotesque fonctionnait selon des structures à l'envers même de celles de Bakhtine. Le foisonnement devient

dissolution, la luxuriance se transforme en pénurie, l'extension en réduction, l'hypertrophie créatrice en déformation, l'excentricité en folie, le déploiement organique en automatisation, l'amalgame vivant en hybridité. [. . .] On peut se demander, devant la radicalité de ce contraste, si l'on n'a pas affaire à deux grotesques inconciliables, à deux époques radicalement distinctes du grotesque, une culture grotesque euphorique culminant à la Renaissance et un grotesque grinçant et solitaire du XVIIIe au XXe siècle.

19 Dominique Iehl 4.

CHAPTER SIX

TEACHING AND SELLING DRACULA IN TWENTY-FIRST-CENTURY ROMANIA

MONICA GIRARD, NANCY-UNIVERSITÉ

The figure of Vlad the Impaler, *voivode* of Walachia in the fifteenth century, has been the subject of much debate, both in Romanian historiography and in western studies. After the publication of Bram Stoker's *Dracula* in 1897, many foreigners claimed that the Romanian *voivode* was the model for the character in the novel. Yet the Romanians have always taken pride in their historical heritage and have defended their national hero despite his evil reputation spread first by the German, Slavonic and Turkish legends in the late fifteenth and sixteenth centuries, then followed by Stoker's *Dracula* in the nineteenth century, and more recently by postmodernist practices including numerous film adaptations of Stoker's *Dracula* and other media spin-offs. Today, however, the Romanians are faced with a moral dilemma: how to promote the Romanian history and culture attached to this complex historical figure without destroying a myth which encourages tourists to take an interest in their country.

I began this study by investigating how Vlad Țepeș is seen by a sample of the Romanian population. Since historical knowledge is acquired first and foremost at school, I asked a specific group of Romanian students what they knew about this historical figure. I posed the same question to three different sets of students from two different high schools, each with a specific profile. After examining and comparing their answers, I realised that their similar remarks probably reflected the information read in textbooks chosen by their teachers. The fact that most of them talk about Vlad Țepeș as a national hero and a symbol of justice is related to characteristics of the *voivode* commonly portrayed in Romanian history textbooks. Consequently, I looked into these different textbooks to see to what extent the pupils' answers were rooted in the information provided by the authors of these textbooks or in the popularity of the Dracula myth itself. I then studied the variety of legends and sources mentioned in the textbooks which have contributed to Vlad Țepeș's reputation abroad, a reputation which is partly at the origin of the development of tourism in Romania.

Romanian students on Vlad Ţepeş: three surveys

Survey 1 was given on 25 October 2005. Ten eleventh-form students aged seventeen from Petrol High School (Câmpina, Romania) answered the following question: "What do you know about Vlad Ţepeş?"[1] Their responses proved that they distinguish between historical reality and myth and are aware of the process of distortion and defamation that the figure of Vlad Ţepeş has undergone when transposed into legend, fiction, and film. The following compiled answers, their exact words translated from Romanian, focus on three major issues: history, fiction, and tourism:

> Vlad Ţepeş was a *voivode* who reigned in the fifteenth century in Transylvania. He was the son of Vlad Dracula. His nickname, Ţepeş, reflects the method with which he punished and killed (by impaling) his enemies: Turks, war prisoners, traitors, thieves, and liars. He was feared by his subjects. He has survived in history as the cruellest but also the fairest ruler. He is seen as the dispenser and the symbol of justice. All the legends associated with him draw on his cruelty and sense of justice. The Hungarian merchants started the rumour that Vlad Ţepeş was a vampire in order to get revenge because he raised their taxes. The vampire in legends is only a distortion of the image of a *voivode*. The legends of the vampire have no real foundation. Because he was bloodthirsty, the legend associated Vlad Ţepeş with a vampire who drank his enemies' blood. The vampire is said to have lived in Bran castle. The novel *Dracula* was written by an Englishman [sic] but nothing is real. Many films have been made about Dracula [examples given: *Nosferatu, Dracula 2000, Van Helsing*]. The action of these films takes place in Transylvania. Our country has become famous thanks to Dracula and lots of foreign tourists come to visit Romania, especially Bran Castle and Sighişoara Castle. Vlad Ţepeş's international fame is beneficial for our country because many tourists come to find out the truth and learn more about the mystery.

It is interesting to note that the whole group of students in Survey 1 stated that the *voivode* reigned in Transylvania. This mistake could confirm the impact on teenagers of myth, legends, fiction, and the film industry over knowledge or historical information acquired at school. The legend and fictional aspects are stressed more by these students as compared to other students' answers in Surveys 2 and 3, as we shall see. They also amalgamate different layers of myth since, in reality, there is no association between vampires and Vlad Ţepeş in fifteenth-century and sixteenth-century legends, which will be shown in the third part of this essay. When talking about legends, a majority of students insisted on the point that "nothing is real," as if they resented the association between the fictitious Dracula and the real Ţepeş and wished to "correct" the legend by strongly denying the assumption that Vlad the vampire is Vlad the national hero. This led me to carry out a subsequent survey about how the students perceive this association and how they respond to the tourists' point of view. The students in Survey 1 gave more importance to the historical figure's international fame, as opposed to, for instance, the students in Survey 3, who focused more on historical facts and precise details.

Survey 2 was given on 5 December 2005. Thirty-one eleventh-form students from Nicolaie Grigorescu High School (Câmpina, Romania) answered the same question: "What do you know about Vlad Ţepeş?" The following answers are again the exact translation of a composite of their own words:

Vlad Ţepeş was *voivode* of Walachia; he had two/three periods of reign in [the] fifteenth century/seventeenth century. His father was Vlad Dracul (order of the Dragon) and his cousin was Radu cel Frumos (Radu the Handsome). He had a "diabolic," "barbarian" method of impalement for corrupt people and *boyars*; hence his nickname. He was cruel, authoritarian, and feared by everybody. He was cruel but fair; he was unforgiving; he was cunning and famous for his war strategies. People mistake him for Dracula, the famous vampire. Western societies associate him incorrectly with Count Dracula, a character created by Bram Stoker, because of his name, "Vlad Dracul." A myth has been developed, associating him with Dracula. Nowadays, tourists visit the Poienari castle where he lived.

Vlad Ţepeş's personality and nickname are the two recurrent details associated with the *voivode*. Compared to the first group, these students were more precise and tried to provide more historical information, even if sometimes the data was not accurate: some of them situated the reign of the *voivode* in the seventeenth century instead of the fifteenth century; others hesitated between two or three reigns; and some of the family links were incorrect, Radu the Handsome being Vlad's brother, not cousin. Overall, they gave the same information as in Survey 1, with the same concern to mark the difference between the historical figure and the fictitious character.

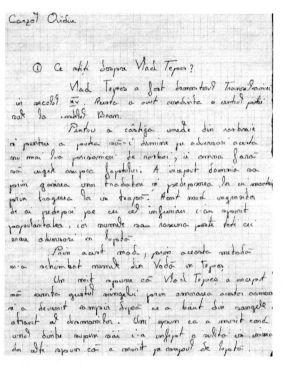

Figure 7-1: Sample Romanian Student Response
(Courtesy of the Author)

Survey 3 was given on 5 December 2005 and concerned twenty-seven twelfth-form students (eighteen years old) from the Nicolaie Grigorescu High School (Câmpina, Romania). Like their counterparts, they answered the question: "What do you know about Vlad Țepeș?" Their answers have been compiled and translated from Romanian:

Vlad Țepeș reigned in 1446, 1456-1462, and 1478. He was *Voivode* of Walachia. His brother, Radu cel Frumos, chased him away from Walachia. He was the son of Vlad Dracul: the name comes from the order of the Dragon, "Dracul" in Romanian. Țepeș was famous for his pitiless punishments of unfaithful *boyars*, traitors, and thieves. His methods shocked his contemporaries but the punishments he inflicted must be put in the context of his time. His nickname, Țepeș, was associated with his method of killing, that is to say impalement. He waged a famous battle against the Turks in winter 1462. In this famous night attack, he disguised himself as a Turk, entered the enemy camp, and slaughtered them. Vlad Țepeș was famous for the wars of independence. The Sultan tried to trap him but he used cunning strategies, such as retreating before the invaders by burning harvests and poisoning wells behind him. He refused to pay taxes to the Turks. He played a big part in the crusade against the Ottomans to insure the autonomy and independence of the Romanians. In 1462 he was exiled to Transylvania but Matei Corvin, the Hungarian king, pressured by the Sas and Secui *boyars*, put him in jail in Buda; Matei Corvin accused Vlad Ţepeş of collaborating with the Turks (he discovered some falsified letters). Supported by Ştefan cel Mare (Stephen the Great, Moldavian *voivode*), he came back to Walachia as a *voivode* but was killed because of the *boyars'* complots. He reigned in the capital, Tirgoviste, but he was buried in Snagov. Famous legends include the one about a gold cup near the well that nobody dared to steal and the story of nailing Turk messengers' turbans to their heads because they refused to take them off in front of him as a sign of respect. Because of his methods of punishment, he became the hero of macabre stories. Dracula and Bran Castle are related to vampirism by foreigners. Influenced by Sas chronicles which describe him in an unfavourable light, and based on real cruelty practiced by Vlad Ţepeş, Bram Stoker created *Dracula*. This novel is fiction, associating Vlad Ţepeş with a vampire from Sighişoara. The Bran castle visited by tourists was not Ţepeş's real place of residence.

The same kind of information is repeated by the students, all of them most certainly influenced by their textbooks. However, the eighteen-year-old students in the last survey gave more historical, more accurate, and less mythic references than those in Surveys 1 and 2. They provided more complex data about the historical figure and put him in a broader geopolitical perspective.

In conclusion, regarding the three surveys, the facts mentioned by the students vary (if only slightly) from one group to another. These differences depend not only on personal knowledge but also on other criteria: differences in age, in the high schools attended (industrial versus general), in the importance of history in their curriculum, in the textbooks used by their teachers and the way information is presented in these textbooks, in the additional information provided by their teachers, and in how recently they have studied the issue in question in their classes. However, there is one consistent characteristic in each of these surveys: the Romanian students, irrespective of age group or high school attended, have practically the same background knowledge about the historical figure Vlad Ţepeş. In other words, they all talk about his methods of punishment (impalement), his cruelty and sense of justice, his legendary war escapades, and his cunningness in battle, and each considers him to be a defender of independence. They are also keenly aware of how the *voivode*'s image has been transposed by the West into fiction, but they always make a point in clearly and carefully differentiating fact from legend.

Vlad Țepeș portrayed in Romanian history textbooks

The textbooks I have taken into account are used by the history teachers in the different high schools in which I carried out the surveys. This variety of textbooks targets students between thirteen and eighteen years old. A very didactic explanation about Vlad Țepeș's personality and role in Walachian history is provided in the seventh-form textbook aimed at the youngest age group examined here. The authors seek to render a balanced portrait of the *voivode*, insisting on two aspects of his reign: Vlad Țepeș was "authoritarian, pitiless with his enemies, but also a courageous fighter against the Ottomans."[2] "Authoritarian" is in fact the key word in Vlad Țepeș's portrayal, being mentioned three times in two paragraphs, along with other adjectives such as "cruel," "merciless," "unforgiving." These negative features paradoxically paint a somewhat positive portrait as they seem essential to the role the *voivode* fulfilled as a defender of the independence of Walachia and who managed to repel the Turkish invaders from his homeland. It is important to underline the fact that there is no mention of "Dracula," neither in relation to his father's rank or inherited distinction,[3] nor to international literature. Instead, the authors talk about historical documents that offer an image of the *voivode* in accordance with the "historical truth." They also mention the German tales relating Vlad's deeds, tales which were largely influenced by Matei Corvin's defamatory policy and which were meant to focus only on the negative traits of the *voivode*. On the other hand, the Russian tales present him as a "great leader."[4] The authors also give details about Vlad Țepeș's internal policy: his reign was marked by his anti-*boyar* policy, his aim being to build a government (*Sfatul domnesc*) which was no longer composed only of noblemen but mainly of devoted dignitaries chosen by himself. This led to limiting the traditional powers of the *boyars* and the strengthening of the central power. It was also marked by the punishments inflicted on thieves, criminals, and those who conspired against him, as well as a more efficient organisation of the army divided into "the big army" (*oastea cea mare*) and "the small army" (*oastea cea mica*), a personal guard composed of mercenaries and his most faithful soldiers.

As far as his external policy is concerned, the textbook refers to Vlad's refusal to pay a tribute of money and young soldiers, which led to the deterioration of his relationship with the Turks. He was intuitive, endowed with strategic intelligence; he knew how to avoid his enemies' traps to capture him and planned guerrilla night attacks in order to surprise the Turks. He successfully thwarted complots and outsmarted his enemies. He is also presented as a victim of the complot devised by Matei Corvin who, despite the financial help from the West to support the fight against the Ottomans, was not willing to support Țepeș and, following other interests in the southeast of

Europe, clearly avoided the Ottoman conflict. The authors talk about a letter meant to compromise Vlad Ţepeş: he allegedly wrote to the Sultan and promised him help to conquer Hungary. The compromising letters, intrigue, and rumours coming directly from the Hungarian court and released through their own propaganda contributed to Vlad Ţepeş's downfall and gave Matei Corvin a reason to incarcerate the Walachian *voivode*. This complot is seen as an unfair outcome of a "life dedicated from beginning to end to the idea of preserving the independence of Walachia."[5]

In the twelfth-form textbook, Medieval Romanian civilisation is put into the larger perspective of a European context.[6] The foreign policy of Transylvania, Walachia, and Moldavia between the fifteenth and sixteenth centuries coincided insofar as the three principalities had a common aim: maintaining their historical borders, and safeguarding their autonomy and political independence. Vlad Ţepeş is part of the same chapter as other *voivodes* such as Mircea cel Bătrîn, Alexandru cel Bun, Iancu de Hunedoara, and Ştefan cel Mare (Stephen the Great); they all fought to protect their countries against the great powers, be they Christian (Hungary, Poland) or Islamic (the Ottoman Empire), all having shared the same dream of expanding their territories and annexing the Romanian principalities.

Vlad Ţepeş's international reputation is also hinted at in the different textbooks. Indeed, in the second paragraph of the chapter devoted to Vlad Ţepeş in the eleventh-form textbook, the authors of the textbook distinguish between the international fame attached to the historical figure, the legend that contributed to his celebrity, and the historical reality.[7] It is interesting to note that in Vlad Ţepeş's case, the starting point for a historical account is the reference to his international celebrity and the literary renown associated with a character in fiction: "His international renown, which has fed a whole literary genre, is that of a villain, a bloodthirsty, power-loving person born to serve evil: a prototype of the devil, Dracula."[8] Unlike this textbook in which "literary renown" is rather vague, the authors of the twelfth-form textbook are more specific about the figure of the Walachian *voivode* in literature, as they clearly mention Bram Stoker's novel. The reference to the Irish author is therefore explicit: "Many specialists have identified [Vlad Ţepeş] with Dracula, Bram Stoker's eponymous character, especially because of the impact of totally unfavourable tales spread by the Sibiu Sas population."[9]

The origin of this reputation, according to the eleventh-form textbook, as well as the seventh-form one, is the legend built and developed by German tales that largely contributed to the myth. These tales emanated from propaganda circulating during the reign of Matei Corvin, the son of Iancu de Hunedoara, and from the Sas (Saxon) population of Transylvania. The Hungarian king's court at Buda launched a slanderous campaign of defamatory rumours against the *voivode*'s person, using to this end the complaints of the Sas merchants about the protectionist trade laws imposed by Vlad Țepeș. His economic policy favoured the Walachian merchants rather than the prosperous Sas towns beyond the Carpathians, especially Brașov and Sibiu. Indeed, in spring 1459, Țepeș annulled the privileges of the Sas merchants, which consisted of buying products directly from the Walachian producers. Instead, they had to exchange goods in established fairs at the Walacho-Transylvanian border and negotiate with Walachian traders. This programme, meant to redress the economic situation of the country and bring prosperity to its inhabitants, was in fact perceived as repression against Sas citizens, who usually supported Walachian heirs to the throne among the various eligible members of the royal family (the throne of Walachia being hereditary but not by the law of primogeniture). As some of the Sas merchants did not comply with these new laws, Vlad Țepeș retaliated militarily in southern Transylvania, impaling a number of Transylvanian Saxon traders captured on Walachian territory and seizing their goods.

The origins of the tales spread by the Sas population are also dealt with in another twelfth-form textbook.[10] The authors talk about Țepeș's aim, which was to establish fair trade based on reciprocity and justice. To be sure, he wanted his Walachian tradesmen to have the same status and rights in Transylvania that the Sas merchants had when they came to Walachia. The Sas traders who did not obey this rule were cruelly punished. "Hence, through their tales spread in western countries, they perpetuated his fame as a tyrant and they came up with the name of Dracula by transforming *"Dragul"* (from his father's legacy of the Order of the Dragon) into *"Dracul,"* a word with a specific semantic weight."[11] His fame as a tyrant therefore started because of the strict economic and protectionist policies, well before the cruel military campaign against the Turks during which he impaled his enemies.

The authors of the eleventh-form history textbook also claim that it was feelings of anger and revenge from the Transylvanian population and its rulers that contributed to the portrayal of a terrifying and wicked *voivode*. The primary sources (Russian, German, Turkish pamphlets) were obviously biased against the Walachian *voivode*. Not only were they politically inspired—all were written after sealing alliances which, depending on points of view, appeared as betrayals or manipulations—these sources also certainly provided mass entertainment, hence the exaggeration meant to make Țepeș's exploits appear extraordinary. What I would call anachronistically the "sensational news stories of the fifteenth century" resulted from the increasingly widespread use of the printing press. The pamphlets were real "bestsellers," reprinted numerous times over the thirty years following Vlad Țepeș's death, proof of their constant popularity.

In all the textbooks under examination, a constant feature is how the authors collectively try to reach a positive portrait of the *voivode* in order to counterbalance the facts and events compiled from various sources. Thus, after briefly mentioning the exaggerated and biased German tales, the authors of the eleventh-form textbook sum up Țepeș's personality by depicting him in an extremely favourable light: "Beyond these exaggerations, he appeared to have been a strong personality, an enemy of disorder, anarchy, dishonesty, and a tireless fighter for the independence of his country."[12] However, the authors do not mention any primary sources on which they base their flattering portrayal. The history textbook seems vague (e.g., "it has been said"; "other sources"[13]), with no bibliographical references to support the authors' remarks. The eulogy of the *voivode* transmitted to the teenagers reflects a certain nationalistic desire to justify his strict reign. The authors enumerate all the aspects which may have contributed to his reputation: Sas inhabitants' anger, conflict with Hungarian interests, the Turks' powerlessness during certain campaigns, and the feelings of frustration and injustice of the *boyars*, who were deprived of their secular role as key decision makers in Walachian society. In this textbook, just as in all the others, the principal merit of Vlad Țepeș appears to be his courageous anti-Ottoman campaign, which prevented Sultan Mohammed II from incorporating Walachia into the boundaries of his growing empire. He is seen as a tireless freedom-fighter, who shielded Christendom from Islam, and the cruelties and atrocities he committed are presented as a necessary evil for his war strategy or justice system.

The Romanian principalities were the last Christian bastions offering resistance to the spread of Islamic influence; they played a strategic geographical, political, military, and religious role in the crusade planned by the Christian powers. Vlad Țepeș is an outstanding figure in Romanian history, the embodiment of the Romanians' aspirations for freedom and independence. The same arguments and historical perspectives taught to teenagers are presented by Romanian historians, including Mircea Eliade, who, in *The Romanians: A Concise History*, sums up Țepeș's personality and bravery in a chapter entitled "The Crusade Spirit: John Corvinus and Stephen the Great," emphasising the *voivode*'s mission to fight against the "pagans" and to defend against Turkish incursions:

> The very year John Corvinus died (1456), the throne of Muntenia was ascended by one of the most bitter enemies of Islam, Vlad, also called the "Impaler," due to the way in which he used to eliminate his foes: the torture of impaling. In 1462 he attacked the Turkish armies garrisoned by the Danube, annihilated them and, according to a contemporary of the event, spread such terror that "he who has succeeded in crossing into Anatolia should consider himself a lucky man." Obviously, such an offence could not pass unpunished. Sultan Mohammed II,

who had conquered Constantinople, could not tolerate an insult coming from a
poor Romanian prince; he attacked Vlad that very year with a huge army
(chronicler Chalcochondil speaks of 250,000 men, but the figure is undoubtedly
exaggerated). Vlad only had 10,000 men, but he knew so well the tactics of
guerilla warfare that ultimately he inflicted great casualties upon the enemy.
Mohammed's army began to suffer from a lack of supplies, as Vlad kept
attacking the supply routes. Eventually, the sultan decided to withdraw his
troops. Unhappily, Vlad's brother, Radu the Handsome, accepted Muslim
sovereignty and usurped his throne. The career of one of the bravest Romanian
princes was thus shortened through an act of felony.[14]

While presenting different aspects of his reign, different points of view,
the unstable domestic political and economic situation and the international
context, the authors of the six textbooks I have examined unanimously agree to
offer the teenagers the portrait of a great national hero, in accordance with
Romanian historiography. The most recurrent qualities enumerated by these
textbooks are his sense of justice, his defence of the independence and
autonomy of his country, his military acumen and prowess, as well as strategic
conception of battles. Ample description of his heroic endeavours against the
enemy who invaded his homeland is given in the majority of these textbooks:
we are told how he thwarted Turkish plots and frustrated his enemies' plans
with his guerrilla warfare and subterfuge. All the textbooks present him as a
unique figure in Romanian history who, in standing against the Ottoman
Empire, contributed to the building of a strong, independent Walachian state.
Vlad Ţepeş appears as one of the greatest symbols of Romanian independence
and nationhood.

A Romanian dilemma: links between the historical
Vlad Ţepeş and the fictitious Dracula

According to Ştefan Andreescu, the information Bram Stoker had when
he "constructed the counterfeit myth of Dracula" was based on medieval
legends about Vlad Ţepeş.[15] Fiction is therefore rooted in legend which, in turn,
draws on the deliberate distortion of the intriguing personality of the real
voivode. There are four types of legends about Vlad Ţepeş based on German,
Slavonic, Romanian, Byzantine, and Turkish sources.[16] These medieval legends
enjoyed wide diffusion throughout Europe in the fifteenth and sixteenth
centuries. Characteristics already put forth by the history textbooks appear in
these legends, obviously in a more biased and exaggerated way. However, I
would like to show that in all the legends and anecdotes examined, there is no
association of Vlad with vampires.

The German tales, based on a brochure published by Matthias Hupfuff in Strasbourg in 1500 and included in Annex I of Ion Stăvăruş's study, talk about Draculea *Voivode*, the "savage tyrant" who committed many "strange, scary, and barbaric deeds."[17] These stories have recurrent elements. The victims included Hungarian and Transylvanian merchants, foreign messengers and ambassadors (French, Italian, Hungarian, Turkish), priests, beggars, liars, gypsies, *boyars*, Christians, Jews, pagans, innocent young and old men, women, and even babies. No one was immune to Dracula's cruelty. Draculea always performs gratuitous, absurd sacrifices by impaling, burning alive, beheading, cutting, slicing, skinning, hanging, mutilating sexual organs, boiling alive, or frying his enemies or his own subjects. The innocence of defenceless victims is stressed in opposition to the *voivode*'s sadistic pleasure of killing and burning, sometimes "while having breakfast."[18] There are numerous details about the number of victims (400 young foreign men who came to Walachia in order to learn the language; three gypsies fried and 300 others who are given the alternative to eat the gypsies or to fight against the Turks; 500 *boyars* impaled because they gave a wrong answer; 600 merchants from Ţara Bîrsei impaled to confiscate their merchandise; 25,000 Bulgarians killed, etc.), as well as an exhaustive description of the methods of killing and of the gory tortures devised. The medieval reader is given minute details about the cruel, heartless sacrifices (for example, the story of simultaneously impaling mothers and babies on the same spike, after having cut off their breasts and inserted the babies' heads in them); the unjustified, ludicrous, disproportionate decisions to have people killed for tiny flaws (for example, the story of the woman who faced the death penalty because she had made a short-sleeved shirt for her husband instead of a long-sleeved one); and the sadistic and cannibalistic tendencies of his punishment gradually reaching their nadir of horror and revulsion (for example, the story about frying children and forcing their mothers to eat them, then cutting off the women's breasts and forcing their husbands to eat them, then impaling them all). The list of tortures accumulated in these thirty-five stories is impressive. In conclusion, the German tales display a *voivode* devoid of humanity, who derives a perverted pleasure from slowly and painfully killing his victims, be they innocent or guilty.

The Slavonic stories about the *Voivode* Draculea transcribed by Ion Stăvăruş in Annex II of his work are based on the oldest manuscript to be found in Leningrad at the Saltikov-Scedrin Public Library. The nineteen stories were written in 1486 and rewritten in 1490. The *voivode*'s religion constitutes a major issue in these stories, which is perfectly relevant from a Slavonic point of view; his renunciation of Orthodox religion under pressure from Matei Corvin, who put him in jail for twelve years, is related in a Manichean way: "He left the light and embraced the darkness"; "he left our orthodox faith and received the Latin deceit."[19] While his portrait is also that of an intolerant, arrogant, and cruel prince, he is not evil incarnate, as he is portrayed in the German stories. He is also capable of compassion, rewards the bravery of his soldiers, priests and merchants who tell the truth, and spares his Christian enemies. His main victims are Turkish, Polish, and Hungarian messengers: he nails their turbans to their heads if they do not take off their turbans, which is seen as a sign of disrespect, and impales the ones who are stupid or dim-witted. Other victims are cowardly soldiers and the poor, who are seen as parasites and a burden on society. Stories about women are frequent: lazy women, adulterous women, young girls who lose their virginity, and widows. The punishment is terrible for them as well, involving mutilation of their sexual organs, cutting off of limbs, skinning, binding, and eventual hanging. The details of his cruelty are as vividly described here as in the German stories. Gruesome facts about the method of impalement are also given: the stake was inserted through the victim's bottom, emerging from his or her mouth. The height of the spear indicated the rank of the victim. The crusade against theft, lies, injustice of priests, merchants and common people appear in most of these stories. Among them appears the legend of the gold cup, which is known by all Romanian students: a gold cup near a well was used by passers-by to drink water. Nobody dared to steal this cup, which was proof of how safe Walachia was and how honest its inhabitants were.

The Romanian stories about Vlad Ţepeş are part of a folkloric oral tradition. Ion Stăvăruş gathered seventeen such stories in Annex III. Although extremely cruel punishments are described, they are meant to be less absurd, less meaningless and less unreasonable than the German and Slavonic stories. They seem to end with a moral, and Vlad Ţepeş is clearly the figure of justice. He is not portrayed in a completely negative light: he punishes his victims (his victims are Turks who plunder Walachia, *boyars* who are traitors, thieves, liars, lazy women, beggars, and dishonest and fawning priests) but, on the other hand, he also punishes *boyars* who are mean to old and poor people, and he is the defender of honest people against greedy merchants. He is described as "exceptionally brave" but also pitiless when punishing "lazy, mean people, and the enemies of his country."[20] He has no mercy for "the unfaithfulness and slyness of the traitors";[21] he is loved and feared by his soldiers; he is the defender of the freedom and independence of his country against the Turks; and he is famous abroad for his bravery and extraordinary deeds. The adjectives used in the stories to describe his qualities are "fearless," "great," "courageous," "very cruel but just," and "cunning and smart."

A recurrent antagonist in these legends is the Turkish Sultan Mohammed II, who hates the Walachian *voivode* and plans to catch him alive. Famous Romanian oral stories, also to be found in the Slavonic tradition, are told from the Romanians' point of view: the story of Ţepeş disguised as a Turk to reach the Turk camp and kill the sultan, the gold cup legend, and the story in which he ordered the sultan's messengers' turbans to be nailed to their heads. The safety of the country is emphasised several times through legends about foreign merchants, along with the *voivode*'s determination to restore order and justice.

Vlad Ţepeş

Sultanul Mehmed al II-lea.
Pictură de Gentile Bellini

(1442–1448), pribeag în Moldova şi Transilvania (1448–1456), prizonier la Vişegrad şi Pesta (1462–1474). Din cei 45 de ani ai vieţii (născut probabil în 1431, ucis în 1476), şansa i-a hărăzit tronului doar 6, cu mult mai puţin decât lui Iancu de Hunedoara (15) şi vărului său, Ştefan cel Mare (47).

Politica internă. Împrejurările concrete ale preluării tronului de către Vlad Ţepeş nu sunt încă pe de-a-ntregul clarificate. Este cert doar că predecesorul său, Vladislav, a fost îndepărtat şi ucis în vara lui 1456 şi că domnia fiului lui *Vlad Dracul* era instituită la mijlocul lunii august. acelaşi an. În ultimii ani, s-a afirmat că întronarea lui Ţepeş a reprezentat episodul decisiv al rivalităţii otomano-ungare pentru influenţă asupra Ţării Româneşti.

La 6 septembrie 1456 el înştiinţa pe braşoveni că este întru-totul credincios regelui maghiar Ladislau „de frica turcilor", care, cum rezultă din alte relatări, pun asupra ţării „sarcini mari cu neputinţă de suportat". Numai trei luni mai târziu însă, la 16 decembrie 1456, *Ladislau de Hunedoara*, fiul lui Iancu, se plânge de necazurile, pagubele şi supărările pricinuite de Vlad, motiv pentru care se şi pregătea un pretendent la Braşov.

Politica internă a lui Vlad Ţepeş a fost determinată de faptul că Ţara Românească era dominată de interminabile lupte pentru putere, repetate schimbări de domni, anarhie internă şi amestec brutal al vecinilor hrăpăreţi.

El a înţeles că ordinea şi stabilitatea politică sunt indestructibil legate de întărirea puterii centrale, de celebrarea domnului ca „mare stăpânitor" şi de

247

Figure 7-2: Vlad Ţepeş and his Turkish Rival, Sultan Mohammed II
from *Istoria românilor din cele mai vechi timpuri pîna la Revoluţia din 1821*
(Courtesy of Editura Didactica şi Pedagogică Bucureşti)

The point of view of the Turkish anecdotes is obviously different from the Romanian folk tales. These anecdotes included by Ion Stăvăruş in Annex IV are extracted from chronicles written by Ţepeş's contemporaries (the Byzantine Laonic Chalcocondil and Ducas and the Ottoman Enveri, Tursun-bei and Aşik-Paşa-Zade). They focus on Kaziklu *Voivode*'s domestic policy and the authoritarian and cruel measures taken by the *voivode* to consolidate his power

when he ascended to the throne, the measures of repression to keep his
neighbours at bay, and the relationship of conflict between the Walachians and
the Turks, especially during the 1461–1462 military campaign.

He is portrayed as the "bloodthirsty tyrant," merciless not only towards
traitors and criminals, but even towards his own people (it is said that when
somebody in a village was guilty, the entire village was impaled, men, women,
and children alike).[22] The disproportionate punishments given by the "violent"
and "evil" "tyrant" or "despot" are recorded in these anecdotes, which mainly
focus on his war campaigns against the Turks, the secret alliances sealed with
the Hungarians against the Ottomans, and his sly methods of attacking by night:
"The bei of Walachia, this cursed son of a bastard, attacked Hamsa-bei at
midnight."[23] The way Țepeș is qualified in the Turkish chronicles is also in
keeping with the way the confrontations are presented; indeed, the religious
aspect is omnipresent, and the Muslims are constantly tricked by being slyly
attacked by the "ghiauri" (non-Muslims). The leader of the *ghiauri*, the enemies,
is a "daring," "damned" "bastard" fighting against the "dazzling and powerful
Emperor," "the Shah of the World," "the Enlightened Shah" who, with the help
of Allah, reduced the number of "damned enemies" and "countless dragon-like
ghiaurs" in the famous night attack initiated by Țepeș-Kaziklu. The Turk's own
chronicles stress bravery and skilful military actions.

In sum, the legends and anecdotes have common features and recurrent
elements that appear and reappear in different sources. The way Vlad Țepeș is
described and the phenomenon of distortion, exaggeration, and amplification of
the historical truth depend largely on the biased point of view of these different
sources. The wide circulation of the stories in different parts of Europe
surrounding Walachia should also be pointed out. The representations vary from
the cruel tyrant to the hero with a strong sense of justice, protector of
defenceless people and of his country. These sensational legends established his
reputation throughout Europe. However, in none of these legends is there any
vampiric association with Vlad Țepeș. The word vampire is never used in any
chronicles, oral stories, or written legends. A different layer of myth was to be
added in the nineteenth century after Bram Stoker's novel appeared and
westerners assumed that Vlad Țepeș was Stoker's inspiration for his vampire
Count.

Today, the Romanians respond in two different ways to the association
between the historical figure, Vlad Țepeș, and the fictitious character, Count
Dracula.[24] Nicolae Stoicescu's *Vlad Țepeș* is but one of the many examples of
historical articles and books about Vlad Țepeș written mainly in the 1970s
when, during the communist period, there was a visible effort to develop a
nationalistic policy.[25] Stoicescu tries to separate Vlad Țepeș, the historical
figure, not only from legends but also from Stoker's fiction. This book is seen

by western critics as part of the communist propaganda at that time to rehabilitate and reinforce Vlad Țepeș's reputation as a national hero. In another survey I carried out in April 2006, only a minority of Romanian students said they disliked the fact that westerners associate Romania with the home of the vampire and that the world's most notorious vampire, Dracula, bears the name of one of Romania's national heroes. These students condemn the denigration of their national hero and resent the fact that he became a horror icon for western nations. This survey included sixty-six students, between the ages of fourteen and eighteen, from two different high schools, Petrol High School and Energetic High School (Câmpina, Romania). The questions asked in this survey were: "As a Romanian, what do you feel when foreigners associate Vlad Țepeș with Dracula? In your opinion, what impact does this association have on the image of your country?" The following composite answer sums up the students' exact words expressing dissatisfaction with the Vlad Țepeș/Dracula association:

> Because of a novelist's rich imagination, foreigners see us all as a bizarre, violent, and barbaric people who have mystic and occult practices. The Vlad Țepeș/Dracula association is only a tourist attraction for foreigners eager to be frightened by horror stories and adventures. I'm offended that Vlad Țepeș is associated with Dracula. It's sad and disappointing that Vlad Țepeș is associated with a vampire. Vlad Țepeș has thus become a notorious serial killer for foreigners. A great Romanian ruler is represented as a vampire and a monster only to attract tourists. We should respect his memory. As a Romanian, I want the tourists to be told the truth. This phantasmagorical association and aberration should not be believed by foreigners. Foreigners should learn more about Vlad Țepeș because their association is detrimental to the image of Romania.

Attitudes have grown more equivocal, however, especially after the Romanian revolution in 1989. According to some of the students in the survey mentioned, uninformed tourists—who do not, cannot, or will not distinguish between Vlad Țepeș and Count Dracula—come and visit Romania and take part in events organised especially for them, such as "Halloween in Eastern Europe," "Christmas with Prince Vlad Dracula," "Brief Encounter," "Journey into Hell and Heaven," "The Magic Mountain," "Jonathan Harker Trail," "In the Footsteps of Jonathan Harker," "The Escape," etc.[26] And yet, the vast majority of students in the survey underlined the positive effects of Dracula tourism on Romania's image and economy. Here is a sample of their answers translated from Romanian:

> Because foreigners are fascinated by the mystery attached to Dracula, they come every year to discover the places supposedly haunted by vampires and to satisfy their curiosity and know more about the sinister deeds of the Romanian *voivode*. This is a valuable resource for tourism, an economic and cultural advantage. Only unusual and interesting things attract tourists. The Romanians are right to

make the most of this fascination foreigners have for Vlad Țepeș and promote tourism, even if this association is far-fetched and people are in fact interested in things that are not true. Thanks to this association, Romania is known worldwide. The link between Vlad Țepeș and Dracula is maybe the only thing some foreigners know about Romania. If it's beneficial for Romania, I really don't mind this association. People will at least know where Romania is situated on a map. As a Romanian, I'm proud of this myth as people around the world are interested in us. I'm happy Romania can attract tourists because our national heritage is brought to the fore. It brings Romania a certain prestige and reputation.

The students' answers reflect today's tourist tendencies of taking advantage of the West's fascination with the Dracula myth in order to develop a profitable business, paradoxically promoting the stereotypes that the Romanians are trying to debunk, as seen in some of the students' disappointed reactions to the Țepeș/Dracula association. Tourist agencies contend with the amalgam between the historical figure and the fictitious character. They play on the tourists' confusion, ready to sell "Dracula" to western tourists. They market that simulacrum not as a representation of the "real" but as the real itself. This practice evinces postmodernism's tendency to produce historicity through the disappearance of the "real" as the tours offered to foreign tourists are not exactly a means to rehabilitate the reputation of Vlad Țepeș, but to reconfirm their stereotypes about vampires drawn from fiction and reinforced by the film industry.

The Romanians are aware of the financial and economic advantages of this phenomenon and, as a result, many tours, as well as a Dracula theme park, have been created to meet the rising demands.[27] As clearly expressed by the students in the survey, many of them are eager to accept the erroneous link made by foreigners between their national hero and Dracula the vampire, conveyed by literature and cinema, especially for commercial reasons. They seem ready to compromise their national history for profit. This attitude is commented upon by a famous Romanian journalist, Octavian Paler, whose opinion, tinged with sarcasm, is cited by Elizabeth Miller: "Dracula is not a Romanian myth. It is a myth that was imposed on us. But since the madness has become world-wide with fan clubs and universities that have departments of vampirology without knowing where Romania is, why should we not transform Dracula into an agent of tourism?"[28] Miller's response captures rather succinctly the ironic situation that such thinking has led to: "Such responses point to the central dilemma facing Romanians eager to promote Transylvania as a tourist destination: how to appeal to the widespread interest in Dracula and vampires, while remaining true to their own history and culture."[29]

Conclusion

I would like to conclude on the Romanian dilemma which cannot be easily resolved because the pride Romanians have for their national hero, Vlad Țepeș (based on knowledge acquired at school and on the information provided by history textbooks), is outweighed by the lucrative appeal of his exploitation through the distorted image of Count Dracula, a vampire. In a postmodernist fashion, the Romanians seem to have embarked on a policy that plays upon the disappearance of the historical in favour of the historicised. This is clearly demonstrated by the majority of students who take pride in the way their history is "consumed" by foreigners, even if they perfectly realise that what is taught at school in history lessons is reduced to a series of clichés and aberrations. They seem ready, however, to participate in the celebration of a simulacrum and displace history with commodity. As Dracula tourism has become part of a calculated mass or popular commercial culture, it would be extremely difficult now for Romanians to go against the tide and promote Romanian history and culture by distinguishing carefully between the two Draculas.

Notes

1 In Survey 1, the students specialize in computer technology and have two history lessons per week; in Survey 2, the students specialize in mathematics and computer technology and have two history lessons per week; in Survey 3 students of social sciences have four history lessons per week. All English translations from the original Romanian sources in this essay are my own.

2 Hadrian Daicoviciu, Pompiliu Teodor, and Ioan Câmpineanu, *Istorie. Clasa a VII a* (București: Editura didactica și pedagogică, 1997), 116. See also Sorin Oane and Maria Ochescu, *Istorie. Clasa a VIII a* (București: Humanitas Educațional, 2000), and Alexandru Vulpe, et al., *Istorie. Clasa a VIII a* (București: Sigma, 2000).

3 "Vlad, fiul Drac*ului*" means Vlad, "the son of Dracul." "Drac" in Romanian means devil, and "ul" is the masculine form of the definite article, "the devil." The final ending "ui" is the genitive marker, "the son of." The name is clearly related to Vlad Țepeș's father's sobriquet, "Dracul," who was awarded in 1431 the Order of the Dragon by the Holy Roman Emperor Sigismund of Luxembourg. The Order of the Dragon was a knightly order dedicated to fighting the Turks.

4 Hadrian Daicoviciu, Pompiliu Teodor, and Ioan Câmpineanu 116. In the third part of this essay, I will examine the Slavonic legends and will show that this is not exactly the case since Țepeș is also endowed with negative features.

5 Hadrian Daicoviciu, Pompiliu Teodor, and Ioan Câmpineanu 118.

6 Nicoleta Dumitrescu et al., *Istoria Românilor: manual pentru clasa a XII a* (București: Humanitas Educațional, 2003).

7 Mihai Manea, Adrian Pascu, and Bogdan Teodorescu, *Istoria românilor din cele mai vechi timpuri pîna la Revolutia din 1821.* *Manual pentru clasa a XI a* (Bucureşti: Editura didactică şi pedagogică, 1992), 247.

8 Mihai Manea, Adrian Pascu, and Bogdan Teodorescu 245.

9 Dumitrescu et al. 38.

10 Iulian Cârţana et al., *Istorie: Manual pentru clasa a XII a* (Piteşti: Editura Carminis, 2000).

11 Iulian Cârţana et al. 40.

12 Mihai Manea, Adrian Pascu, and Bogdan Teodorescu 246.

13 Mihai Manea, Adrian Pascu, and Bogdan Teodorescu 247.

14 Mircea Eliade, *The Romanians: A Concise History* (Bucharest: Roza Vinturilor, 1997), 32-33.

15 Ştefan Andreescu, *Vlad Ţepeş (Dracula)* (Bucureşti: Minerva, 1976), 275.

16 My study is based on Ion Stăvăruş's book, *Povestiri medievale despre Vlad Ţepeş— Draculea* (Bucureşti: Univers, 1993), 123-70.

17 Ion Stăvăruş 124.

18 Ion Stăvăruş 125.

19 Ion Stăvăruş 138.

20 Ion Stăvăruş 143.

21 Ion Stăvăruş 143.

22 Ion Stăvăruş 162.

23 Aşik-Paşa-Zade, "Chronicles of the Ottoman Dynasty," in Ion Stăvăruş, 165.

24 See, for example, Mihai Ungheanu, *Răstălmacirea lui Ţepeş. "Dracula"—un roman politic?* (Bucureşti: Editura Globus, 1992); Georgina Viorica Rogoz, *Istoria despre Dracula* (Bucureşti: NOI Media Print, 2004); and Daniel Tiberiu Apostol, *Dracula: mit sau realitate* (Braşov: Editura Muzeului Bran, 2005).

25 Nicolaie Stoicescu, *Vlad Ţepeş* (Bucureşti: Editura Academiei Republicii Socialiste Romania, 1978). See also Lucian Boia, *Istorie şi mit în conştiinţa româneasca* (Bucureşti: Humanitas, 1997), and Denis Buican, *Avatarurile lui Dracula; de la Vlad Ţepeş la Stalin şi Ceausescu* (Bucureşti: Scripta, 1993).

26 These examples of tours and events are quoted from a brochure ("Transylvania Uncovered: Your Invitation to Another Europe") found at a tourist information centre in London, England.

27 See, for example, the following websites which promote Dracula tours:
http://www.travelworld.ro/en/romania_itinerary.php?id_circuite=21 (2 Jan. 2006);
http://www.romtour.com/prince_vlad_dracula_the_true_story.htm (2 Jan. 2006);
http://www.visit-romania.ro/sectiuni/engleza/searchofdracula/searchofdracula.htm (2 Jan. 2006);
http://www.infohub.com/TRAVEL/SIT/sit_pages/13091.html (2 Jan. 2006).

28 Elizabeth Miller, *A Dracula Handbook* (Xlibris, 2005), 157.

29 Elizabeth Miller 157.

Part III: Postmodernism in Coppola's *Bram Stoker's Dracula*

CHAPTER SEVEN

DRACULA: TRADITION AND POSTMODERNISM IN STOKER'S NOVEL AND COPPOLA'S FILM

JEAN MARIGNY, UNIVERSITÉ STENDHAL-GRENOBLE III

After a first perusal of *Dracula*, a modern reader might find it superficial or even childish because of its Manichean approach. The plot could be readily summed up as the story of a devilish vampire, obviously embodying absolute evil, who plagues a group of worthy Englishmen. Thanks to the courage and virtue of his adversaries, helped by a wise Dutch university professor, he is finally eliminated and public order is restored. If we read the book more closely, however, we can pick up quite a few contradictions, and the plot appears more intricate than it first seemed. We may have different readings of the novel and indeed psychoanalysts, sociologists, historians, and even political scientists have given their own—and sometimes contradictory—versions of the story. To some extent, *Dracula* is a paradoxical novel. The same remark can be made about the various films that were made from Stoker's novel. Coppola's own adaptation of *Dracula* is no exception. Not only does the film emphasize the contradictions in the novel but brings to the story and its main characters a paradoxical interpretation of its own. This essay, therefore, is meant to study the paradoxes in Stoker's novel and Coppola's film and to show that, while using traditional themes, they have quite a modern, even postmodern, approach.

The first paradox in Stoker's novel is that it is both in keeping with the spirit of the eighteenth-century English Gothic novel and firmly rooted in late nineteenth-century modernity. The story of this young English solicitor's clerk, who goes to the very heart of a mountainous country in Central Europe to meet an eccentric Count living in an old remote castle, indeed reminds us of Walpole's *The Castle of Otranto* or Ann Radcliffe's *The Mysteries of Udolpho*. Stoker has even adopted the manner and style of eighteenth-century epistolary novels. At the same time, the author repeatedly reminds us that his own story takes place in modern times. Dr. Seward is a disciple of Charcot, whose theories, at the end of the nineteenth century, were at the forefront of psychiatry, itself a brand-new science; he uses a phonograph to record his observations; Harker uses a Kodak camera to take pictures of the estates he offers for sale; Mina Harker writes in shorthand, a new technique of writing, and uses a typewriter, a recent invention, to record her husband's notes. Unlike the heroines of Gothic novels who were always under the protection of a parent and had no experience of adult life, Mina stands for the emancipated New Woman who takes her destiny upon herself. She has an occupation—she is a schoolteacher—and she does not depend on her husband. In her relationship with Jonathan, she often plays the part normally assigned to the husband in Victorian society. As far as the narrative framework is concerned, it is made up of a kaleidoscope of documents, extracts of diaries, letters, etc., quite in the manner of Gothic novels, but Stoker introduces such elements of the modern civilization, such as newspaper clippings and telegrams.

At the outset, *Dracula* can be read as an edifying novel, in conformity with the tenets of this literary genre. This should not surprise us when we know the author's personality: Stoker was supposed to be a good Victorian, a good husband, a good father, and an indefatigable, honest worker. Like most of his contemporaries, he would blame loose manners and see sexuality as the root of all evil. In an article published in *The Nineteenth Century Magazine* in 1908, he writes: "A close analysis will show that the only emotions which in the long run harm are those arising from sex impulses, and when we have realised this we have put a finger on the actual point of danger."[1] After regretting the excessive freedom enjoyed by novelists, Stoker castigates those who appealed to the "base appetites" of their readers, and he asserts that in the struggle between good and evil, what he calls "the war between God and the Devil," it is necessary to set up a system of censorship which should be as severe as the one already exercised over drama, to prevent the country from falling into decadence: "To prevent this, censorship must be continuous and rigid."[2] Being himself a novelist, Stoker felt it as a duty to set an example, to practise self-censorship, and to set his writings in keeping with established morality. *Dracula*, on the whole, appears as a moralising tale, in accordance with the ethical tenets of Victorian society. The fight between good and evil is illustrated by the conflict opposing Count Dracula, a devilish character who challenges God and the established order and ignores pity, to the other characters: pious, virtuous, honest men and women. Thanks to wise Professor Van Helsing, good ultimately prevails: Dracula is eliminated, and the two female victims he had tainted are restored to their innate purity. Lucy, who dies after tragic circumstances, stands as a martyr, but when the blissful stake releases her soul, she becomes again the pure maiden she was before: "There, in the coffin lay no longer the foul Thing that we had so dreaded and grown to hate [...] but Lucy, as we had seen her in her life, with her face of unequalled sweetness and purity" (*D* 192). Mina can likewise see that the infamous mark on her forehead has disappeared after the vampire's demise "See! the snow is not more stainless than her forehead! The curse has passed away" (*D* 326).

There are, however, surprisingly bold erotic passages in the novel, like the scene in which Harker has to face the three vampire women (*D* 42-43) or when Dracula bares his chest, opens a vein with his nails, and compels prudish Mina to lick the blood oozing from the wound (*D* 253). We may wonder why Stoker did not use the self-censorship he had advocated for other writers, but the real point is to know whether he really was the severe moralist he pretended to be. He has often been described as a flawless individual, a faithful husband, and a relentless worker. Naturally enough, his first biographers quote the conclusion of his death certificate, which indicates that the cause of his death was "exhaustion," to make him a sort of martyr to his work. On the contrary, Daniel Farson, the writer's grandnephew, asserts in his biography, *The Man Who Wrote Dracula* (1975), that if we read the whole certificate we realize that Stoker died in fact of an untreated syphilis he had caught in France during a European tour of the Lyceum Theatre.

Whatever we may make of it, we can at least say that in *Dracula*, this moral fable where evil is punished and virtue rewarded, everything is not simply black and white. The characters who are supposed to be virtuous have their own weaknesses. Such is the case, first and foremost, of Van Helsing, the "anti-Dracula," considered as the one who has the necessary skill, wisdom, and virtue to fight evil. Jack Seward, his disciple, is full of praise for him:

> He is a philosopher and a metaphysician, and one of the most advanced scientists of his day; and he has, I believe, an absolutely open mind. This, with an iron nerve, a temper of the ice-brook, an indomitable resolution, self-command and toleration exalted from virtues to blessings, and the kindliest and truest heart that beats [. . .]. (*D* 106)

And yet, this fount of knowledge, coupled with a humanist demeanor, has sometimes a disconcerting and even unpleasant attitude. His way of speaking is ridiculous: unlike Dracula, who speaks grammatically-correct English, Van Helsing uses broken English, which spoils the solemnity of what he says. In his relationship with other people, he is often abrupt, authoritative, contemptuous, and self-reliant. As a physician, at Lucy's bedside he confines himself in an absurd attitude of secrecy, refusing to reveal his diagnosis to the other characters, including Dr. Seward. The result of such a policy is disastrous.[3] When he orders garlic flowers to be put in the patient's bedroom, he does not explain why. As a result, Mrs. Westenra, seeing that Lucy cannot bear the smell of these flowers, removes them from the room, unwittingly endangering her daughter's life. From the very beginning, Van Helsing has obviously understood what Lucy is suffering from, and yet, not only does he not confide in anybody, but he also proves unable to prevent her death in spite of the many blood transfusions he orders from several donors (which may be very dangerous from a medical standpoint). After Lucy's death, he even commits the mistake of delaying the beheading of the corpse, as he has intended to do, and it is not until the girl, who has become a vampire, jeopardizes the lives of several children that he decides to do so. Sometimes, we might even put Van Helsing's sanity in doubt, especially in the passage where he bursts out laughing as he goes to Lucy's burial. We can also wonder at the fact that this learned professor, coming from Protestant Holland, always uses consecrated hosts and cites Latin prayers, both central to the Roman Catholic creed. It is also surprising that a renowned scientist should praise superstition as the best way to fight evil (*D* 284). It strikes us at last to see that, apart from Van Helsing, the only character who knows everything from the outset is mad Renfield, whose apparently incoherent words are sometimes full of wisdom. Van Helsing himself says, "Perhaps I may gain more knowledge out of the folly of this madman than I shall from the teaching of the most wise" (*D* 225). Like Shakespeare in *King Lear*, Stoker inverts usual standards, and finally it is the madman who speaks the truth. We can notice as well that Renfield, the faithful servant of Dracula, the devil incarnate, often quotes the Bible.

Among Dracula's other adversaries, Jonathan Harker himself is paradoxical. He is introduced in the novel as a brave, serious and virtuous character, but there are a few flaws in his personality. In the famous scene when he faces the three vampire women of Dracula's Castle, this model of virtue seems to be ready to fall to temptation:

> I could feel the soft, shivering touch of the lips on the supersensitive skin of my throat, and the hard dents of two sharp teeth, just touching and pausing there. I closed my eyes in a languorous ecstasy and waited—waited with beating heart. (*D* 43)

Back in England, after his terrible experience in Transylvania, Harker becomes apathetic. He shirks his responsibilities and proves unable to protect his own wife. He even becomes ridiculous when he sleeps deeply while Dracula, a few steps from his bed, is initiating his wife to vampirism. The other "good" characters of the story, Arthur Holmwood and Jack Seward, are pleasant enough, but they have no striking personalities. Only Quincey Morris appears as an exception. Dr. Seward praises him warmly:

> What a fine fellow is Quincey! I believe in my heart of hearts that he suffered as much about Lucy's death as any of us; but he bore himself through it like a

moral Viking. If America can go on breeding men like that, she will be a power
in the world indeed. (*D* 156)

Some critics of *Dracula* have read this last sentence as a kind of prophecy of the
Cold War.[4] According to them, Quincey Morris, by eliminating a danger from
Eastern Europe, stands for young America coming to the rescue of old Western
Europe. In any case, this character deserves the reader's admiration at the end of
the novel when he gives the vampire a mortal blow, at the cost of his own life.
Apart from Quincey Morris, the male characters of the novel have rather a
passive attitude concerning the story's events, and we feel that Mina, the only
female protagonist after Lucy's death, is Dracula's sole opponent, who
continually shows her courage and level-headedness. Van Helsing does not
hesitate to praise her for these qualities:

> She has man's brain—a brain that a man should have were he much gifted—and
> woman's heart. The good God fashioned her for a purpose, believe me, when He
> made that so good combination. Friend John, up to now fortune has made that
> woman of help to us [. . .]. (*D* 207)

When compared with the novel's protagonists, Dracula appears
physically and morally as a sort of giant, and yet he is the only character in the
novel who never expresses himself in writing. He appears only in the main
episodes of the plot, but at the same time he is constantly in the reader's mind
because everybody speaks of him. He is perfectly hateful and his behaviour is
often revolting, especially when he throws a living baby in a bag to the three
vampire women (*D* 43). Unable to have any sympathy for him, the reader
cannot identify with Dracula. And yet Dracula is a fine-looking man. Physically,
he is very tall and, at least at the beginning, is endowed with the nobility and
authority of a patriarch. He has a natural elegance and speaks refined English,
which sets him in vivid contrast with Van Helsing and his pidgin. Unlike the
Professor, whose hesitations are sometimes harmful, Dracula knows exactly
what he wants to do, and we cannot but admire the skillful scheme he has set up
to settle in the very heart of England in order to conquer the world. Van Helsing
himself pays him a tribute: "Oh! If such an one was to come from God, and not
the Devil, what a force for good might he not be in this old world of ours" (*D*
279). Besides, Dracula shows undeniable courage when he accepts to fight alone
against all his adversaries, and he can take the liberty of challenging and even
making fun of them. To his adversaries, who have tried in vain to catch him, he
is both ironic and threatening:

> "You think to baffle me, you—with your pale faces all in a row, like sheep in a
> butcher's. You shall be sorry yet, each one of you! You think you have left me

without a place to rest; but I have more. My revenge is just begun! I spread it over centuries, and time is on my side." (*D* 267)

In spite of his devilish nature, which should normally arouse our reproof, Dracula, to some extent, commands our admiration, like Satan in Book X of Milton's *Paradise Lost*. At the end of the novel, he is finally vanquished, because, in this kind of literature, good must prevail over evil, but we feel as if the story might have quite another dénouement. In other words, Stoker probably intended to write a moral fable, but as he turned his villain into a kind of hero, his demonstration is not entirely convincing, at least from the Victorian standpoint. In *Dracula*, the official ethics and the positivism of Victorian society are often called into question: evil is sometimes made attractive, virtue is not always rewarded, medical science is challenged, and madness prevails over reason and wisdom. Stoker's conformist, and even moralising style hardly conceals the contradictions of a society which is crushed by the restraint of all kinds of taboos and which, more or less consciously, longs for freedom. It is probably this paradox which sets *Dracula* apart from the conventional literature of its time. Apparently based on the aesthetic principles of eighteenth-century Gothic novels, *Dracula* belongs in fact to modern literature, as Lance Olsen defines in *Ellipse and Uncertainty: An Introduction to Postmodern Fantasy*:

> Modernism was the prevalent cultural mode between the 1880's and the 1930's. It signals a reaction against the Victorian and naturalist modes. In other words, it is a reaction against the dominant assumptions of the nineteenth-century, post romantic sensibility, a reaction that negates the belief in materialism fostered by Marx, Darwin, and the scientific method based on Newtonian mechanics. It attacks the bourgeois mentality that gained power steadily through the eighteenth and nineteenth centuries.[5]

By subverting the moral and even aesthetic codes of Victorian literature, by giving the reader more freedom to have his own opinion, by making his characters far more complex than they seem, Stoker indeed foreshadows postmodern literature, and it is probably one of the reasons why *Dracula* is so widely read today. Coppola's film, different as it may be from the novel, nevertheless illustrates the modern and even postmodern import of the novel.

Francis Ford Coppola's adaptation of Stoker's novel is also quite paradoxical because it is apparently faithful to the text while completely altering its meaning. It must be noted that, when the film was released in the United States, it bore two different titles, *Bram Stoker's Dracula*, which seemed to indicate that the film director intended to respect the writer's scheme, and *Dracula: The Untold Story*, which implies, quite on the contrary, that the film was meant to tell a different story. If we exclude the prologue and the end of the film, we may consider Coppola's film to be rather faithful to the plot of the novel. Except for a few television films which are close to the novel, most of the feature films which appeared before Coppola's *Bram Stoker's Dracula* have taken great liberties with Stoker's story. Murnau, for instance, had not requested Stoker's widow for the permission to make use of the plot and characters of *Dracula*. Consequently, he had to give his film another title, *Nosferatu*, and he had to change the names of all characters: Dracula became Count Orlock; Van Helsing, Professor Bulwer; Jonathan and Mina Harker, Jonathan and Ellen Hutter; and Renfield, Knock. The plot was set in Germany and not in England. In his new version of *Nosferatu*, Werner Herzog also situated his film in Germany, but as he no longer had copyright problems, he could restore the original names of his characters. Terence Fisher situated his film in an unspecified country of continental Europe, which allowed him to dispose of the *Demeter* episode. To go from Dracula's country to the place where the main protagonists lived, one had just to cross a border.

In the various film adaptations of *Dracula*, some passages of the novel either disappeared or became unrecognizable, while the main protagonists were mixed up and minor characters suppressed. In both *Nosferatu* films, for instance, it is Mina who succeeds in eliminating the vampire, at the cost of her own life, by making him forget the sunrise and thus be exposed to the rays of the morning sun. In Terence Fisher's *Dracula*, it is Van Helsing who turns the Count into ashes by opening the curtains shading the windows. In John Badham's film, the final episode takes place on board a ship, and Dracula is hoisted to the top of a mast, thus exposed to the sunlight. In all these examples, the character of Quincey Morris is merely deleted as his presence in the plot is no longer necessary. The brave Texan appears only in Philip's Saville television film, *Count Dracula*, where he is confused with Arthur Holmwood, and in Jess Franco's *El Conde Drácula*.

Film directors also tended to change some elements of the plot completely. In Tod Browning's *Dracula*, Harker disappears and is replaced by Renfield; in Terence Fisher's *Dracula*, Harker remains as a prisoner in Dracula's castle and, having become himself a vampire, must be eliminated by Van Helsing; in Herzog's *Nosferatu* Harker succeeds the vampire in spreading the plague throughout the world. Van Helsing himself, who plays a major role in the novel, appears as an old man in both versions of *Nosferatu* who understands nothing and is even killed by Dracula in John Badham's *Dracula*. Very often, the roles of the protagonists are entirely changed. In both versions of *Nosferatu*, Renfield is Harker's employer, and it is he who sends him to Dracula's castle before he falls into madness. There is an exchange in the roles of Mina and Lucy in the films made by Fisher, Badham, and Herzog, and in Badham's film Mina is Van Helsing's daughter. In short, it would be tedious to give here the full list of inaccuracies in *Dracula*'s film adaptations.

Unlike his predecessors, Coppola made a point of using all the events in the plot of the novel and respecting their order of succession: Harker's voyage and stay in Dracula's castle, the *Demeter* episode, the Count's landing at Whitby, Lucy's illness and Van Helsing's arrival in London, Mina and Jonathan's wedding in Transylvania, Lucy's death, her becoming a vampire and her being beheaded by Holmwood, the destruction of Dracula's crates at Carfax Abbey by Van Helsing and his aides, Mina's initiation to vampirism by the Count, Renfield's death, the final pursuit as far as Dracula's Castle, the destruction of the three female vampires by Van Helsing, the elimination of Dracula at the cost of Quincey Morris's life, and Mina's release from her curse. The dialogues are rather faithful to the text of the novel as well, and many are verbatim quotations. Coppola even uses episodes which were never represented before in the earlier *Dracula* films, such as the escape of the wolf Bersicker from the zoo, or the scene in which Jonathan and Mina, in a cab, come across a rejuvenated Dracula in a street of London. The metamorphosis of the old man who welcomes Harker at the door of his castle into a young dandy who strolls in the streets of London may appear as exaggerated, and yet in the novel Stoker insists on the vampire's becoming younger and younger. At the beginning of the novel, as Dracula's prisoner, Harker notices a first change when he sees the Count for the first time in his coffin: "There lay the Count, but looking as if his youth had been half renewed, for the white hair and moustache were changed to dark iron-grey; the cheeks were fuller, and the white skin seemed ruby-red underneath [. . .]" (*D* 53). Later, when he sees him again in London, he is surprised of the new change in the Count's appearance. Dracula is then described as a "tall, thin man, with a beaky nose and black moustache [. . .]" (*D* 155).

If Coppola had not deliberately added episodes of his own to the plot, like the prologue, the meeting of Dracula and Mina in London, and the final love scene—all of which completely change the meaning of the story—we might have said that his film was the most faithful adaptation of the novel ever made. Besides, Coppola is the first film director who made a point of representing all the protagonists of the story: all of them appear with their true names, including Quincey Morris, so often ignored in other films. Of course the names of a few minor characters, like Mrs. Westenra or Lord Godalming, are not even mentioned in the film, and Hawkins, Harker's employer, appears only once; but they do not play an important part in the novel either. If we except the three main protagonists—Dracula, Mina, and Van Helsing—we may consider that the other characters appear as they are represented in the novel. Renfield, for instance, often under-represented in films, is given by Coppola his full import. The only inaccuracy in the film is that he is Hawkins's former employee. Jonathan Harker, Arthur Holmwood, and Quincey Morris are in keeping with their models in the novel. As far as Lucy is concerned, Coppola has somewhat exaggerated a feature of her personality by making her a liberated woman who takes pride in her sexual experiences, but on the whole, she is as Stoker portrayed her.

Van Helsing, Dracula, and Mina, however, are completely unorthodox, as if Coppola, inspired by the paradoxes in the novel, had taken fun in inverting the roles. In the part of the film taking place in London, Dracula, the "villain" of the story, is depicted as a romantic young lover, who can be at times overwhelmed by emotion and who appeals more and more to the spectator's sympathy, while Van Helsing, supposed to embody wisdom and virtue, quite on the contrary is more and more disconcerting to the spectator because of his brutal and even vulgar attitude. In his portrayal of the vampire as he appears at the very beginning, Coppola is no more accurate than his predecessors. Stoker describes the Count as a "tall old man, clean shaven save for a long white moustache" (*D* 21), with "eyebrows [...] very massive, almost meeting over the nose, and with bushy hair, that seemed to curl in its own profusion" (*D* 23), while in both versions of *Nosferatu*, the vampire is bald and has the face of a devil with very long incisors. Tod Browning's *Dracula*, as embodied by Bela Lugosi, is a man in his forties, with an entirely shaven face and black, flat hair. Christopher Lee in Terence Fisher's film is about the same age as Lugosi, but his eyes are bloodshot, and his eye-teeth protrude. And John Badham's Dracula, played by Frank Langella, is a handsome youth whose countenance is by no means sinister. The only film in which Dracula appears as depicted in the novel is Jess Franco's *El Conde Drácula*, in which Christopher Lee, at last, has the white hair and long white moustache described in Harker's diary. Coppola shows us a clean shaven old man, dressed in brightly-coloured nightgowns, and with an extravagant hairstyle. In the second part of the film, Dracula, played by the same actor, Gary Oldman, is entirely different: he has become a young dandy, with a small moustache and goatee, wearing sunglasses and dressed in fashionable clothes.

Coppola's Van Helsing, as well, is quite different from his counterpart in the novel. Stoker describes him as a patriarch always speaking in a solemn tone, in spite of his broken English, and using the name of God in nearly all his sentences. In the most classical adaptations, Van Helsing, featured by Edward Van Sloan in Browning's film and by Peter Cushing in Terence Fisher's *Dracula*, appears as a self-reliant, but courteous scholar, who takes up the full responsibility of what he is doing. On the contrary, Coppola's Van Helsing appears as a coarse, brutal character who indulges in dubious jokes. His broad-brimmed hat makes him look like an adventurer rather than a respectable university professor. He is sometimes simply hateful when, for instance, he smells Mina as if she were a delicacy and goes waltzing with her, just after poor

Lucy's burial, or again when he carves a piece of meat with gusto, immediately after he has beheaded the girl's corpse, as if that horrible deed had given him an appetite. Later, in Transylvania he voluptuously kisses Mina, then under the influence of the vampires. Eventually, after he has beheaded the three vampire sisters, he proudly carries their heads like trophies before throwing them into the precipice. Coppola has obviously intended to demystify this character. Mina herself in Coppola's film, who in the novel is a virtuous, brave wife and who always thinks of her dear Jonathan, becomes a coquette who likes male compliments and finally deceives her husband.

The real paradox of Coppola's film is that, while following Stoker's plot accurately and giving each of the characters the part he or she was supposed to play in the novel, it tells a totally different story. At the beginning of the novel, Dracula alludes to his warlord ancestors, in particular a heroic *voivode* who spent his life fighting the Turks. The modern reader immediately recognizes the *voivode* as Vlad Ţepeş (the Impaler), the historical Dracula (1431–1476), a warlord of Walachia who is considered as the liberator of his country. Later, Van Helsing implies that Count Dracula might really be the same Vlad Ţepeş, who, having turned into a vampire after his death, would have survived for centuries: "He must, indeed, have been that Voivode Dracula who won his name against the Turk [. . .]" (*D* 212). But it is a mere hypothesis, which is never proved in the novel. Coppola takes up this hypothesis at its face value: in the prologue of his film, the actor Gary Oldman, who plays the role of the Count, appears as Vlad Ţepeş. Furthermore, Coppola, taking his inspiration from a real episode of the *voivode*'s life (that is, the suicide of his wife, who leaped into the River Argeş at the foot of Poienari fortress), imagines that Vlad, mad with pain, challenges God himself and thus becomes a vampire. This new element completely changes the story, as Mina Harker proves to be the reincarnation of Dracula's wife, and Dracula is still desperately in love with her.[6]

The idea of Dracula as a lover is not new. Other filmmakers have used it before Coppola (e.g., Murnau, Herzog, Badham, and Dan Curtis). In Badham's *Dracula*, Mina even falls in love with the vampire. Yet Coppola changes the meaning of the events related in the novel to bear out this idea. For instance, the scene of Mina's initiation to vampirism by the Count was described as a kind of rape by Stoker; in the film, it becomes a mere exchange between consenting partners, with Mina deliberately drinking her lover's blood to become a vampire in order to share his fate. What is new in Coppola's conception is that Mina's love will finally allow the vampire to recover his initial purity and be saved from damnation after he is beheaded. The novel does not allow such interpretation; Mina is not attracted to Dracula. Quite on the contrary, she fears and loathes him. She is horrified by the vampire's kiss on her throat: "And oh, my God, my God, pity me! He placed his reeking lips upon my throat" (*D* 251). In the novel, Dracula is clearly not in love with Mina. He wants to turn her into a vampire merely for the sake of having a useful instrument at his service. When he offers her his own blood in a kind of parodic desecration of the Eucharist, he says "[you shall be] my bountiful wine-press for a while; and shall be later on my companion and my helper" (*D* 252). Unlike Coppola's hero, Stoker's Dracula is impervious to love. It is what one of the three vampire women says at the beginning of the novel: "You yourself never loved; you never love" (*D* 43). Coppola quotes this sentence in his film, but he makes his vampire hero reply: "I shall love now" (*BSD* 60).[7]

Finally, when Dracula in the novel turns into dust after he is stabbed by Quincey Morris, this tragic end is described as a deserved punishment, whereas in Coppola's film, Dracula, transfigured by Mina's love, becomes a human being again before dying. At the very moment when Mina kisses his mouth, the dying monster recovers his human features, like the Beast in Mme Le Prince de Beaumont's tale. Thus, the story told by Coppola is closer to "Beauty and the Beast" than to Stoker's novel. Coppola, incidentally, makes reference to Jean Cocteau's 1945 masterpiece, *La Belle et la Bête* (*Beauty and the Beast*), when Dracula turns Mina's tears into pearls. We may notice as well that the pair of lovers represented in a fresco on the ceiling of the castle in the film' tableau is exactly in the same position as Jean Marais and Josette Day in the epilogue of *La Belle et la Bête*. As compared to his predecessors who had adapted Stoker's Dracula rather loosely while respecting the story on the whole, Coppola has paradoxically adapted the novel quite accurately, while changing the meaning of the story completely. Coppola obviously intended to offset the duality of his hero, and it is probably the reason why the old man who welcomes Harker at the beginning and the young dandy who appeals to Mina in London are so different, physically and morally.

Coppola's rather unusual treatment of *Dracula* can be considered postmodern in the sense that it is a deconstruction of traditional horror films. Terror is no longer the main interest of the film, and traditional roles are reversed: the so-called hero of the story (Van Helsing) appears as a dubious character, whereas the villain (Dracula) is glorified at the end; the relationship between the predator and his "victim" (Mina) becomes a love affair; and no moral conclusion can be drawn at the end as the conventional fight between good and evil has proved meaningless. The main character is closer to Anne Rice's postmodern vampires than to Gothic villains. The film itself is a kaleidoscope of images in which the spectator is sometimes lost. Whereas Coppola's film has sometimes been hailed as a masterpiece of postmodern cinema, it has also been severely criticized. Nina Auerbach, for instance, wrote that

[. . .] the fundamental illogic of Coppola's kaleidoscopic cinematography, and of
Oldman's Dracula himself, suggests that a postmodern Dracula maybe a
contradiction in terms. Audiences who believe absolutely in Anne Rice's Louis
and Lestat seem to relish in a perpetual state of visual and ontological
decomposition. It may be that Coppola has killed Dracula at last and that he will
fade out with the twentieth century.[8]

Whatever its detractors may say, Coppola's *Dracula*, a kind of lyrical and
baroque poem to eternal love, is an original film which will be a landmark in the
history of twentieth-century cinema. Thanks to the beauty of its
cinematography, the originality of its screenplay, and, generally speaking, its
brilliant inspiration, Coppola's film is a monument which pays tribute to the
novel it simultaneously deconstructs. Such a tribute shows, if need be, that
Stoker's *Dracula*, like Mary Shelley's *Frankenstein*, is far more complex and
elaborate than it seems on first reading, and above all closer to modern—and
perhaps postmodern—literature than to the Gothic tradition which was supposed
to inspire it. If it is true that the novel may seem old-fashioned to the modern
reader because of its pathos and grandiloquence, it has kept today all its powers
of attraction. *Dracula* challenges time and fashions because it is a masterpiece
of fantastic literature.

Notes

---

1 Qtd. in Daniel Farson, *The Man Who Wrote Dracula* (London: Michael Joseph, 1975),
209.
2 Daniel Farson 208.
3 See Jean Marigny, "Secrecy as a Strategy in Dracula," *Journal of Dracula Studies* 2
(2000), available at http://blooferland.com/drc/images/02Marigny.rtf (10 Jan. 2007).
4 See Gabriel Ronay, "USA: Dracula and the Cold War," *The Dracula Myth: The Cult of
the Vampire* (London and New York: W. H. Allen, 1972), 164-170.
5 Lance Olsen, *Ellipse of Uncertainty: An Introduction to Postmodern Fantasy* (New
York and London: Greenwood Press, 1987), 7.
6 Van Helsing, in Coppola's conception, might also be the reincarnation of the priest
who curses Dracula in the prologue, as both characters are played by the same actor
(Anthony Hopkins).
7 The line in the screenplay reads: "Yes—I too can love. And I shall love again."
8 Nina Auerbach, *Our Vampires, Ourselves* (Chicago and London: The University of
Chicago Press, 1995), 209, 16n.

CHAPTER EIGHT

POSTMODERN VERBAL DISCOURSE IN COPPOLA'S *BRAM STOKER'S DRACULA*

JEAN-MARIE LECOMTE, NANCY- UNIVERSITÉ (I.U.T.)

Speech as a formal component of film has rarely been studied. It is all the more surprising as most films rely on verbal language and its screen modalities (dialogue, voice-overs, off-screen speech, diegetic written signs, etc.) to anchor images and to further plot, character, and theme.[1] Film genres are usually tied to specific speech styles and language aesthetics, although directors and their screenwriters adapt these conventions to suit both cultural sensibilities and authorial intentions. Filmic speech has yet to become an independent field of study with its own methodology and theoretical tools. Its scope is eclectic and interdisciplinary, drawing on linguistics, stylistics, discourse analysis, and film studies. Within that broad approach, the subject of postmodern discourse in Coppola's *Dracula* raises many difficulties.[2] First, "postmodern" is to be understood here in its temporal sense referring to a Hollywood cinema born roughly in the 1980s and departing from modernity by being less politically articulate and addressing the senses rather than the intellect.[3] And second, "verbal discourse" describes the form and function of filmic speech taken either in isolation as text, or, more satisfactorily, integrated into the overall cinematic style of the film as "visual sound." It is a matter of choice (stylistic, semantic, and phenomenological) made by Coppola, together with his screenwriter and his team, to give the hearer-viewer a particular aural and phenomenological experience, addressing both the ear and the eye. My aim is to show that the filmmaker's choices partake of the aesthetics and poetics of postmodern film discourse.

The aesthetics of postmodern soundscape

Dracula starts with a historical prologue and a voice-over narrative anchoring animated images. It throws us back to the earliest days of cinema when magic lantern projections needed a storyteller, but Coppola's hidden narrator is obviously more complex. A voice without a face transcending images is often endowed with divine powers.[4] Anthony Hopkins's, however, comes short of what Sarah Kozloff calls the classical invisible storyteller by coming in and out the screen in different guises as the extra-diegetic storyteller, the Orthodox priest and Van Helsing the metaphysical philosopher.[5] Hopkins's distinctive vocal timbre haunting several bodies could, in theory, call attention to itself as a form of metalepsis.[6] It does not break the illusion in this particular case because a gossamer thread holds the three cinematic personae together: the actor's voice inhabiting several screen bodies acts like an occult sonic presence, challenging Dracula's mystic bodies and uncanny voices.

Although a postmodern allusion to Hannibal Lecter's sinister phonic image is perhaps intended here,[7] the opening voice-over is more akin to a film noir technique where an acousmatic character sets up a close, almost intimate vocal relationship with the viewer.[8] We are reminded of the dead man's commentary in Billy Wilder's *Sunset Boulevard*, sharing his confessional narrative with the spectator, and we feel on his side of the aural space, in a kind of dark limbo.[9] Together with Mina's and Jonathan's epistolary voice-overs, the plurivocal storytelling in Coppola's *Dracula* envelop viewers in a surreal soundscape, like a many-voiced Scheherazade mesmerising the audience.

The significance of voice-over discursive levels

Vampire movies always tread on thin ice; they constantly teeter on the edge of parody through overexposure. Already in 1935, *Mark of the Vampire*, Tod Browning's remake of his own *Dracula*, was wrapped up by an illusion-breaking epilogue showing Bela Lugosi in his vampire outfit and telling Luna, his associate, that "this vampire business has given [him] a great idea for a new act."[10] Browning already felt that the genre had exhausted its horror potential, as the disenchantment caused by the fake Dracula's closing lines shows. Dialogue in horror movies tends to be difficult to integrate as speech may easily dispel the climate of fear, induced by visuals and sound effects. In *Dracula, Prince of Darkness*, the unimaginative dialogue sounds silly and redundant.[11] This Hammer picture is saved from burlesque solely by the silent and elusive presence of Christopher Lee's Dracula. In the late seventies, John Badham directed a successful version of *Dracula* by avoiding all manners of Gothic effects that threatened his vampire with ridicule: out went fangs, bats, coffins, garlic, and crosses.[12] The film's language was ironed-out accordingly, and most of the usual rituals associated with the vampire myth were meticulously done away with to prevent disbelief.

The virtual world of vampires comes across a postmodern audience as camp, kitsch, or vaguely ridiculous; direct dialogues within that remote universe may appear either too realistic, archaic, or simply absurd. When contemporary speech jars with visuals representing a Victorian past, irony—this most didactic figure of speech—raises its modernist head, that is, a Gorgon shunned by postmodern cinema which aims above all at diverting and entertaining audiences, not alerting and educating them. Speech trying to mirror the language of the age of Dracula (both fifteenth century and Victorian) puts the viewer in the place of a distant overhearer, his rightful place in classical Hollywood cinema.[13] A mock period dialogue style can easily become burlesque and equally interfere with viewer involvement that remains, despite claims to the contrary, an essential tenet of postmodern entertainment in its neo-classical variety.[14] In Coppola's *Dracula*, direct, synchronous dialogue is balanced and often displaced by voice-over narration (extra-diegetic authorial, diegetic epistolary, diegetic telepathic, inner speech) that takes over the soundtrack. Apart from the limited "add-on value"[15] of the extra-diegetic narrator's comments, most of the voice-over discourse of the film expresses the internalised speech of Mina, Jonathan, and Dracula, verbalising diary entries, fragments of letters, and private thoughts. These literary voices ghosting the postmodern screen appeal to the affective ear of the viewer. They ensure that the hearer-viewer is personally addressed to in a virtual sound space, between screen space and the "real world." This linguistic "in-betweenness" is peculiar to Coppola's vampiric world. It creates an intimate, subjective soundscape— voices from without, often reinforced by sound motifs. This shifts the role of the viewer from overhearer or eavesdropper to confidant. This in-between soundspace comes to the attention of the hearer when Dracula, in the guise of a young prince, watches Mina walking in the streets of London. He addresses her in direct speech: "See me. See me, now!" (*BSD* 76). But the point of audition is outside the diegetic world, for neither Mina nor the passers-by react to his voice. This swift, surreal mobility of speech, transcending visuals, crossing all cinematic frontiers (diegesis, screen, shot, sequence) "vampirises" subjectivities and energises the verbal power of postmodern film.

As these voices overlaying the screen tend to speak a literary language, they are vested with the authority of a written text, heralding the decay of the spoken word and rediscovering the efficacy of literature. Equally in *Interview with the Vampire*, a 1994 Hollywood production, the undead hero (Brad Pitt) recalls, in voice-over, his picaresque adventures through centuries, in explicit David Copperfield fashion.[16] Should we conclude that, in the world of effete postmodern images, the text alone matters? Perhaps not, but we may wonder whether contemporary *auteurs* are not too conscious of their literary masters. Dracula's speech in particular departs from the Hollywood canon of realism (even found in the horror genre) and stands out as strangely stylised.

Vampiric tropes

It is difficult to refer to a dialogue genre specific to horror movies. Sarah Kozloff has pointed out the features of film dialogue common to a genre (in Westerns or melodramas, for example). The language of individual filmmakers may also exhibit formal characteristics as essential as their visual style (e.g., the Coen Brothers or John Cassavetes[17]). But language in the horror genre is not easily reducible to formulas, however flexible. Keeping to Hollywoodian Draculas, one may venture to select out fragments of "vampire discourse" that are common to the Dracula sub-genre. Bela Lugosi, the 1931 vampire archetype, spoke in a foreign accent, with a very slow delivery, carefully picking out each word. His discourse is constructed to sound over-polite and is laden with cryptic sentences. His main rhetorical tropes are metaphor, paradox, enigma, and silence. As a figure of speech personified, Browning's Dracula is a monstrous anti-logos playing upon a refusal to speak, contradiction, and figurative language. Examples abound. When Renfield climbs up the stairs of the castle, Dracula alludes to the spider spinning its web for the unwary fly and juxtaposes a literary enigma: "the blood is the life." Oblique discourse drives Renfield mad. "To die, to be really dead, must be glorious" rejoins the Transylvanian Count to Lucy's Gothic/Romantic speech. Nearly all of Lugosi's utterances have a rhetorical twist. The rhetoric of John Badham's vampire, half a century later, is similar but considerably toned down. "I have buried many friends and I, too, am weary. I am the last of my kind, descended from a conquering race. My family was its heart's blood, its brains, its swords. But the war-like days are over," Dracula announces to Lucy, in a calm, ice-cold voice. His style lies more in schemes or syntactic arrangement and in prosody than in florid tropes. He has no foreign accent, but he briefly speaks to Lucy in Romanian to seduce her, for the vampire has suddenly turned romantic lover.

From the vantage point of language style and content, Coppola's *Bram Stoker's Dracula* appears closer to Bram Stoker's text in representing dialogue with Harker in the famous castle sequences. Visually, Gary Oldman's vampire bears little or no resemblance with the Count portrayed by Stoker, but his lines display no semantic creativity or variation. In adapting scenes from the novel, cinematic codes may take liberties with the original, but linguistic codes remain faithful to its dialogue lines. In addition, true to the postmodern trope of hyperbole, Coppola's Prince Vlad heightens nearly each rhetorical trait to make it more "spectacular" to the ears. But the scope of these Victorian vampiric tropes is drastically limited to the verbal transactions between Jonathan and Dracula in the Gothic Transylvanian setting. Thereafter, verbal discourse runs its own original course.

Dracula: foreignness made beautiful

The movie confronts the viewer-hearer with an immediate convention of the horror genre, that of the polymorphic body and voice. Dracula's body polymorphism is taken for granted even in the era of primitive special effects of the early thirties, where he would turn into a giant bat or materialise out of vapour. Badham's vampire keeps visual polymorphism to a minimum, ever conscious of the ridicule that overexposure of the bat/wolf/vapour would trigger. Yet the filmmaker does come up with a visually-striking snaking movement down a wall—a trick that, incidentally, Coppola shamelessly plagiarises (or filmically nods to). Coppola's vampire goes through so many shapes and forms, monstrous or otherwise, that, surfeited, the viewer may sicken and so die. But there are interesting developments in the use of vocal polymorphism. The vampire can muster an impressive semiotic range. Cultural polyglossia and the ability to call upon various modes of communication (ranging from distorted voice, animal groans, and primitive cries to the polished speech of a prince) are his vocal imprints.

Polyglossia deserves more than a passing remark here, as it seems to be a characteristic of the postmodern soundtrack in general. Traditionally, Hollywood has considered that film heroes would naturally speak English and has only occasionally tolerated a foreign accent, provided it was not too intrusive. Foregrounded foreign accents or tongues had comic or satirical potential. Lucy, in Browning's *Dracula*, makes fun of Lugosi's eastern accent, threatening for a moment the horror potential of the vampire. In the 1979 Dracula version, Langella speaks perfect Standard English, and he briefly whispers a few sweet words in Romanian, which enhances his romantic appeal to love-struck Lucy. Since then, Hollywood has had a remarkable change of linguistic and ideological heart, enlisting and even prizing foreignness in film heroes. Recently, *The Passion of Christ*, which has been shot like a horror movie, boasts a soundtrack with an exotic language, relegating English to subtitles.[18] A strong Spanish accent, like that of Antonio Banderas, is aesthetically desirable in postmodern Hollywood.

The function of diglossia in Coppola's *Bram Stoker's Dracula* is possibly related to the idea that the speaker's native tongue stands for his or her affective language (expressing the heart and soul), while English as a learnt language corresponds to acculturation and civilised logos. This is certainly borne out in *Bram Stoker's Dracula*. Whenever the Prince switches to his native tongue, his dialect works like a subterranean language linking past and present, stirring emotions in Mina and soothing beasts. English is mainly used as a transactional or argumentative vernacular and is never pragmatically successful, often leading to verbal confrontation. Foreignness, sounding a deeper affective note, is looked on favourably in the Hollywood of the post-1990s. This is the new age of affective cinema, devoid of the "tear-jerking" overtones of classical melodramas. The vampire's "style switching" can be associated with a mystical sound motif that reverberates in the limbo of the viewer's language consciousness.[19] Even in Dracula's English, there are degrees of foreignness that are subtly exploited by Gary Oldman's voice.

Vocal and body mutability

From the dawn of sound, matching body with voice has always been coded in Hollywood, any departure from an expected norm being the ruin of a character or an actor. It is well known that voices carry cultural, ideological, and sexual overtones, and their inhabiting bodies have the same implications. What voices started to inhabit monstrous bodies in early horror movies is a fascinating field of study beyond the scope of this essay. Early talking human monsters are almost always foreigners, their English being possessed of a monster within. With the notable exception of Mr. Hyde in 1932, their physical appearance remains hardly atypical, only vaguely disquieting.[20] But their speech is definitely fearsome, so much so that monstrosity could be defined solely in terms of speech and vocal features. In the days of silent cinema, human monsters had to be visually nightmarish (e.g., Nosferatu, the Phantom of the Opera) and reduced linguistically to a few intertitles. Coppola's new vampire is a compound of both silent and talking Draculas, and the filmmaker plays consciously upon this cinematic mutability. The vampire's dumb shadow is like "a symphony in grey": he groans and raves in his werewolf or reptilian self, talks like a novel as an elderly Count, and socialises like a Victorian dandy. All these guises tend to cancel each other and lose the name of fear. What started as a horror movie ends up being an erotic melodrama incorporating fabulous elements. The vampire softens into a neo-romantic lover and, for an undead monster, espouses a new lyrical phraseology.

Figures of evil discourse

One of the first statements of Draculea *qua* historical figure is a performative one that creates the allegorical figure of Dracula, the

personification of death. The filmic Prince is primarily a linguistic creation and
no more, and, as a text, he incorporates many lines from Bram Stoker's novel.
These lines have been dutifully relayed by many Hollywood screenwriters and
repeated verbatim by actors in their own tone and timber. But there are subtle
variations within this textual model. Coppola introduces many variants in the
cinematic representation of his vampire that amount to ideological shifts, and
therein lies the postmodern novelty. The Dracula myth is culture-bound because
it tells us how a community faces death at a given point in time. In the twentieth
century, cinema expressed that attitude most powerfully. And the way a culture
deals with death speaks volume for its ideology.

At no time does Tod Browning give the viewer a full exposition as to
the motivation, teleology, and overall modal functions (knowledge, belief,
desire, etc.) of his vampire. Lugosi's Dracula impersonates man's age-old fear
of death and dying, especially in one's prime (vampires prey exclusively on the
virginal young). Browning's basic Hollywoodian message is that you must face
death, defeat the fear of death, and not be seduced by its gaze, an essential
American belief at the time. The filmmaker stresses the role of willpower,
science, and reason to dispel the age-old spectre. In the thirties, Thanatos could
still be looked in the eye, and Van Helsing, as the conscience of the age, would
not flinch from it. In the Dracula world of Tod Browning, only wise old men
can lead the ideological battle; women are weak and unreliable because of their
sentimental outlook.

Andy Warhol's *Dracula* departs from the myth and shows the fall of
the House of Dracula, the end of an old order that has become socially and
sexually incompetent.[21] In that Dracula of the 1970s, death has been evacuated
by a new soft-porn hedonism. Van Helsing has metamorphosed into a young
Adonis who deflowers every virgin courted by the inept vampire, who throws
tantrums like a spoilt child. This is a reflection of the iconoclastic ideology of
the 1970s, which turned old fears into derision, a sort of artistic Bacchanalia
that, in the end, proved intellectual truancy.

Badham's undead Count brings us closer to Coppola's in semiotic and
linguistic development. The vampire's sensual hand caressing Mina's on a
moonlit beach is a visual metonym that ushers in a more desirable Death. The
hand of death grasps the willing hand of life: Mina is sick and dying and her
Keatsian self is "half in love with easeful death." Later, Lucy dances with
Dracula in a cinematic dance macabre and laughs under the jealous eye of her
fiancé. The film gives an ambiguous view of Dracula as an allegory of both love
and death. Yet Lucy makes a conscious, existentialist choice to rebel against her
father and lover. Badham makes it clear that Lucy (unlike Mina) is never under
a spell and is determined to follow her own light and be Dracula's lover. A
feminist twist is introduced in the old myth—an ideological intimation that the

New Woman will elect the course of her own sentimental life, even unto death. Lucy is clearly the main narrative spring, upstaging a frail-looking Van Helsing and the Pickwickian physician, Dr Seward. Her will power remains strong, even under the withering gaze of Dracula. Old death carries no sting in the comforting presence of new womanhood.

The three faces of death

It seems that Coppola tries to incorporate all the ideological facets of previous Dracula allegories and attitudinal reactions to them. In teleological terms, like the 1930 vampire, he aims at making the young and foolish his disciples and encounters the old wily Van Helsing. He cuts erotic capers like Warhol's soft-porn fop lusting after virgins, and he falls under the spell of redemptive feminine love, like Badham's suave Thanatos. Coppola's hero reflects the three faces of death of western culture: the monstrous Victorian figure spirited away by an alliance of pseudo-science and religion (Dracula vs. Van Helsing), the medieval phantasm of death lusting after life-blood (Dracula raping Lucy), and the romantic sad knight exorcised by the mystique of feminine love (Prince Draculea in love with Mina). What makes him postmodern is that he is a compound of the various allegories of death throughout the history of western art and culture. When it comes to his discourse, he obviously becomes a more complex allegory. In other words, as a verbal allegory, the postmodern Dracula is not that easily reducible to a mixture of figures past.

The voice of disenchanted mankind

Coppola introduces a reason for death (or Dracula) to plague the lives of mankind. In a verbal move, unusual in vampire movies, the Prince of Darkness provides the viewer with the whys and wherefores of vampirism. All Dracula myths are underpinned by the biblical doxa that death is the blight laid on man and woman for their transgression; therefore, the blame falls on them. Coppola subverts this premise and puts the blame on God's arbitrary justice. God has wronged Draculea, the warrior, in his flesh and blood by denying him true love for a woman, so he has rebelled and pledged to take revenge on God's creatures. This resonates well with postmodern audiences, who have been steeped in the modern worship of Love yet angered by the chaotic spectacle of planetary wars and arbitrary cosmic events. The disillusioned cry of all mankind seems to be distilled in the crusading Knight's grieved interrogation: "Is this my reward for defending God's church?" (*BSD* 18). And his antichristic pledge: "I shall rise from my own death to avenge hers with all the powers of darkness!"

(*BSD* 19). As a result, Coppola's Dracula should be interpreted as the resurrected Antichrist, the forlorn spirit of man labouring under a sense of cosmic wrong. No cinematic visuals can impart abstract thought, and the spectator gathers the ideological drift of the movie solely by listening to Dracula's discourse. So much for the visual "grammar" of cinema.

The reluctant vampire

The vampire also echoes a sensitive chord in the heart of western ideology. When he claims that "the happiest man on earth is the one who finds [. . .] true love" (*BSD* 44), he expresses a tenet of neo-romantic thought that is today tinged with materialist humanism: human love is more redeeming than divine love. That is why the movie is closer to fabulous tales like *Beauty and the Beast*[22] or *Pandora and the Flying Dutchman*,[23] a Hollywood movie based on the legend of a seventeenth-century adventurer who, after killing his wife in a jealous fit, curses God and his fate. He dies and resurrects as an immortal sailor on a ghost ship wandering the seas. He can only be saved from his tormented restlessness by the love of a woman. Centuries later, anchoring off the coast of a Spanish harbour, he falls in love with a *femme fatale* (Ava Gardner), who happens to be the reincarnation of his seventeenth-century wife. Her sacrificial love gives him eternal peace. Similarly, Dracula is given peace by Mina's love "in the presence of God." Dracula is a sensitive, reluctant vampire when it comes to Mina, his true love, which makes him more like a neo-romantic beast hankering for beauty. Although one should not stress too much the shallow philosophy of Coppola's *Bram Stoker's Dracula*, it is nevertheless interesting to note how it tallies with postmodern viewers' expectations of love, sex, and death in their humanistic, neo-romantic dimension. Another aspect of the complexity of that vampire can be derived from his unusual dialogic interaction with other characters and how it is screen-managed.

The ghost talks: the visual dynamics of Dracula's film dialogue

So far, I have assumed that filmic speech could be analysed as text (narrative voices, rhetoric, and ideological discourse). When language comes alive as cinematic dialogue, it undergoes many changes and turns into a specific mode of communication. The horror genre raises many difficulties for the writer of film dialogue, which is a stylised imitation of realistic speech as social semiotic (differing from the norms of speech representation in novels and dramas). Although film conversation has (mercifully) little to do with everyday exchanges, writing a dialogue for fictional characters involves necessarily certain choices in terms of social interaction. Language puts characters on a social map, whether they are Western villains, melodramatic heroines, or phantasmic vampires. Furthermore, the study of film language as social interaction must take on board art direction and camera work, which screen-manage dialogue and make it an audio-visual experience. Friedrich W. Murnau's *Nosferatu* is, for the most part, a silent figure, a flickering shadow on a screen. He does not yield easily to social comment and retains his eerie potential even today. Tod Browning's Dracula ceases to be a frightening psychic or surreal representation as soon as he enters into social talk with spectators in the opera house, especially in that stagy, medium-shot style of the early talkies. Talk kills ghosts, as Oscar Wilde demonstrated all too well.[24] In Hollywood movies, a garrulous spectre, like the Ghost in Mrs Muir's house, always ends up being a loser in the cut and thrust of dialogic interaction.[25] The dead in cinema ought to remain figures of elective mutism, yet Coppola's vampire is a master of discourse. His desire to seduce, to control, and most of all to bare his heart sets him apart in the gallery of vampires. His confessional voice marks him out as a new Dracula. In that respect, he is the father of postmodern confessional vampires, the likes of Louis or Lestat in *Interview with the Vampire* or Max Schreck, the metaleptic Nosferatu of E. Elias Merhige's *Shadow of the Vampire*.[26]

Dialogue enables the Count to give a social voice to evil, to integrate adverse discourse into the body politic for rehabilitation purposes. The first verbal exchange of Coppola's vampire occurs after he has appeared in the asynchronous guise of an epistolary voice. This cinematic convention kindles the viewer's desire to see the visual source of the sound, but that event has another important purpose, that of electing Jonathan and (later) Mina as his main addressees in two-shot dialogue scenes. As social man, Dracula never talks to anybody else, except, briefly, to the vampiresses and, in an inhuman shape, to Van Helsing. The opening conversation with Harker in the castle consists nearly entirely of textual lifts from the Victorian novel and reflects Bram Stoker's original tenor of discourse: the vampire asserting and transmitting the language of power and control. He stands for a symbolic order that equates verbal mastery with verbal mystery. His insistence on hierarchy, family, caste, and status, interspersed with figurative epigrams and enigmas, meets no pragmatic resistance from Jonathan, whose mercantile and literal discourse is submissive. For a late Victorian readership, the world of the vampire was a vivid allegory of their medieval past, revivified by the Pre-Raphaelites that had held it in both fear and fascination. They had to lay that cultural ghost to rest; they put a metaphorical axe through its heart and made their entry into the twentieth century. For moviegoers in the early 1930s, Dracula was the ghost of their western past from which they had to sever links, especially the romantic phylum personified by starry-eyed Mina. For postmodern audiences of the early 1990s, the vampire was but a complex, polysemic, and confused abstraction that had suffered from overexposure.

The Americanisation of evil

The Americanisation of Dracula, the evil undead, is what characterises the pragmatic and discursive evolution of Coppola's Count. Discourse shifts from the Victorian model of power domination between the old aristocrat and the young middle-class clerk to the reversal of roles and relationships in the dialogues between Mina and the vampire Prince. Early on, Mina takes verbal control in many ways, especially at the micro-level of conversational turns where she handles "toppers" ("If you seek culture, then visit a museum: London is filled with them," *BSD* 78), contrary assertions ("How can you call this science?" *BSD* 83) and mild mockery ("A prince no less!" *BSD* 78). At this stage, Mina is closer to a feminist voice with modernist overtones. But the main postmodern shift occurs not on a dialogic level but on a cinematographic level. Having dragged Mina in a corner of a London cinematograph, Dracula metamorphoses into the evil-good vampire and his "beastly selves" (be it AIDS, death, sex, violence, evil, animality, or all these rolled into one) are visualized as a wolf. The kinesic allegory of Mina's petting the wolf is unmistakable: she acknowledges, soothes, and falls in love with that obscure object of fear, which is not so much polysemic or polymorphic as preverbal. Its many faces and voices in Coppola's movie precisely cancel themselves out or, in postmodern parlance, constantly displace one another and find no semantic stability. Dracula stands for a dreadful cinematic flux, an abstract audio-visual nightmare, arrested and made stable by the hand of woman.

Americanisation of that abstract fear comes with a whimper, a sigh, a kiss, and a tear. Coppola tackles the poly-semantic nightmare with affective cinematography. From then on, the film will be hard put to resist the melodramatic pull, that gremlin that haunts any Hollywood production. This "sissifying" strain, so characteristic of postmodern discourse, will mostly manifest itself on a verbal level, not in Coppola's cinematography.[27]

Dialogue in melodramas wavers between heightened self-expression and repressed emotions.[28] The language of melodrama seeps into the dialogue scenes between Mina and Prince Dracula, but the visuals interfere and set up a counterpoint of dissonance that pulls back the movie into the realm of horror ambivalence. The restaurant scene, when Mina and the Prince drink absinthe, provides one instance of an embedded allegory, a trope commonly found in melodramatic discourse: the star-crossed lovers talk in parables, bringing together past and present to refer to their subterranean love. The *mise en scène* of the dialogue and the visual style are quite intricate. On paper, the dialogue is an imitation of fairy tale phraseology. When it is brought to the screen, it is integrated with cinematographic metaphors that run contrary to the language of love. The tableaux-like composition of the dialogue scenes, together with the contrived posturing of the characters, the superimposed "flashback" pictures, and the claustrophobic lighting give an early cinema feel and a late-Victorian aesthetic denseness to the sequence. This would certainly fit in well with the language of idealised love. But visual symbolism, pattern of editing, body language, shifting points of view, and shot scales reveal a dark side to the ideal of love and over-emphasise lust. In the stylised opening shots—an extreme close-up view of an eye and an overhead shot of a decanter filling a cup—the formal figure of the circle functions as an opening into which the male gaze and the intoxicating fluid can permeate. The closing shot of this inceptive sequence lingers on Mina's sensual mouth absorbing the absinthe-soaked lump of sugar. The shots dissolve into one another, a very apt editing metaphor, given the obvious "fluid-and-fill" symbolism of the whole sequence.

Later, in a similar editing pattern, the Prince's male gaze penetrates into Mina's life-blood through the inlet of her eyes. The camera intent on the male character's eyes and his relative facial immobility creates a sense of disquiet. Mina's body movements and posturing conjure up an ambivalent ballet of attraction and evasion. The geometrical lines drawn by their body and gaze alignment never bring them into close, face-to-face contact (until the final scene where they are seen dancing in a candle-lit room.) During brief tantalising moments, their faces do turn towards each other and their lips nearly brush one another, only to be frustrated by Mina's suppressed desire.[29] Coppola's visual aesthetics here tend to break down the barriers between good and evil. The evil, libidinous eye of the dead Count is as intense as it is pathetic when tears flow down his dead cheeks. Mina is both tantalising and inhibited, wavering between two axiological poles yet resisting male invasiveness. This cinematic play of seduction is intercut by a shot of Jonathan (the official fiancé) escaping from his prison. The parallel editing here interferes with the erotic thrust of the parlour sequence, thus articulating the taboo theme. What is clearly shown by the interplay of visual metaphors and film dialogue is the conventional neo-romantic nature of the verbal language compared with the complex cinematography of the sequence. What semantics is imparted by the spoken content, though, tends to "dumb down" the disturbing ambivalence suggested by the images. "Language as non-commitment" or "consensual discourse" seems to be a feature of postmodern discourse, while images are allowed to impact the viewer.

Yet, in the bed sequence when Mina arouses the divided vampire, the power of language comes into its own again, but with a difference. Mina, the woman, articulates the dangerous words "make me yours" (*BSD* 135). This is not safe sex (or text). But in the world of Coppola's *Bram Stoker's Dracula*, Mina certainly sets the ideological tenor of discourse. Whether her words are challenging, sentimental, subversive, or eventually therapeutic (in the closing sequence), she robs both Van Helsing and the male vampire of real verbal power. She is both the light and the word, quite literally the cinematic light and speech on the screen. But in the end, while her voice is soothing, her body discourse is ambivalent and aggressive: after saying, in angelic voice-over, the Christian words of redemption, her hand violently cuts off the phallic head of male evil, the source of all diseases. In all other Dracula versions, this symbolic gesture was the privilege of a man. Here, Mina, in one fell swoop, reverses the ancient myths of Eve and Pandora. Had she not dealt the final blow, the film, ending with her therapeutic discourse, would have merely sounded a neo-classical note. Mina ceases to be a guiding light—Van Helsing's ideal woman—and becomes instead an annihilating force. Viewers can hardly fail to notice the final dissonance between Mina's verbal and gestural communication.

Conclusion

The linguistic and verbal component of Coppola's motion picture is a complex stream of dialogues, monologues, a-synchronous storytellers, foreign speech, and other sundry vocalisations. Nearly all the medium's possibilities in terms of cinematic discourse have been harnessed, like a summing-up of what can be achieved. This eclecticism and inventiveness partly reflect the various levels of discourse found in Bram Stoker's novel, but it also circumvents the difficulties raised by writing film dialogue for horror movies. The hearer-viewer is confronted with several narrative and discursive stances, until the very end when Mina's viewpoint dominates. Film discourse carries overtones of abstract thought that visual codes cannot express. The evolution of the Count's discourse runs from the traditional language of evil duplicity to the language of Hollywood melodrama in the dialogue scenes with Mina. The vampire gradually loses the tenor of discourse, and Mina takes over as the main vocal master and voice-over narrator. A new cinematic duplicity, in both aural and visual codes, arises. Mina's verbal discourse exerts an ambivalent dialogic and perlocutionary influence on the Prince. Ultimately, kinesic codes, to borrow Keir Elam's term, and verbal behaviour are not easily reconciled in Mina and her realm of postmodern ambivalence.[30]

Notes

1 Sarah Kozloff, *Overhearing Film Dialogue* (Berkeley: University of California Press, 2000).

2 *Bram Stoker's Dracula*, dir. Francis Ford Coppola, perf. Winona Ryder, Gary Oldman (Columbia, 1992).

3 Laurent Jullier, *L'écran post-moderne* (Paris: L'Harmattan, 1997), 71-96.

4 Michel Chion, *La voix au cinéma* (Paris: Éditions de l'Étoile, 1982), 29.

5 Sarah Kozloff, *Invisible Storytellers—Voice-over Narration in American Fiction Film* (Berkeley: University of California Press, 1988).

6 A filmic metalepsis occurs where the real world breaks into the world of screen illusion (for example when a character suddenly drops his screen persona and reverts to the person he or she is in life).

7 *The Silence of the Lambs*, dir. Jonathan Demme, perf. Jodie Foster, Antony Hopkins (Orion Pictures, 1991).

8 Michel Chion 25.

9 *Sunset Boulevard*, dir. Billy Wilder, perf. Gloria Swanson, William Holden (Paramount, 1950).

10 *Mark of the Vampire*, dir. Tod Browning, perf. Bela Lugosi (Universal, 1935), and *Dracula*, dir. Tod Browning, perf. Bela Lugosi (Universal, 1931).

11 *Dracula, Prince of Darkness*, dir. Terence Fisher, perf. Christopher Lee (Hammer Films, 1966).

12 *Dracula*, dir. John Badham, perf. Frank Langella, Kate Nelligan (Universal, 1979).

13 Sarah Kozloff, *Film Dialogue* 21

14 Laurent Jullier 26.

15 Sarah Kozloff, *Film Dialogue*, 17.

16 *Interview with the Vampire*, dir. Neil Jordan, perf. Tom Cruise, Brad Pitt (Greffen Pictures, 1994).

17 See Todd Berliner, "Hollywood Movie Dialogue and the 'Real Realism' of John Cassavetes," *Film Quarterly* 52.3 (Spring 1999): 2-16, and Paul Coughlin, "Language Aesthetics in Three Films by Joel and Ethan Coen," available at http://www.thefilmjournal.com/issue12/coens.html (6 July 2006).

18 *The Passion of Christ*, dir. Mel Gibson, perf. James Caviezel (Icon Pictures, 2004).

19 In sociolinguistics, "style switching" refers to a multilingual speaker's ability to switch from one language to another in multi-code situations.

20 *Dr. Jekyll and Mr. Hyde*, dir. Rouben Mamoulian, perf. Fredric March, Miriam Hopkins (Paramount, 1931).

21 *Blood for Dracula*, dir. Paul Morrissey, perf. Udo Kier (CFS Kosutnjak, 1974).

22 *La Belle et la Bête*, dir. Jean Cocteau, perf. Jean Marais, Josette Day (DisCina, 1946).

23 *Pandora and the Flying Dutchman*, dir. Albert Lewin, perf. Ava Gardner, James Mason (MGM, 1951).

24 *The Canterville Ghost*, dir. Jules Dassin, perf. Charles Laughton (MGM, 1944).

25 *The Ghost and Mrs Muir*, dir. Joseph Mankiewicz, perf. Gene Tierney, Rex Harrison (Twentieth-Century Fox, 1947).

26 *Shadow of the Vampire*, dir. E. Elias Merhige, perf. John Malkovich (Lions Gate Films, 2000).
27 This emotive streak is admittedly more prevalent in the discourse of the press than in contemporary films.
28 Sarah Kozloff, *Film Dialogue* 235-66.
29 The screenplay states: "He kisses her tenderly, passionately" (*BSD* 98). The actual scene in the film does not follow the screenwriter's directions.
30 Keir Elam, *The Semiotics of Theatre and Drama* (London: Methuen, 1980), 57.

CHAPTER NINE

THE VISION OF RELIGION IN FRANCIS FORD COPPOLA'S *BRAM STOKER'S DRACULA*

JACQUES COULARDEAU, UNIVERSITÉ PARIS DAUPHINE UNIVERSITÉ PARIS I PANTHÉON SORBONNE

Francis Ford Coppola's *Bram Stoker's Dracula* gives one the impression of being heavily religious in its iconography but that such icons are rather commonplace and reduced to an excessive presence of Catholic symbols, particularly crosses of all types: one Maltese cross (we could wonder if it is not a cross patty), Latin crosses (a lot), one Greek cross, one Celtic cross, one clechy cross, and one botonny cross, plus quite a few crucifixes, one enormous altar crucifix, and one wayside Calvary cross. Among this inventory, one would expect to find a Rosy Cross, since the film deals with controversial religious themes and vampires at a time when Christendom was menaced by the Moslem Turks. But there is no Rosy Cross, no allusion then to the Templars, to Mary Magdalene, the Caballah, the Rosicrutians, the Gnostics, or any other deviant branch of Christianity.

And yet the film is religious from beginning to end, with an opening sequence that is pure religion, but I doubt that Francis Ford Coppola was conscious at the time of making a deeply religious film, in spite of its opening sequence. In this essay, then, I will discuss why the film has such a religious nature and try to assess the level of awareness Francis Ford Coppola may have had about the subject. In so doing, I will address an essential question: does the film represent the standard vision of the vampire as an enemy, a monster to be destroyed for our own good, or does it attempt to do something else? In other words, is Francis Ford Coppola in line with Stephen King, who sees the vampire as a monster to be destroyed and nothing else, or does he share the view of Anne Rice, who sees the vampire as a lovable monster (if a monster at all), and an extremely *human* being (even if it is no longer a human being), who can be seen as a reincarnation of Jesus Christ since the vampire, too, has the power to save humanity? Or is Francis Ford Coppola following his own line of thinking, if one at all?

The last question I address is one about religion in general in the film. Does it constitute a motivation, a solace, an escape, a damnation, a protection, a weapon, or a salvation? And what, if either of these, is Coppola's Christian rooting, particularly in the film's numerous references to the Bible? Assessing the film's Christian dimension reveals its postmodern nature as none of these questions can be answered very easily: all are open and refuse to be closed. Monster or non-monster, Christian or non-Christian, a crusade against Dracula or a pilgrimage to apotheosize him? All choices are open; no option is final and absolutely sure.

The first sequence: the past

The first sequence of *Bram Stoker's Dracula*, even before its opening credits, is meant to set the historical background, which is highly religious. Christendom is under attack by the Ottomans, or Turks, who have been stopped by Count Dracula, a member of the Sacred Order of the Dragon at the end of the fifteenth century. The film opens in the year 1462, when the religious symbols of the cathedral in Constantinople are changed for those of a mosque. The first cross of the film, probably a Maltese cross, is hurled to the ground, shatters, and is then replaced by a crescent, the only crescent to be featured in the film, notwithstanding the crescent-shaped decoration adorning the helmet of a Turkish soldier. Though Coppola does not provide the historical details, we are to understand that the cathedral is Hagia Sophia (Saint Sophia's) in present-day Istanbul.

Sophia means "wisdom" in Greek, an essential doctrine in early Christianity. One of the apocryphal gospels is even known as the Gospel of the Sophia of Jesus Christ. But this "power and wisdom of God" is Christ, as Paul says in 1 Corinthians 1:25. This wisdom of God, as opposed to the wisdom of man (that is, of the flesh), is central to the Gospel of Mary Magdalene, as well as to much of St. Paul's writings. The fall of Saint Sophia's is thus a religious symbol that carries us far inside the Christian faith.

What is also noteworthy is that Sophia was the Goddess of Wisdom for the Mediterranean world in the first century. The bride of God himself, she was a Goddess who was either adulated or rejected entirely. Some also see her as the Irish Sheela-na-gig, the Great Mother, the Mother of all things, but also the Goddess of Death and the underworld. Yet we must not forget that this very Sophia was designated, via the Atbash cipher, as Baphomet by the Templars— [taf][mem][vav][pe][bet] for "Baphomet" in Hebrew, which is read from right to left, becomes [alef][yud][pe][vav][shib], or Sophia, a Greek word written in Hebrew from right to left—and that this reference was seen as a gnostic element in that order. The Templars in this very first sequence—though the absence of a Rosy Cross or a Templars cross is rather surprising here—are engaged in the Crusades against the Muslims, which is in agreement with the film's timeframe; that the debate over the death or survival of Jesus, his relationship with Mary Magdalene, and the fate of his bones, etc. was popular at the time the film and video came out in 1992 and 1994, respectively, may have contributed to Coppola's decision to frame Stoker's novel within this historical context. What is more, the Maltese cross is a direct allusion to the various orders that used this cross as a symbol, orders that were connected to the Holy Land, the Crusades, etc.

This one image in the film thus transmits to the audience multiple layers of meaning, even if the reference to Constantinople, a name actually used by the voice-over, sends us back to the triumph of Pauline theology under Emperor Constantine. All of that need not be expressed, however, as it is part of the West's historical unconscious. We are dealing instead with the subliminal dimension of the film and its animated images. The medium is the message more than the message itself, or the message *qua* message is entirely determined by the medium, as Marshall McLuhan has argued.[1] As such, we are led to "read" Coppola's film in light of his postmodern theory since its religious meaning is purely subliminal, expressed not so much in its words but rather in its images alone. And by not being expressed in words but rather in the simple swapping of religious symbols atop a place of worship that we are supposed to recognize—which could even promote an Islamic reading of this scene, as I will discuss later on—Coppola avoids choosing sides.

On the eve of the battle, Dracula prepares himself in the chapel of his castle with Orthodox priests. The altar of this chapel is dominated by a cross that should be a crucifix but is not. At the crosspoint is a large round boss. The two arms, or branches, and the column, or trunk, are decorated with some kind of carving (a bas relief carved into the stone but not out of the stone). While it is impossible to make out the details, on each side of the cross can be seen an angel standing in the shadow, and they resemble two eagles because of their wings and two candelabra with nine candles each. Nine and nine make eighteen. Nine is an allusion to the ninth hour that marked Christ's death ("When the sixth hour came there was darkness over the whole land until the ninth hour," Mark 15:33), but it is also considered in its triplicate as the symbol of Satan. Here, only two nines are provided, but eighteen divided by three is six. If six is positive because it is Solomon's number, its triplicate is negative: "[. . .] the number of the beast: it is the number of a man, the number 666," Revelation 13:18).[2]

The visual reference to dualism (the two candelabra and the two angels) and the more abstract reference to ternarism are essential but very complex. Dualism is a reference to gnosticism, but also to the dual nature of the Old Testament God (God and God's spirit in Genesis 1:1-2), whereas ternarism is a reference to the Trinity, the triple nature of the New Testament God (God, the Holy Spirit, and the Son of God, though we must note that the phrase "Son of God" came later and that Jesus used the phrase "Son of Man" to describe himself, though he spoke frequently of his Father, even if Jewish tradition spoke of God as *the* father). And yet this ternary nature is perverted into some diabolical reference, though to reach it we may need to use dualism: twice nine is eighteen, which is three times six, which is twice three, just as nine is three times three. This complex intertwining of binary and ternary elements is once again part of our historical and here religious subconscious, widely reinforced by Shakespeare's and subsequent English poets' language and poetry. Two centuries before Shakespeare, Chaucer had already used this basic opposition in the English language: the binary iambic rhythm versus the disruptive ternary element (the three temples of the final "tournament" in "The Knight's Tale," for example, that cover up two temples to goddesses versus one temple to one god, and are the reverse sexual image of two knights fighting to the death over one woman).[3]

It is on this background that Dracula takes leave of his wife, Elisabeta. When he goes out of the castle, the army is seen waving spears and two crosses. The ensuing battle is brutal but ends in victory with a Turkish soldier sliding down the spear on which he was impaled and with the crescent-like decoration on his helmet undulating as his body descends. Dracula then kisses a botonny cross and says in his own language (the English translation appearing in subtitles): "God be praised. I am victorious" (*BSD* 15). The subtitles emphasize the clearly religious message here. In fact, the whole end of this sequence will be punctuated by such subtitles, with God appearing as the righteous and effective motivation for the war.

Then the sequence speeds up. Dracula returns home and finds his wife dead in the chapel on the steps to the altar. We have just seen her commit suicide by jumping from the castle into the moat. She finds solace neither in religion nor God. Dracula is confronted by three priests carrying crosses, one of whom says to him: "She has taken her own life, my son. Her soul cannot be saved. She is damned. It is God's law" (*BSD* 18). Even after death, religion and God fail to console, and Dracula curses them. As such, the altar, its cross, its two angels, and its two nine-candle candelabra become bad omens for him. Dracula grows angry and incites damnation: "Is this my reward for defending God's church?" (*BSD* 18). He knocks down the holy-water stoup, spreading the holy water across the floor (the first flooding). He brutally pushes one priest away, prompting them to yell: "Sacrilege!" (*BSD* 19). Dracula then draws his sword and stabs it in the boss at the crosspoint of the cross: one cross against another cross since the sword is a cross of its own. This image is extremely symbolic. He stabs the very heart of the cross, hence Christ's heart, and when it starts bleeding, it is Christ's heart that is bleeding. In other words, he is shedding Christ's blood in his wrath. This blood quickly spreads (the second flooding), first to an angel who has Jonathan Harker's head (foreshadowing his presence in the next scene), then to a candle, and finally across the entire floor. Dracula takes the chalice and dips it into the blood emerging from the cross. All this is colored by Dracula's declaration: "I renounce God! I shall rise from my own death to avenge hers with all the powers of darkness" (*BSD* 19). When he brings the chalice to his lips, he says again: "The blood is the life and it shall be mine!" (*BSD* 19). When the blood finally reaches Elisabeta's corpse. Dracula roars out, falls, and disappears from the frame.

This sequence has deep significance as for the vision of religion conveyed by the film. Religion and the cross lead to the blood rite, but the negation of religion perverts the blood rite from Christ's salvation to human damnation brought on by the desire to avenge human injustice. The reference here to the powers of darkness is essential to give the diabolical dimension of Dracula, who appears thus as the Antichrist: by renouncing God as he drinks Christ's blood, he becomes the Beast. From a sacred dragon, Dracula turns into the dragon of the Apocalypse, and the cross becomes the door to darkness.

Coppola's desire to push limits but refusal to choose sides in the holy wars lends the film its postmodern appeal, for this sequence could be read perfectly well from a Moslem point of view: pride at first in the Ottoman expansion, then disgust and even hatred with the brutality of the Christian reaction and Dracula's war methods. This is clearly expressed visually in the two crescents, the first one during Saint Sophia's deconsecrating (or profaning, per the traditional Christianized meaning of the word), and the second one undulating on the helmet of the impaled Turkish warrior. Once again, no words are used to provide us with an interpretation of this scene; only these images vehicle the message.

Religion as protection

As soon as Jonathan arrives in Transylvania, stepping off the stagecoach to wait for the Count's carriage, a girl, probably a gypsy, as shown by her headdress, gives him a small crucifix to wear around his neck and says: "For the dead travel fast" (*BSD* 32). With Jonathan in the background, the camera foregrounds the back of a very particular roadside Calvary. The cross is covered at the top with two boards that form a triangle, and at the crosspoint there seems to be some rags hanging. We then hear wolves howling, and we see the cross with Jonathan's eyes from in front. The storm's lightning enables us to clearly see what appears to be some kind of heavily toothed animal maw.

The first element we retain is the triangle over the cross. We cannot of course measure the angles of the triangle, but the visual proportions are common enough in our geometrical culture and world: either 30°-30°-120°, which leads us to the hexagram, or David's star, or 36°-36°-108°, which are in the pentagram series (18°, 36°, 54°, 72°, 108°).[4] On the cross, we have a body properly nailed to it, but the head is that of a wolf, and a voracious and monstrous wolf at that. Christ has thus become a wolf: a bad omen for Jonathan (and for the viewer), but also a simple statement that God, Christ, and religion offer no protection at all because Christ is nothing but a wolf, or has been transformed into a wolf in the territory Jonathan is entering. But Jonathan, the good salesman that he is, does not react at all.

Later on in the castle, the crucifix he has received from the gypsy girl protects Jonathan from Dracula while he is shaving in his room. The reflection of Jonathan's crucifix in the razor blade Dracula is holding, and then the same reflection in Dracula's black pupil, forces Dracula to step back from what appears to be his easy prey. Again, when Jonathan wanders about the castle and enters a bedroom in which he is approached, sexually and hungrily, by three women, one of them, who has appeared between his legs and is crawling up his chest, sees the crucifix. She screeches, and the crucifix melts and disappears. It has provided him no protection whatsoever this time. Is it because of the obvious sexual desire—and pleasure—that Jonathan experiences at this moment, or is it for some other reason? I tend towards the former, the sexual desire explanation, because similar results occur later on with Mina and Lucy: if you desire the vampire, you cannot but fall in his (or her) mesmerizing trap, and religious icons can no longer protect those who renounce its chaste principles.[5]

When Jonathan escapes, the haven that saves him is a women's monastery, the monastery of the Sisters of the Blessed Sacrament (perhaps a reference to the Compagnie du Saint Sacrement of the seventeenth century, which was considered as being slightly marginal or even heretical to canonical law). He sees it looming in the night rain in the form of two luminous crosses: a Latin cross on the door, and a Greek cross on the window of the entrance, thus joining the two Christian traditions of pre-Reformation Europe. Mina will soon receive a letter from Sister Agatha, go to Romania, and marry Jonathan in the monastery. During their Orthodox wedding ceremony, Mina and Jonathan partake of the blood rite of the Holy Communion, with Coppola emphasizing their drinking the consecrated wine, hence Christ's blood, a blood rite that is often considered as being a direct allusion to, if not recuperation of, the wine rites of Bacchus or Dionysus, a Greek god who is also himself the son of God,

Zeus. This communion and blood rite has to be thought of in parallel with Dracula's drinking of the blood of the cross in a chalice at the beginning of the film. But is their religious devotion a form of protection? I do not believe so, since Mina will ultimately be seduced by Dracula, and in fact has already been seduced in London by his young personification, Prince Vlad, all the while Jonathan was recuperating in the monastery. The blood rite is too late, and its protection ineffective.

The failure of religion

The film's essential message, then, is that religion completely fails us, or will fail us. It certainly failed Lucy. Her name, LVX or LUX, means light, but also Luke, and the first-ever representation of Mary as an icon or as a carved image, according to the eastern or western traditions. As such, she is Lucifer, the fallen angel of light. She is also Lug, the Celtic god of metalwork—a sword maker in a way—and light, whose name is found throughout Europe. And yet she is seduced by Dracula in the most traditional vampiric way. Her victimization is necessary to assess Mina's later in the story. Once she has been transformed into a vampire, she uses sex and sex appeal to entrap her human victims. When she is finally killed, and Dracula escapes, we find that nothing has protected her, the least of which her religious name. The men with their guns are fooled, the garlic is ineffective, and Dracula remains at large. Even though Lucy leaves her crucifix on her pillow the first time she goes out at night to meet Dracula in the labyrinth, her desire has already trumped the religious icon's effectiveness in protecting her, as it had been early with Jonathan and the three female vampires. Even when she becomes one of the undead and the men assemble to hunt her in her tomb, they kill her in the most common of ways: a stake through the heart (we can note that there is no mention of wood here since it is metal) and the final beheading. She is thus destroyed, but in no way by religion or with an obvious religious dimension, since even the beheading, which is a biblical allusion, is not clearly made religious in the scene. The religious allusion is—or may be—only made clearer by the viewer's historical unconscious.

But religion fails in another way. It fails to stop the dark forces from entering in the first place. We could even argue that religion in the film frees the dark forces to go on with their business. Dracula, for instance, is shown and declared the master of the wind and of the sea (like the spirit of God hovering over the watery abyss in Genesis 1:2). He can start and command a storm, and even travels in a boat that bears a significant name: *Demeter*. Demeter is one of the names of the triple goddess, another religious tradition that bores very deep in westerners' minds. The triple goddess is essential to English literary tradition as early as Shakespeare's thrice-crowned goddess: Hecate, the Goddess of the Dead; Selene, the Goddess of the Night and the Moon (the inconstant moon and its three phases); and Diana, the Goddess of the Day, the forest, and animal life. But Demeter recalls another level of realization of the triple goddess, this time more Germanic. This time, it is Elisabeta who carries the allusion through her name: "beta" links her to the three Bethen: Ambeth (Mother Earth), Wilbeth (the Sun), and Borbeth (the Moon). The suffix "bethen" is connected to two roots: /bett/ refers to the mother-earth on which we used to sleep (bett = bed in English), and /beten/ refers to praying or calling the goddess (beten = to pray in English). These three Bethen have survived in folklore even today in Austria and were even the sources of Shakespeare's three weird sisters in *Macbeth*, where the name Macbeth itself is derived from this root.

This reference to the triple goddess is essential because it shows Dracula as the heir of an older tradition than Christianity, that is to say paganism, which is a biased word inherited from the Christian tradition. Older religions are centered on a cult to nature: the night and the day, as well as the earth, the sun, and the moon. They are deeply ternary in the fact that they do not concentrate on only the sun and the moon, the night and the day, but on three astral spheres—the sun, the moon, and the earth—and thus cannot be reduced to night and day. That could explain why Dracula can go around in the daytime, even if his powers are weaker: he is not only a night animal. The world is not simply all black or all white, evidenced in the albino wolf that escapes from the London Zoo, symbol of the night as much as of the day, of darkness as much as of light. Coppola's turning Stoker's grey Bersicker wolf white could be understood as an inversion of the old Christian tradition of eradicating paganism in our civilization. As such, Coppola's film seems to posit not a post-religious phase in human development, but definitely a post-Christian phase in which all objectives that had been set by Christianity twenty centuries ago have more or less been made irrelevant in our world. And yet, this film, like all films and animated images, is subliminal: with dead images it creates the illusion of movement, and with dead ideology it nourishes the unconscious need of a scapegoat.

As with Lucy, religion ultimately fails Mina. Short for Wilhelmina, (the feminine form of Wilhelm, or protection by will), Mina will be seduced by Prince Vlad, a younger embodiment of Dracula. We cannot deny that Elisabeta and Mina are visually the same person since they are the same actress—once again, the visual element becomes the message. Coppola manipulates the audience here into going beyond the myth, the tradition, the social and cultural habits, just as he had done in forging Jonathan's likeness on the altar cross in Dracula's chapel. Coppola weaves links and lines that trespass limits and add a visual dimension that cannot be carried by the novel alone. He thus produces a vision of love as crossing traditions and centuries, of love as being universal because it is truer than religion. For this reason, Mina-Elisabeta is seduced by Prince Vlad. Though he is a little awkward at first due to his lack of practice of courting in modern society, he is helped a lot by his suggestive powers that force her out of her fear and into his trap. This is very clear when the white wolf appears, transforms the cinematograph into a shadow puppet show that evokes, through its dominant red color and shapes, the war against the Turks of the beginning of the film. But this wolf is controled by Prince Vlad and also by Mina, who does not seem surprised at all when she caresses the wolf.

Here again, though, nothing can protect us from this natural force that Vlad-Dracula represents: the call from the earth, the primeval forest, the triple goddess, the three Bethen. For that reason, Coppola introduces another example of the failure of religion, and even of science and civilization in general. Renfield, who is completely outside the nascent psychiatry of the time (a new classification will have to be invented for such a case, as Dr. Jack Steward says), unites Ambeth (one of the three goddesses dedicated to the earth) by the root /am-/ or /an-/ (meaning earth and also mother, and, what is more, through Renfield's own name) with the worm that lives in this earth. It is not coincidental, then, that he eats an orange worm the first time he has a discussion with his doctor. Religion fails Renfield, though, because he fell into Dracula's trap when he went to Transylvania in the first place, because he now escapes human and even scientific control, and because he is endowed with the power to communicate with Dracula, his Master. The film is very careful to avoid the term "Lord" that Stoker uses in the novel (cf. *D* 245) and to only use the term "Master" so as not to mix Dracula and Jesus in this particular context. But we could queer this reference and put forward the symbolic dimension of the worm-penis living in the earth-(Ren)field-womb. I would insist here on the importance of using the term "penis" instead of "phallus" because for Jacques Lacan, a major figure in post-structuralist and postmodern criticism, everyone has a phallus, including women of course, since the phallus is not a sex organ but a construct or a reconstruct of one's own self: the Ideal of the Ego, the virtual model and target everyone builds in their minds to guide themselves or to be guided by on the road leading to being and becoming fully realized individuals.

Perhaps the most striking example of the failure of religion can be seen in Dracula's living in Carfax Abbey in London. This Abbey is of course no longer consecrated since Henry VIII closed all religious orders in England. Yet it is a religious symbol, a Catholic symbol, and those who are fighting against Dracula are not Catholics but Protestants, from England, from the United States, and from the Netherlands. This division of Christianity after the Reformation is thus present in the powerlessness of Christianity against Dracula. If we consider this religious schism in light of the previous one between the Orthodox and

Catholic churches, we come to the conclusion that the splitting of Christianity into its three main branches over the centuries is responsible for its failure to protect. Once again, this is not stated explicitly in the film but only alluded to: Orthodox Christians stopped the Turks initially, but the Turks were able to advance because the Crusades, fought only by the Catholics, were a failure. Because Catholicism will itself split in two again during the Reformation, the church will fail in preventing Dracula from entering the West, from invading the Christian world. Ironically, it is the breakaway Protestant branch that will put a stop to Dracula, but not in any religious way, orthodox or unorthodox.

Religion as a weapon

If religion alone cannot protect us, maybe it can provide us with the weapons necessary to defend ourselves. Here the film, especially with Van Helsing, the great specialist on matters such as these, becomes over-wrought. The first thing he tries to get is knowledge from various books in libraries, and it is here that he learns of the history of Dracula. This knowledge is tied from the very start to black and morbid humor. As he says to his medical students in the Netherlands:

> The diseases of the blood, such as syphilis [. . .]. The very name, venereal diseases, the diseases of Venus, imputes that they are of divine origin and that they are involved in that sex problem about which the ethics and ideals of Christian civilization are concerned. In fact civilization and syphilization have advanced together. (*BSD* 88)

In a way, religion is said to provide us with knowledge, but the implementation of that knowledge is not very religious. Religion itself is no help, nor is its knowledge, except when it describes the living customs of the vampire for the hunters to adapt their methods.

The cross as religious icon and epistemological weapon is contradictory in the film. Here, a crucifix is melted by a female vampire, a cross is set on fire by Dracula himself, and Lucy recoils when confronted with a cross and obediently lies down in her coffin berated by Van Helsing, who repeats over and over again: "This is the Holy Cross. We are strong in the Lord, his power, his might. Lord God is upon us [. . .]."[6] Altogether the cross has limited power, and the little power it does have invested in it from time to time is the result of fear, disgust, or repulsion in the vampire. The cross is thus not dangerous per se in a vampire's eyes, but rather a provocation, an obscenity. To show his distaste, Dracula stamps his foot on the floor, and the cross catches fire.

The wafer, too, has extremely limited power. It only marks a vampiric being with a slight superficial burn that is used by Coppola dramatically in the last sequence to show Mina's vampiric nature and infection, and her sudden liberation of this infection after she kills Dracula. Similarly, the holy water used in the Carfax Abbey cannot counter Dracula, who escapes in the shape of a green vapor. Nor can Latin incantations exorcize the vampire. As a matter of fact, standard weapons like swords and guns are more effective in fighting Dracula and protecting one from harm than are all of the religious paraphernalia mentioned, a fact Coppola marginalizes in the film.

If religion cannot provide us with real protection or real weapons, then how can the vampire be defeated? The film, like the novel, is explicit in its answer. The first vampire, Lucy, is destroyed with a stake through her heart (I have already pointed out that it was metal and not wood, let alone ash) and a good cutlass stroke to the neck. The second batch of vampires that are destroyed are the three female vampires in Dracula's castle. Once again, they are kept at bay with a circle of fire and not crumbled wafers or holy water; and they are liquidated on the following morning with a sword that beheads them all. Van Helsing throws their three heads into the abyss and the river—the same river where Elisabeta committed suicide and to which Jonathan escaped. In other words, in receiving the three severed heads, the river has symbolically been purified of Elisabeta's suicide. I say symbolically here and not religiously since suicide can never be purified in religion.

But how can Dracula himself be killed? He can be killed if he is captured before sundown, when he becomes powerful again. This fails, of course, for when he is attacked with weapons and his throat is half slit, and a sword is plunged into his heart, he is still not completely dead. He lay helpless in the chapel on the altar steps, in the same place and position where he had found the dead Elisabeta, but in a completely inverted situation (symbolic regeneration): Mina, Elisabeta's reincarnation, is looking down upon him and is going to complete the task. But Mina's motivation here is not at all to destroy the monster (as the "Crew of Light" wishes to do in the novel), but rather to save his soul, to liberate him from the powers of darkness and from his damnation. She will press the sword through his heart and cut off his head, but her actions are motivated by love.

This execution is possible because, when she had the opportunity to drink his blood, he reacted so that she would not drink enough to make her transformation complete. She remained a human being despite her vampiric characteristics. On the other hand, Dracula had rediscovered love, which made him prevent her from over-drinking, so that she was only "baptized" into vampirism, as Van Helsing says. Love, and not religious belief, returns his humanity to him, hence his ability to die. He can die in shared love and thus be saved, salvaged, regenerated, and resuscitated to the eternal life of the soul.

Coppola's ending, however, raises a problem of interpretation. What is the meaning of the beheading? What does it bring to the film? We may think of David and Goliath at first, but that biblical story does not fit here because we systematically have, in the prior beheading episodes, a sexual divide between the beheaded and the beheader. Moreover, in this last case, it is a woman who is doing the beheading. Answers to this problem may best be explained with reference to the book of Judith in the Old Testament. Judith is a Jewish widow in Bethulia, an unknown city that controls "the only means to access to Judaea" (Judith 4:7), and decides, on the order from "Joakim the high priest resident in Jerusalem at the time" (Judith 4:6), to save Israel of sure destruction when the general-in-chief of the Assyrian army, Holofernes, comes in the name of Nebuchadnezzar to punish the tribes, Israel among others, for not having answered his call some time before in his campaign against Arphaxad. Judith criticizes the elders and other people in the town who only lament and beg God for help, a God that should be neither coerced nor cajoled as she says (Judith 8:17). She then leaves the elders and the town and calls upon Holofernes to pardon her because she rejects her coward tribe. Flattered, Holofernes falls into her sexual trap; she gets him drunk, so that she will not be soiled, and cuts off his head with his own scimitar and brings it back to Bethulia. This steels the Jews in battle, and they defeat the general-less Assyrian army.[7]

There are striking similarities between the stories of Judith and Mina in Coppola's film, echoed in Jonathan's declaration at the end when Mina enters the chapel with the dying Dracula: "Let her go. Now her time has come" (*BSD* 161).[8] Similar, too, is Mina's apparent betrayal of her fellow human beings. But the main difference is that there is real love between Mina and Dracula, and that she will behead him not to destroy him but to absolve him, that is, not to bring her fellow human beings to fight and defeat an army, but to destroy the possibility of there ever being such a war in the first place. As Van Helsing says, speaking of Dracula to Mina: "His salvation is his destruction" (*BSD* 139).[9] Van Helsing's meaning is thus not negative, in the way a drunken man may be emasculated by a woman; rather it bespeaks the salvation of a reprieved soul by a woman in the name of and thanks to mutual love. The biblical reference does not bring the meaning into the tale but tremendously reinforces that meaning through the contrast.

But once again the reference is not explicit. It is part of our culture, or at least it has to be in order to be understood (so that we can understand this understood meaning in the film). To many in Coppola's audience, not all of these religious allusions reach a conscious level. For many, the beheading scene would no doubt recall action films that abound in beheadings, such as *Highlander* for example, even if in Russell Mulcahy's film the fighters are necessarily men. But a contemporary audience is able to look beyond the sexual divide as if it were meaningless, which it never is of course, even if this meaninglessness is in itself meaningful in a postmodern perspective.

The film and today's religious debates

Coppola's film is not concerned with the raging debate on Jesus' bloodline, his relationship to Mary Magdalene, or even the Templars; such concerns emerged a decade later with Dan Brown's *Da Vinci Code*, the bestseller that set the whole religious landscape on fire.[10] Yet the film is in concert with the literary debate over the nature of vampires taking place at the time between two of the most recognizable names in fantastic and horror literature.[11] Stephen King in his *'Salem's Lot* (the novel came out in 1975, the TV mini series that became the first film in 1979, and *Return to 'Salem's Lot* in 1987[12]) gives the standard image of the vampire: a monster that has to be destroyed by any means. The films produced from this novel are even pushing this image of the vampire to such an extreme that it has nearly become farcical. Anne Rice, on the other hand, has built her Vampire Chronicles (including the first three novels, *Interview with the Vampire*, 1976; *The Vampire Lestat*, 1985; *The Queen of the Damned*, 1988; as well as in the more recent novels dedicated to her cast of vampires[13]), around a historical lineage of the undead, who witness humanity's evolution cross the many centuries that they live, keeping their human personalities beyond their death and rebirth. Coppola draws from both Gothic masters in his film, starting with the traditional image of the vampire (though not reduced to the caricature of the monster that King uses), and moving slowly toward human regeneration through Mina's reincarnation of Elisabeta. Dracula becomes a witness of the past who recovers his humanity though his destruction, which is also his salvation. Coppola surely could not have been ignorant of these contemporary portrayals of vampires and thus consciously positioned his Dracula in between the two paradigms.

Yet Coppola's film does carry religious import and does have an impact on the present religious debate that widens the scope of the film more than makes it appear archaic. The first element is the apocalyptic vision, but a real apocalypse: the Turks' destruction of Christianity. The response to this apocalypse is another apocalypse, reduced visually to the impaled bodies of Vlad Țepeș's victims writhing on their stakes. The color of these apocalypses is of course red, the color of blood, fire, anger, and Dracula's armor. This apocalyptic vision is even transferred onto the chapel scene when Dracula causes the blood from the cross to flood the church (the image of the flood is dominant in John's *Book of Revelation*, in all possible material realizations). The reference to the dragon at this moment, Dracula being a member of the Order of the Dragon, is also an allusion to the dragon in the Apocalypse. But the reference is inverted: the dragon is on the side of the church, and it is this inversion that may pervert the tale. The dragon turns against the church either because he is a dragon and cannot be anything but the Beast in a standard reading of the *Book of Revelation*, or because the church is the real beast that betrays him, its most loyal servant. In the *Book of Revelation* is a story of a pregnant woman who is protected from on high against "a huge red dragon which had seven heads and ten horns, and each of the seven heads crowned with a coronet. Its tail dragged a third of the stars from the sky and dropped them to the earth" (*Revelation* 12:3-4). And it is only when the dragon fails at capturing the pregnant woman that "the dragon delegates his power to the beast" (*Revelation* 12:17). In applying this story to Coppola's film, Dracula becomes the beast when the church fails to protect Elisabeta against the Turks and against her eventual suicide. The pattern is similar but inverted since Dracula is not after the woman but the Turks, not serving his own interest but serving the interest of the church, and not coveting the woman but in love with her; the woman is not protected and sent to some haven but rather left unprotected and abandoned to her death.

In addition to the purifying powers of love, damnation and salvation provide the film its major themes. Damnation is obvious in Dracula's desecration of the chapel, having committed an unpardonable sacrilege. But damnation is constantly present for other characters as well, particularly Lucy and then Mina. Here the vision is simply puritanical: evil, as represented by Lucy after her transformation, has to be destroyed. But unlike with Dracula, Lucy is not given a choice. She is mesmerized into falling and being damned, in the same manner as Mina. Neither is given a choice (save Dracula's later insistence that Mina not drink too much from his breast), and choice is the necessary element for goodness to carry any meaning. As Milton demonstrates in *Areopagitica* or *Paradise Lost*, if there is no possible choice, man is not responsible for the acts he commits, good or evil. Those acts thus have no ethical value. Regarding Lucy, we decide that what she is doing is evil, and we destroy her to save ourselves. Her salvation, if she is indeed damned from the start, is not even taken into account. There is no considering her fate among the men who accept to hunt her down, including her husband.

On the other hand, Mina is given a choice because Dracula limits her damnation, and she takes full responsibility for her fate when she is confronted with killing Dracula. In Miltonian terms, her acts are absolutely ethical, positive or negative, because she chooses to do what she does. Here we have the reversal of Christ's story. Apart from the fact that Dracula drank Christ's blood pouring from the cross and became a vampire because of the way he got that blood, he has to die to be saved, to shed his blood to be liberated of the damnation of which he is victim. By dying, he does not save anyone except himself, though we could say he saves the world from the damnation he represents for human beings, which would be the traditional puritanical view that deprives man of free choice. On Mina's side, she has to kill Dracula in order to save him, to save herself, and to save the world. Christ's fate is inverted once again. Salvation is no longer a story of a man who is killed to save mankind but a woman who kills to protect humanity. This inversion is Coppola's fundamental Christian message in the film.

Conclusion

On one side is the Lamb, Christ. He is a willing victim who sacrifices himself to save humanity from damnation. By being shed, his blood saves others, and the blood rite that comes from it is to remind us of his sacrifice. On Judgment Day, however, the Lamb will kill in the name of God to rid the world of sin, evil, and the Beast and enable those who can be saved to live in the messianic Jerusalem. The Lamb is thus delivering fire, hail, rain, floods, and plagues onto the world to destroy the whole of sinning humanity and to preserve its saints. Distinguishing good from evil can only be achieved in death, according to the Pauline doctrine.

On the other side is Dracula, who cannot be understood alone. He has to be taken in connection with his love for Mina-Elisabeta. He starts as a blood shedder, and a particularly cruel one at that. He then makes the choice to become a monster out of spite and anger, what Mary Magdalene would call "foolish wisdom" or "wrathful wisdom" (Gospel according to Mary Magdalene 8:19). Then he has to be sacrificed to be saved. His blood saves him and eventually the one he loves since he will not be able to destroy her. His death saves humanity of his own menace. In other words, he is a complete Antichrist. When Dracula is finally saved, there will be no need for his second coming.

This Christian metaphor of the salvation of the Antichrist is punctuated with religious elements to emphasize the idea that the Antichrist can only be countered by love, and there we reach the real Christian meaning of Coppola's film. Evil can only be reformed through love: not Jesus' universal love, but a sexual love, even if the two protagonists are now beyond sexuality.

Was Coppola conscious of all this complexity of meaning in producing *Bram Stoker's Dracula*? If we follow the "Making of . . ." documentary added to the 1994 video version of the film and later to the DVD, then certainly not. Throughout the long documentary the religious question is reduced to a minimum. Apart from Dracula being referred to as the Devil or Mephistopheles, there is little evidence (save a couple of quotations from the film itself) to suggest Coppola was forthright in his religious intent. In fact, the documentary concentrates on the working methods of Coppola as a director more than on the meaning of the film. In 1992, the situation was not ripe for an earnest religious debate on the film. The fact that the film was shot in 1992 may explain why some of the religious meaning in it is left more to innuendo, subliminal allusions, or understood references. Audiences had not yet discovered the Opus Dei. The film's religious meaning seems to be nearly incidental, which is regretful because its myths are universal and absolutely crucial to the history of humanity and the invention of religions. Religions, all of them, have one primeval objective: to protect the believers against blood-curdling and blood-thirsty violence by cultivating human ethics in human beings. Dracula, the myth of the vampire, of the blood drinking tyrant or monster, is always present in religious mythologies. He is there in the *Book of Revelation*, and in Isaiah and Ezekiel. He is Bel or Baal, the dragon, the Beast, the monster omnipresent in so many of the later books of the Old Testament that it is impossible to exclude them from the field of dragon-cultivating mythologies. Even Moses' bronze serpent appears as a form both of punishment and of protection from God, who is called a "seraph," derived from the angel "seraphim," which is represented as a winged dragon (Numbers 21:1-9).

And it is this dimension of mythologies in general that merges all human religions into a universal religious consciousness, even subliminal awareness, that makes the film a film of its time, the postmodern time, a time in which references are intertwined and lack historical objectivity. Maybe something is still rotten in the state of Denmark, but something is definitely queer in the imagination of our time.

As for Coppola's intention, I can only put forward hypotheses. Coppola, though, seems to use the cinematographic medium as a way to convey meaning through images, always keeping the various sides balanced so that the film remains understandable, in one way or another, by all members of the audience. It is a commercial necessity, of course, one that corresponds to the spirit of our day. Maybe this spirit has been created by the commercial intentions of the medium (where the medium is the message), or the spirit of the day has emerged from history itself and has invested the medium with its essence (where the message is the medium). Does postmodernity emerge from the market economy in the field of ideas, ideologies, and cultural constructions, or does it come from the slow and steady evolution of the human species in its historical adventure? We cannot know for sure. We might even say that this market economy can be seen as part of this historical adventure in what some identify as a dialectical though not antagonistic relation. For sure, great filmmakers like Francis Ford Coppola go along with the spirit of their time, trying to satisfy their own artistic needs in addition to the commercial needs of their audiences. In *Bram Stoker's Dracula*, Coppola attempts to connect as many people in the audience as possible beyond their various divides—sexual, social, economic, cultural, artistic, religious, or whatever.

Notes

1 See Marshall McLuhan, *Understanding Media: The Extensions of Man* (London: Routledge, 1964).

2 Some commentators have claimed that 666 is the total of the number values of "Nero-Caesar" (in Hebrew).

3 See Steve Ellis, ed., *Chaucer: An Oxford Guide* (Oxford: Oxford University Press, 2005).

4 Richard Andrews and Paul Schellenberger, *The Tomb of God: Unlocking the Code to a 2,000-year-old Mystery* (London: Time Warner Books, 1996).

5 Queer theory can help explain the sexual dimensions of the film, for while Dracula is not gay, there is no real sexual limit to his thirst; he drinks out of necessity, male and female victims alike. Jonathan, on the other hand, has limits since he is attracted to the female vampires, in the same way Lucy and Mina are drawn to Dracula. Anne Rice will use this sexually-ambivalent tradition widely with her vampire Lestat de Lioncourt, who definitely has a gay, or a campy, side. Coppola uses this gay element parsimoniously but effectively, which is also how we should view the queer in the film.

6 This line does not appear in the screenplay.

7 See École Biblique de Jérusalem, *La Bible de Jérusalem* (Paris: Les Éditions du Cerf, 1998), and Alexander Jones, ed., *The Jerusalem Bible: Reader's Edition* (Garden City, NY: Doubleday, 1966).

8 The line in the screenplay reads: "Let her go. Our work is finished here. Hers is just begun."

9 The line in the screenplay reads: "Your salvation is his destruction."

10 See, for instance, Robert Eisenman, *James: The Brother of Jesus* (London: Watkins Publishing, 2002).

11 See Peter Haining, ed., *The Vampire Omnibus* (London: Orion Books, 1995); Byron Preiss, ed., *The Ultimate Dracula* (London: Headline Book Publishing, 1992); and Alan Ryan, ed., *The Penguin Book of Vampire Stories* (London: Penguin, 1987).

12 Stephen, King, *'Salem's Lot* (New York: Doubleday, 1975).

13 These nine novels, all published by Knopf, are: *The Tale of the Body Thief* (1992), *Memnoch the Devil* (1995), *Pandora* (1998), *The Vampire Armand* (1998), *Vittorio, The Vampire* (1999), *Merrick* (2000), *Blood and Gold* (2001), *Blackwood Farm* (2002), and *Blood Canticle* (2003).

SELECT BIBLIOGRAPHY

Abraham, Nicolas, and Maria Torok. *The Shell and the Kernel: Renewals of Psychoanalysis*. Vol. 1. Trans. Nicholas T. Rand. Chicago and London: University of Chicago Press, 1994.

Andreescu, Ştefan. *Vlad Ţepeş (Dracula)*. Bucureşti: Minerva, 1976.

Andrews, Richard, and Paul Schellenberger. *The Tomb of God: Unlocking the Code to a 2,000-year-old Mystery*. London: Time Warner, 1996.

Anon. "*Dracula*, by Bram Stoker." *The Bookman* 12 August 1897: 129.

Anon. "*Dracula*, by Bram Stoker." *Glasgow Herald* 10 June 1897: 10.

Anon. "*Dracula*, by Bram Stoker." *Manchester Guardian* 15 June 1897: 9.

Anon. "For Midnight Reading." *Pall Mall Gazette* 1 June 1897: 11.

Apostol, Daniel Tiberiu. *Dracula: mit sau realitate*. Braşov: Editura Muzeului Bran, 2005.

Arata, Stephen D. *Fictions of Loss in the Victorian Fin de Siècle*. Cambridge: Cambridge University Press, 1996.

—. "The Occidental Tourist: *Dracula* and the Anxiety of Reverse Colonization." *Victorian Studies* 33 (1990): 621-45.

Auerbach, Nina. *Our Vampires, Ourselves*. Chicago and London: The University of Chicago Press, 1995.

Ballesteros-Gonzáles, Antonio. "Count Dracula's Bloody Inheritors: The Postmodern Vampire." *Dracula: Insémination. Dissémination.* Ed. Dominique Sipière. Amiens: Sterne, 1996. 107-19.

Barber, Paul. *Vampires, Burial, and Death: Folklore and Reality*. New Haven and London: Yale University Press, 1988.

Baudrillard, Jean. *Simulacra and Simulation*. Trans. Sheila Faria Glaser. Ann Arbor: University of Michigan Press, 1994.

Blinderman, Charles. "Vampurella: Darwin & Count Dracula." *Massachusetts Review* 21 (1980): 411-28.

Boia, Lucian. *Istorie şi mit în conştiinţa româneasca*. Bucureşti: Humanitas, 1997.

Boner, Charles. *Transylvania; Its Products and Its Peoples*. London: Longman, 1865.

Booth, William. *In Darkest England and the Way Out*. London: International Headquarters of the Salvation Army, 1890.

British Medical Journal 1 (1887): 344.

Brown, Keith. "Villains and Symbolic Pollution in the Narratives of Nations." *Balkan Identities: Nation and Memory*. Ed. Maria Todorova. London: Hurst, 2004. 233-52.

Buican, Denis. *Avatarurile lui Dracula; de la Vlad Țepeș la Stalin și Ceausescu*. București: Scripta, 1993.

Byron, Glennis. Introduction. *New Casebooks: Dracula*. Ed. Glennis Byron. London: Palgrave; New York: St. Martin's Press, 1999. 1-21.

Calmet, Dom Augustin. *Dissertation sur les revenants en corps, les excommuniés, les oupires ou vampires, brucolaques*. Paris: Jérôme Million, 1986.

Cantlie, James. *Degeneration amongst Londoners: A Lecture Delivered at the Parkes Museum of Hygiene, January 27, 1885*. London: Field & Tuer, [1885].

Cârțana, Iulian, Gheorghe Dondorici, Emil Poama, Elena Emilia Lica, Octavian Oșanu, and Relu Stoica. *Istorie: Manual pentru clasa a XII a*. Pitești: Editura Carminis, 2000.

Chion, Michel. *La voix au cinéma*. Paris: Éditions de l'Étoile, 1984.

Condouriotis, Eleni. "Dracula and the Idea of Europe." *Connotations* 9.2 (1999–2000): 143-59.

Coppola, Francis Ford. Afterword. *Bram Stoker's Dracula: A Francis Ford Coppola Film*. Fred Saberhagen and James V. Hart. New York: Signet, 1992. 299-301.

Coppola, Francis Ford, and James V. Hart. *Bram Stoker's Dracula: The Film and the Legend*. New York: Newmarket, 1992.

Corbin, Alain. *Le Miasme et la Jonquille: L'Odorat et l'Imaginaire social, XVIIIᵉ-XIXᵉ siècles*. Paris: Flammarion, Champs, 1986.

—. *Le Temps, le désir et l'horreur: Essais sur le XIXᵉ siècle*. Paris: Flammarion, Champs, 1998.

Corbin, Carol, and Robert A. Campbell. "Postmodern Iconography and Perspective in Coppola's *Bram Stoker's Dracula*." *Journal of Popular Film and Television* 27.2 (Summer 1999): 40-48.

Craft, Christopher. "'Kiss Me with Those Red Lips': Gender and Inversion in Bram Stoker's *Dracula*." *Speaking of Gender*. Ed. Elaine Showalter. New York and London: Routledge, 1989. 216-42.

Curl, James Stephens. *The Victorian Celebration of Death*. Stroud: Sutton, 2001.

Davison, Carol Margaret. *Anti-Semitism and British Gothic Literature*. Houndmills, Basingstoke, and New York: Palgrave, 2004. 120-27.

—, ed. *Bram Stoker's Dracula: Sucking through the Century, 1897–1997*. Toronto and Oxford: Dondurn, 1997.

Daicoviciu, Hadrian, Pompiliu Teodor, and Ioan Câmpineanu. *Istorie. Clasa a VII a.* Bucureşti: Editura didactica şi pedagogică, 1997.

Derrida, Jacques. *Spectres of Marx: The State of the Debt, the Work of Mourning, and the New International.* Trans. Peggy Kamuf. London and New York: Routledge, 1994.

Dijkstra, Bram. *Idols of Perversity: Fantasies of Feminine Evil in Fin-de-Siècle Culture.* New York: Oxford University Press, 1988.

Dumitrescu, Nicoleta, Mihai Manea, Cristian Niţa, Adrian Pascu, Aurel Trandafir, and Mădălina Trandafir. *Istoria Românilor: manual pentru clasa a XII a.* Bucureşti: Humanitas Educaţional, 2003.

École Biblique de Jérusalem. *La Bible de Jérusalem.* Paris: Les Éditions du Cerf, 1998.

Eisenman, Robert. *James: The Brother of Jesus.* London: Faber & Faber, 1997; reprt. London: Watkins, 2002.

Eliade, Mircea. *The Romanians: A Concise History.* Bucharest: Roza Vinturilor, 1997.

Ellis, Steve, ed. *Chaucer: An Oxford Guide.* Oxford: Oxford University Press, 2005.

Farson, Daniel. *The Man Who Wrote Dracula.* London: Michael Joseph, 1975.

Fleming, K. E. "*Orientalism*, the Balkans, and Balkan Historiography." *American Historical Review* 105.4 (2000): 1218-33.

Florescu, Radu R., and Raymond T. McNally. *Dracula, Prince of Many Faces: His Life and His Times.* Boston, Toronto, and London: Little, Brown, 1989.

Foucault, Michel. *The History of Sexuality.* Vol. 1: *An Introduction.* Trans. Robert Hurley. London: Penguin, 1984.

Frayling, Christopher. *Vampyres: Lord Byron to Count Dracula.* London and Boston: Faber & Faber, 1991.

Gelder, Ken. *Reading the Vampire.* London: Routledge, 1994.

Genette, Gérard. *Palimpsestes: La littérature au second degré.* Paris: Éditions du Seuil, 1982.

Gibson, Matthew. "Bram Stoker and the Treaty of Berlin," *Gothic Studies* 6.2 (Nov. 2004): 236-51.

Glenny, Misha. "Only in the Balkans." *London Review of Books* 29 April 1999: 8-13.

Glover, David. *Vampires, Mummies, and Liberals: Bram Stoker and the Politics of Popular Fiction.* Durham and London: Duke University Press, 1996.

Goldsworthy, Vesna. *Inventing Ruritania: The Imperialism of the Imagination.* New Haven: Yale University Press, 1998.

Haggard, H. Rider. *Allan Quatermain.* 1887. Oxford: Oxford University Press, 1995.

Haining, Peter, ed. *The Vampire Omnibus*. London: Orion, 1995.

Haining, Peter, and Peter Tremayne. *The Undead: The Legend of Bram Stoker and Dracula.* London: Constable, 1997.

Halberstam, Judith. "Technologies of Monstrosity: Bram Stoker's *Dracula*." *Victorian Studies* 36.3 (Spring 1993): 333-52.

Hall, Donald, ed. *Muscular Christianity: Embodying the Victorian Age.* Cambridge: Cambridge University Press, 1994.

Halliday, Michael. *Language as Social Semiotic*. London: Arnold, 1978.

Harpham, Geoffrey Galt. *On the Grotesque: Strategies of Contradiction in Art and Literature.* Princeton: Princeton University Press, 1982.

Hatton, Joseph. *By Order of the Czar. The Tragic Story of Anna Klostock, Queen of the Ghetto.* London: Hutchinson and Co., 1890.

Hawley, Michelle. "Harriet Beecher Stowe and Lord Byron: A Case of Celebrity Justice in the Victorian Public Sphere." *Journal of Victorian Culture* 10.2 (Winter 2005): 229-56.

Haynes, Michael. "The Rhetoric of Economics: Cold War Representation of Development in the Balkans." *The Balkans and the West: Constructing the European Other, 1945–2003*. Ed. Andrew Hammond. Aldershot, England and Burlington, VT: Ashgate, 2004. 26-39.

Holte, James Craig. *The Fantastic Vampire*. Westport and London: Greenwood Press, 2002.

Hughes, William. *Beyond Dracula: Bram Stoker's Fiction and its Cultural Context.* Basingstoke: Macmillan, 2000.

Hurley, Kelly. *The Gothic Body: Sexuality, Materialism and Degeneration at the Fin de Siècle.* Cambridge: Cambridge University Press, 1996.

Hutcheon Linda. *The Politics of Postmodernism*. 2nd ed. London and New York: Routledge, 2002.

Huxley, T. H. "On the Physical Basis of Life." *The Fortnightly Review* 1 February 1869: 129-45.

Iehl, Dominique. *Le Grotesque*. Paris: PUF, 1997.

Jameson, Fredric. *Postmodernism, or, The Cultural Logic of Late Capitalism*. Durham: Duke University Press, 1991.

Jelavich, Barbara. *History of the Balkans*. 2 vols. New York: Cambridge University Press, 1983.

Jones, Alexander, ed. *The Jerusalem Bible, Reader's Edition*. Garden City, NY: Doubleday, 1966.

Jullier, Laurent. *L'écran post-moderne*. Paris: L'Harmattan, 1997.

Karadja, Constantin I. "Incunabulele povestind despre cruzimile lui Vlad Țepeș." *Închinare lui Nicolae Iorga*. Cluj: Editura institutului de istorie universală, 1931. 202-7.

Kayser, Wolfgang. *The Grotesque in Art and Literature.* 1957. Trans. Ulrich Weisstein. Bloomington: Indiana University Press, 1963.

Keir, Elam. *The Semiotics of Theatre and Drama.* London: Methuen, 1980.

King, Stephen. *'Salem's Lot.* New York: Doubleday, 1975.

Kostova, Ludmilla. "Claiming a 'Great Briton' for Bulgaria: Reflections on Byron's Bulgarian Reception (1880s–1920s)." *Byron: Heritage and Legacy.* Ed. Cheryl Wilson. New York: Palgrave, forthcoming.

—. "Love and Death Across Cultures: Richard Henry Savage's *In the Old Chateau, a Story of Russian Poland* and Late Nineteenth-Century American Images of Eastern Europe." *Dialogues: American Studies in an International Context.* Ed. Milena Katzarska. Plovdiv: Zombori, 2002. 199-206.

—. "Theorising Europe's 'Wild East': *Imagining the Balkans* and *Inventing Ruritania.*" *The European English Messenger* 10.1 (Spring 2001): 71-73.

Kozloff, Sarah. *Invisible Storytellers: Voice-over Narration in American Fiction Film.* Berkeley: University of California Press, 1988.

—. *Overhearing Film Dialogue.* Berkeley: University of California Press, 2000.

Latman, Audrey. "Spilled Blood: AIDS in Francis Ford Coppola's *Bram Stoker's Dracula.*" *Latent Image* 10 (Winter 1993): n. pag. Available at http://pages.emerson.edu/organizations/fas/latent_image/index.htm (15 Oct. 2006).

Lavigne, Carlen. "Sex, Blood and (Un)Death: The Queer Vampire and HIV." *Journal of Dracula Studies* 6 (2004): n. pag. Available at http://blooferland.com/drc/images/06Carlen.rtf (2 Feb. 2007).

Leatherdale, Clive. *Dracula: the Novel and the Legend.* Westcliff-on-Sea: Desert Island Books, 1995.

Le Bon, Gustave. *The Crowd: A Study of the Popular Mind.* New Brunswick and London: Transaction, 1997.

—. *Psychologie des foules.* Paris: Quadrige/PUF, 2002.

Leech, Goeffrey. *Style in Fiction.* London: Longman, 1981.

Longinović, Tomislav Z. "Vampires Like Us: Gothic Imaginary and 'the serbs.'" *Balkan as Metaphor: Between Globalization and Fragmentation.* Ed. Dušan Belić and Obrad Savić. Cambridge, MA and London: The MIT Press, 2002. 39-60.

Ludlam, Harry. *A Biography of Dracula.* London: Foulsham, 1962.

Lumpkin, John R. "AIDS: Facts for Life." Illinois Department of Public Health Press Release, 30 Oct. 1992: 1-2.

—. "AIDS: Facts for Life," Illinois Department of Public Health letter, Jan. 1993: 1.

Lyotard, Jean-François. *The Postmodern Condition: A Report on Knowledge.* 1979. Trans. Geoff Bennington and Brian Massumi. Minneapolis: University of Minneapolis Press, 1988.

Manea, Mihai, Adrian Pascu, and Bogdan Teodorescu. *Istoria românilor din cele mai vechi timpuri pîna la Revoluția din 1821. Manual pentru clasa a XI a.* București: Editura didactica și pedagogică, 1992.

Marigny, Jean. "Secrecy as a Strategy in Dracula." *Journal of Dracula Studies* 2 (2000). Available at http://blooferland.com/drc/images/02Marigny.rtf (10 Jan. 2007).

—. *Vampires: The World of the Undead.* London: Thames & Hudson, 1994.

Maudsley, Henry. *Body and Will: Being an Essay Concerning Will in Its Metaphysical, Physiological & Pathological Aspects.* London: Kegan Paul, Trench, 1883.

McGunnigle, Christopher. "My Own Vampire: The Metamorphosis of the Queer Monster in Francis Ford Coppola's *Bram Stoker's Dracula.*" *Gothic Studies* 7.2 (Nov. 2005): 172-84.

McLuhan, Marshall. *Understanding Media: The Extensions of Man.* London: Routledge, 1964.

Meade L. T. [Elizabeth Thomasina Smith]. *The Siren.* London: F. V. White & Co., 1898.

Mearns, Andrew. *The Bitter Cry of Outcast London.* London: Clarke, 1883.

Miller, Elizabeth. *A Dracula Handbook.* n.c.: Xlibris, 2005.

—. *Dracula: Sense and Nonsense.* Westcliff-on-Sea: Desert Island Books, 2000.

Miller, William Ian. *The Anatomy of Disgust.* Cambridge, MA and London: Harvard University Press.

Moses, Michael Valdez. "The Irish Vampire: *Dracula*, Parnell, and the Troubled Dreams of Nationhood." *Journal x* 2.1 (1997): 67-111.

Murray, Paul. *From the Shadow of Dracula: A Life of Bram Stoker.* London: Jonathan Cape, 2004.

Newsholme, Arthur. *Hygiene: A Manual of Personal and Public Health.* London: George Gill & Sons, 1892.

Nordau, Max. *Degeneration.* 1895. Lincoln and London: University of Nebraska Press, 1993.

Oane, Sorin, and Maria Ochescu. *Istorie. Clasa a VIII a.* București: Humanitas Educațional, 2000.

Olsen, Lance. *Ellipse of Uncertainty: An Introduction to Postmodern Fantasy.* New York and London: Greenwood Press, 1987.

Olteanu, Pandle. *Limba povestirilor slave despre Vlad Țepeș.* București: Editura Academiei, 1961.

Pick, Daniel. "'Terrors of the Night': *Dracula* and Degeneration in the Late Nineteenth Century." *Critical Inquiry* 30 (1988): 71-87.

Preiss, Byron, ed. *The Ultimate Dracula*. London: Headline, 1992.

Punter, David. *The Literature of Terror: A History of Gothic Fictions from 1765 to the Present Day*. London: Longman, 1980.

Pykett, Lyn. *The "Improper Feminine": The Women's Sensational Novel and the New Woman Writing*. London: Routledge, 1992.

Reade, Brian. *Aubrey Beardsley*. Woodbridge: Antique Collectors' Club, 1998.

Rice, Anne. *Interview with the Vampire*. New York: Knopf, 1976.

Rickels, Laurence A. *The Vampire Lectures*. Minneapolis and London: University of Minnesota Press, 1995.

Rogoz, Georgina Viorica. *Istoria despre Dracula*. Bucureşti: NOI Media Print, 2004.

Ronay, Gabriel. *The Dracula Myth: The Cult of the Vampire*. London and New York: W. H. Allen, 1972.

Rosset, Clément. *Impressions fugitives. L'Ombre, le reflet, l'écho*. Paris: Les Éditions de Minuit, 2004.

Roth, Phyllis A. "Suddenly Sexual Women in Bram Stoker's *Dracula*." In Glennis Byron, 30-42.

Ryan, Alan, ed. *The Penguin Book of Vampire Stories*. London: Penguin, 1987.

Rymer, James Malcolm. *Varney the Vampyre; or The Feast of Blood*. 3 vols. Available at http://etext.lib.virginia.edu/toc/modeng/public/PreVar1.html (8 Oct. 2006).

Samouillan, Jean. *Des dialogues au cinéma*. Paris: L'Harmattan, 2004.

Savage, Richard Henry. *My Official Wife*. Leipzig: Bernard Tauchnitz, 1891.

Senf, Carol A. *Dracula: Between Tradition and Modernism*. New York: Twayne, 1998.

—. "A Response to 'Dracula and the Idea of Europe.'" *Connotations* 10.1 (2000–2001): 47-58.

Skal, David J. *Hollywood Gothic: The Tangled Web of Dracula from Novel to Stage to Screen*. Rev. ed. New York: Faber & Faber, 1990, 2004.

Smith, Andrew. "Bringing Bram Stoker Back From the Margins." *Irish Studies* 9.2 (2001): 241-46.

Stade, George. Introduction. *Dracula by Bram Stoker*. New York: Bantam Classics, 1981. v-xiv.

Stăvăruş, Ion. *Povestiri medievale despre Vlad Ţepeş—Draculea*. Bucureşti: Univers, 1993.

Stead, Evanghélia. *Le Monstre, le Singe et le Fœtus: Tératogonie et décadence dans l'Europe fin-de-siècle*. Paris: Droz, 2004.

Stevenson, Robert Louis. *The Strange Case of Dr Jekyll and Mr Hyde*. 1886. London: Penguin, 2002.

Stevenson, Thomas and Shirley Murphy, eds. *A Treatise on Hygiene and Public Health*. 3 vols. London: Churchill, 1893–96.

Stoicescu, Nicolae. *Vlad Țepeș*. București: Editura Academiei Republicii Socialiste Romania, 1978.

Stoker, Bram. "The Censorship of Fiction." 1908. *A Glimpse of America and Other Lectures, Interviews and Essays*. Ed. Richard Dalby. Westcliff-on-Sea: Desert Island Books, 2002. 154-61.

Stoker, Bram. *Dracula: A Norton Critical Edition*. Ed. Nina Auerbach and David J. Skal. New York and London: Norton, 1997.

—. *The Lady of the Shroud*. 1908. London: Alan Sutton, 1994.

—. *Personal Reminiscences of Henry Irving*. 2 vols. London: Heinemann, 1906.

Thomas, Ronald R. "Specters of the Novel: Dracula and the Cinematic Afterlife of the Victorian Novel." *Victorian Afterlife: Postmodern Culture Rewrites the Nineteenth Century*. Eds. John Kucich and Dianne F. Sadoff. Minneapolis: University of Minnesota Press, 2000. 288-310.

Thorne, Tony. *Countess Dracula: The Life and Times of Elisabeth Báthory, The Blood Countess*. London: Bloomsbury, 1997.

Trotter, David. "The Politics of Adventure in the Early British Spy Novel." *Spy Fiction, Spy Films and Real Intelligence*. Ed. Wesley K. Wark. London: Frank Cass, 1991. 30-54.

Todorova, Maria. *Imagining the Balkans*. London and New York: Oxford University Press, 1997.

Trudgill, Eric. *Madonnas and Magdalens: The Origins and Development of Victorian Sexual Attitudes*. London: Heinemann, 1976.

Tunzelmann, G. W. de. *Electricity in Modern Life*. New York: Collier, 1902.

Ungheanu, Mihai. *Răstălmacirea lui Țepeș. "Dracula"—un roman politic?* București: Editura Globus, 1992.

Valente, Joseph. *Dracula's Crypt: Bram Stoker, Irishness, and the Question of Blood*. Urbana and Chicago: University of Illinois Press, 2006.

Vassé, Claire. *Le dialogue: du texte écrit à la voix mise en scène*. Paris: Éditions Cahiers du Cinéma, 2003.

Vulpe, Alexandru, Radu Păun, Radu Băjenaru, and Ioan Grosu. *Istorie. Clasa a VIII a* București: Sigma, 2000.

Williams, Anne. *Art of Darkness: A Poetics of Gothic*. Chicago and London: The University of Chicago Press, 1995.

Winter, Alison. *Mesmerized: Powers of Mind in Victorian Britain*. Chicago: University of Chicago Press, 1998.

Wohl, Antony S. *Endangered Lives: Public Health in Victorian Britain*. London: Dent, 1983.

Wolff, Larry. *Inventing Eastern Europe: The Map of Civilization on the Mind of the Enlightenment*. Stanford: Stanford University Press, 1994.

Zanger, Jules. "A Sympathetic Vibration: Dracula and the Jews." *English Literature in Transition* 34.1 (1991): 33-54.

SELECT FILMOGRAPHY

La Belle et la Bête. Dir. Jean Cocteau. Perf. Jean Marais, Josette Day. DisCina, 1946.

Blood for Dracula. Dir. Paul Morrissey. Perf. Udo Kier. CFS Kosutnjak, 1974.

Bram Stoker's Dracula. Dir. Francis Ford Coppola. Perf. Winona Ryder, Gary Oldman. Columbia, 1992.

The Canterville Ghost. Dir. Jules Dassin. Perf. Charles Laughton. MGM, 1944.

Dr. Jekyll and Mr. Hyde. Dir. Rouben Mamoulian. Perf. Fredric March, Miriam Hopkins. Paramount, 1931.

Dracula. Dir. John Badham. Perf. Frank Langella, Kate Nelligan. Universal, 1979.

Dracula. Dir. Tod Browning. Perf. Bela Lugosi. Universal, 1931.

Dracula. Dir. Terence Fisher. Perf. Christopher Lee, Peter Cushing. Hammer Films, 1958.

Dracula 2000. Dir. Patrick Lussier. Perf. Christopher Plummer, Gerard Butler. Carfax Productions, 2000.

Dracula, Prince of Darkness. Dir. Terence Fisher. Perf. Christopher Lee. Hammer Films, 1966.

El Conde Drácula—Les nuits de Dracula. Dir. Jess [Jesus] Franco. Per. Christopher Lee, Herbert Lom. Spain/West Germany/France/Italy, 1970.

The Ghost and Mrs. Muir. Dir. Joseph Mankiewicz. Perf. Gene Tierney, Rex Harrison. Twentieth-Century Fox, 1947.

Highlander. Dir. Russell Mulcahy. Perf. Sean Connery, Christoper Lambert. Twentieth-Century Fox, 1986.

Interview with the Vampire. Dir. Neil Jordan. Perf. Tom Cruise, Brad Pitt. Greffen Pictures, 1994.

Love at First Bite. Dir. Stan Dragoti. Perf. George Hamilton, Susan Saint James, Richard Benjamin, Arte Johnson. MGM, 1979.

Mark of the Vampire. Dir. Tod Browning. Perf. Bela Lugosi. Universal, 1935.

Nosferatu, eine Symphonie des Grauen. Dir. Friedrich W. Murnau. Perf. Maw Schreck. Jofa-Atelier Berlin, 1922.

Nosferatu, Phantom der Nacht. Dir. Werner Herzog. Perf. Isabelle Adjani, Klaus Kinski. Gaumont, 1979.

Pandora and the Flying Dutchman. Dir. Albert Lewin. Perf. Ava Gardner, James Mason. MGM, 1951.

The Passion of Christ. Dir. Mel Gibson. Perf. James Caviezel. Icon Pictures, 2004.

The Satanic Rites of Dracula. Dir. Alan Gibson. Perf. Christopher Lee, Peter Cushing. Hammer Films, 1974.

Shadow of the Vampire. Dir. E. Elias Merhige. Perf. John Malkovich. Lions Gate Films, 2000.

The Silence of the Lambs. Dir. Jonathan Demme. Perf. Jodie Foster, Antony Hopkins. Orion Pictures, 1991.

Sunset Boulevard. Dir. Billy Wilder. Perf. Gloria Swanson, William Holden. Paramount, 1950.

Van Helsing. Dir. Stephen Sommers. Perf. Hugh Jackman, Kate Beckinsale. Universal, 2004.

CONTRIBUTORS

Associate Professor at Nancy-Université—C.T.U., in France, **Dr. John S. Bak** teaches courses on translation, American drama, and American Gothic. His articles on Tennessee Williams have appeared in such journals as *Theatre Journal, Mississippi Quarterly, Journal of American Drama and Theatre, The Tennessee Williams Literary Journal, American Drama, Journal of Religion and Theatre, South Atlantic Review, Cercles*, and *Coup de Théâtre*. He has recently completed a book entitled *Ernest Hemingway, Tennessee Williams and Queer Masculinities*.

Currently visiting lecturer at the Université Paris Dauphine and the Université Paris I Panthéon Sorbonne, **Dr. Jacques Coulardeau** has taught in six universities (including the University of California at Davis). His research has connected him with many institutions and journals in a dozen countries, including *Théâtres du Monde* and *Duels en Scène* in Avignon, and *Cercles* in Rouen, France. At present, he is working on several projects with the University of Avignon in the field of drama, with the University of Brest in linguistics, and with the Buddhist and Pali University of Dambulla in Sri Lanka on the transation of Pali into English.

Dr. Françoise Dupeyron-Lafay is Professor of nineteenth-century British literature at the Université Paris XII. She has published widely on Victorian fiction and specialises in Victorian Gothic and literature of the fantastic. She heads the CERLI (Centre d'Etudes et de Recherches sur les Littératures de l'Imaginaire), a multidisciplinary research centre on literature of the fantastic and science fiction. Her publications include *Le Fantastique anglo-saxon. De l'Autre Côté du réel* (1998), *Le Livre et l'image dans les œuvres fantastiques et de science-fiction* (2003), *Détours et hybridations dans les œuvres fantastiques et de science-fiction* (2005), and *Les représentations du corps dans les œuvres fantastique et de science-fiction: figures et fantasmes* (2006).

Dr. Monica Girard, Romanian by birth, is Associate Professor of British literature in the English Department of Nancy-Université in France. In 2003, she defended her Ph.D. thesis, "A Voice of One's Own: Examining Virginia Woolf's Literary Allotropes, *Melymbrosia* (1908) and *The Voyage Out* (1915)." She is currently working on several articles exploring the genesis of Virginia Woolf's first novel from the multiple perspectives of genetic criticism, feminism, narratology, stylistics and linguistics. She is also interested in postcolonial and postmodernist British literature.

Professor of Gothic Studies at Bath Spa University, England, **Dr. William Hughes** has published widely on Stoker and on *Dracula*. His publications include *Beyond Dracula: Bram Stoker's Fiction and its Cultural Context* (2000), *Bram Stoker: A Bibliography* (1997, revised 2004 with the assistance of Richard Dalby) and an annotated edition of Stoker's 1909 *faux* vampire novel, *The Lady of the Shroud* (2001). With Andrew Smith he has co-edited three collections of essays—*Bram Stoker: History, Psychoanalysis and the Gothic* (1998), *Empire and the Gothic: The Politics of Genre* (2003) and *Fictions of Unease: The Gothic from Otranto to The X-Files* (2002, with Andrew Smith and Diane Mason). His current research includes another collection of essays, *Queering the Gothic*, again edited with Andrew Smith, a critical guide to *Dracula*, a new edition of *Dracula* for Sulis Press, and a monograph on Mesmerism and the Victorian Popular Imagination. He is the editor of *Gothic Studies*, the refereed journal of the International Gothic Association.

Dr. Ludmilla Kostova is Associate Professor of British literature and cultural studies at St. Cyril and St. Methodius University of Veliko Turnovo, Bulgaria. She has published widely on eighteenth-century, romantic and modern British literature and has organized seminars and panels on travel writing and cultural encounter. Her book *Tales of the Periphery: The Balkans in Nineteenth-Century British Writing* (1997) has been frequently cited by specialists in the field. Together with Corinne Fowler, she edited a special issue on ethics and travel of *Journeys—The International Journal of Travel and Travel Writing*, vol. 4.1 (2003).

Dr. Jean-Marie Lecomte is Associate Professor in the Department of Communication Studies of the Institute of Technology at Nancy-Université. He specialises in stylistics, Victorian literature, and early cinema. He has written on Gerard Manley Hopkins, the birth of the Hollywood talkies, filmic speech in monster movies, and early Afro-American musicals. Currently, he is completing *Language and Style in Early Sound Film*.

Dr. Jean Marigny is Professor emeritus at the Université Stendhal-Grenoble 3 (France), where he created a research centre on the fantastic, the GERF (Groupe d'Etudes et de Recherches sur le Fantastique). He is a specialist of the vampire in literature. His major works include *Sang pour sang, le réveil des vampires* (1993), which was translated into English as *Vampires, the World of the Undead* (UK, 1994), *Vampires, Restless Creatures of the Night* (USA, 1994), and *Le Vampire dans la littérature du XXe siècle* (2003), which won a literary award, Le Grand Prix de l'Imaginaire, in 2004.

Dr. David Punter is Professor of English at the University of Bristol, where he is also Research Director for the Faculty of Arts. He has published extensively on Gothic and romantic literature; on contemporary writing; and on literary theory, psychoanalysis and the postcolonial. His books include *The Literature of Terror*; *The Hidden Script: Writing and the Unconscious*; *The Romantic Unconscious: A Study in Narcissism and Patriarchy*; *Gothic Pathologies: The Text, the Body and the Law*; *Writing the Passions*; *Postcolonial Imaginings: Fictions of a New World Order*; *The Influence of Postmodernism on Contemporary Writing*, as well as four small volumes of poetry. He has recently completed a book on the concept of modernity, as well as the new edition of *Metaphor* in the New Critical Idiom series.

Dr. Nathalie Saudo is Associate Professor of English at the Université de Picardie. She has published articles on *Dracula*, degeneration and the influence of scientific discourse on fin-de-siècle British literature.

INDEX

Williams, Anne, 24, 30, 148
Winter, Alison, xxiii, 29, 59, 144, 145,
    148
Wohl, Antony, 52, 58, 148

Wolff, Larry, 29, 148

Zanger, Jules, 29, 148